Hitler's Girls

Hitler's Girls

DOVES AMONGST EAGLES

TIM HEATH

Pen & Sword

MILITARY

First published in Great Britain in 2017
and reprinted in 2018 and again in this format in 2019 by
Pen & Sword MILITARY
An imprint of Pen & Sword Books Ltd
Yorkshire – Philadelphia

Copyright © Tim Heath, 2017, 2018, 2019
ISBN: 978 1 52674 297 1

Printed and bound in the UK by CPI Group (UK) Ltd, Croydon, CR0 4YY

Pen & Sword Books Limited incorporates the imprints of Atlas, Archaeology,
Aviation, Discovery, Family History, Fiction, History, Maritime, Military, Military
Classics, Politics, Select, Transport, True Crime, Air World, Frontline Publishing, Leo
Cooper, Remember When, Seaforth Publishing, The Praetorian Press, Wharncliffe
Local History, Wharncliffe Transport, Wharncliffe True Crime and White Owl.

For a complete list of Pen & Sword titles please contact
PEN & SWORD BOOKS LIMITED
47 Church Street, Barnsley, South Yorkshire, S70 2AS, England
E-mail: enquiries@pen-and-sword.co.ok • Website: www.pen-and-sword.co.uk
Or
PEN AND SWORD BOOKS
1950 Lawrence Rd, Havertown, PA 19083, USA
E-mail: Uspen-and-sword@casematepublishers.com
Website: www.penandswordbooks.com

For my Paula, my love, my best friend, my rock, and for women and young girls the world over who are still suffering violence, exploitation and inequality.

Contents

Acknowledgements

I would like to acknowledge the following contributors to this work: Anna Dann, Anita von Schoener, Amy Richardson, Brigitte Schüttenkopf, Carly Hendryks, Dora Brunninghausen, Dana Schmidt, Gabrielle Haefker, Horst Frank, Helga Stroh, Helga Bassler, Helena W. Wessel, Inge Scholl, Kirsten Eckermann, Melissa Schroeder, Sophia Kortge, Theresa Moelle, Heidi Koch, Helena Vogel, Ingeborg Schalle, Olga Kirschener, Martina Schepel, Theobald Hortinger, Barbie Densk, Helene Rischer, Elsa Lantz, Dana Henschell, William Anderson, Richard Marshall, Otto Krische and Anita Skorz, all without whom this book would never have been possible.

I would also like to extend my heartfelt thanks to Claire Hopkins, History Editor at Pen & Sword Books Limited, for her help and support given throughout its production and for making *Hitler's Girls* a reality.

I must also give heartfelt thanks to copy editor and author Gerry van Tonder who has gone above and beyond his duties on this project, Lenny Warren and the Militaria Collectors Network, and Ian Tustin and Lynne Powell of the *Vale Magazine*.

Introduction

The youth that graduate from my academies will terrify the world!
—*Adolf Hitler 1930s*

It was during the course of a visit to the German military cemetery at Cannock Chase in Staffordshire, England, in November of 1997, that the idea for *Hitler's Girls* was conceived. It was a freezing cold, wet and windy morning. I had arrived late at the cemetery, with a view to photographing some graves as part of a research programme being conducted at the time.

I was distracted halfway through my work by the arrival of a group of visitors, which I soon discovered had come from Germany on one of the many excursions organised by the German War Graves Commission at Kassel. Some of the visitors, drawn away from their intended reason for being there, became curious as to what this mad Englishman could possibly be doing – trying to take photographs and write notes in such dreadful weather conditions. After a few minutes, one of the German visitors came over, and after some introduction and handshaking, a conversation developed.

As the weather worsened and snow began to fall, we moved into the small reception area of the building where we could continue talking in relative comfort. By this time, the party of German visitors were trekking back and forth to their luxury coach, clutching freshly cooked hotdogs and cups of steaming, hot coffee. Once inside they began to hand out the food and drinks to each other.

One of the female visitors said to me, 'You must be frozen, and what are you doing to be out here on such a dreadful day?'

She then insisted that I have a hotdog and cup of hot coffee before introducing herself:

'My name is Kirsten Eckermann and I have come to England for one week with my husband and sister to visit her husband's grave, he had served with the Luftwaffe and was killed over England in 1943.'

Naturally the subject of the war became unavoidable. The conversation soon drifted into a period of time that many elderly Germans are still either desperately trying come to terms with or to forget.

I asked Kirsten about her home life and schooling. How had the war affected her and her family, and what it had been like in general to be raised in Hitler's Third Reich? I was very surprised by many of the things she had told me, even more so by the fact that young girls and women also had to join the Hitler Youth. They had no choice, and many had been intimidated into joining.

I had not really had any previous understanding or knowledge of the role of female youth in Nazi Germany. I had previously known little about the two main female Hitler Youth organizations: the *Jung Madel* (young maidens) for ten to fourteen-year-old girls, and its senior equivalent, the *Bund Deutscher Madel* (League of German Maidens/BDM) for fourteen-to-eighteen-year-old girls. I did not possess any real understanding of the many unique problems faced by the female youth of Germany or the expectations placed upon their young shoulders by the sometimes contradictory attitudes of their parents and that of the Nazi education system. This frequently led to violence in the home, as girls strived to become independent of their parent's strict control.

Kirsten went on to explain that the initial role of German girls under Nazi rule was strictly a passive one, where girls and females in general were confined to the two main functions of motherhood and housekeeping. With the outbreak of war in 1939, and the later unsustainable losses in both human and material resource, the Nazis were forced to dictate changes in policy with regard to the role of its female youth. Kirsten explained that from late 1943 up until the total collapse and surrender of the Third Reich, girls were incorporated into the military. Here they were given detailed instructions on how to use rifles, machine guns, make booby traps, and use anti-tank weaponry. It was all in what amounted to a vain attempt to prevent what was an inevitable Allied victory over Nazi Germany.

It is difficult for many to comprehend that young girls often fought side by side with Wehrmacht soldiers old enough to be their fathers, or formed into some quite effective fighting groups of their own, which in turn would inflict casualties upon the invading Allied forces. Female guerrilla units had been specially formed, seeing combat in and around the Warsaw area against the Red Army in 1944.

It soon became clear to me that the kind of information being exchanged here was that of a highly important nature, and should be documented.

I then asked Kirsten if she would be interested in helping me with a view to perhaps producing a book. She agreed to help me as much as she could. We exchanged addresses and shook hands, and Kirsten agreed to talk to some of her friends back in Germany who might also be able to help with information for the proposed book. Subsequently, the work of producing a feasible manuscript was started, along with masses of interviews, via telephone, the Internet and by letter. I also started my search through various archives both here in the UK and in Europe.

Hitler's Girls encapsulates the kind of material that was only made accessible and possible by perseverance, familiarity and friendship with the women concerned, all of whom having chosen to stay silent for all these years. Many have very genuine reasons for keeping quiet. It was only through my work with the German War Graves Commission at Kassel that these women were convinced that I should be the one to tell their stories, memories and anecdotes for the first time. Many of the women gave me the freedom of their old diaries and journals. The translations provided unique and historically valuable information. As some of the contributors had actually met the likes of Adolf Hitler, Goering and Himmler, their journals have yielded new and previously unpublished material concerning these high-ranking figures of the Third Reich.

It is not a pretty picture. Some of the contributors to this work suffered the ordeal of rape and seeing their friends brutally murdered at the hands of Russian soldiers. Some of the work contained within this book, therefore, may disturb and horrify the reader.

I hope, however, that this book represents in no small way the voice of a generation of German women and girls that must be heard. Many are now well into their twilight years, and with the passing of each year, another one passes away. Soon they will all be gone forever, taking their stories with them. It is therefore my ardent wish that this publication, aided by its straightforward approach to the reader – whatever his or her interests – will be easily understood and assimilated.

What I personally have learned from 1997, when I first began working on the project, has certainly enlightened me to the extent where I had to change many of my own personal perceptions on what I had believed life would have been like for young girls and women under Hitler and his twelve-year Reich. Many were likened to doves thrown amongst eagles.

Chapter One

The Third Reich is Born

After what can only be described as an extraordinary series of social and political events, including the death of German president Paul von Hindenburg on 2 August 1934, Adolf Hitler became Führer, or leader, of Germany and the Third Reich was conceived. Hitler acted quickly to ensure he seized total power in Germany. He appointed loyal Nazis to various positions within the new government and replaced all labour unions with the Nazi-controlled German Labour Front, or *Deutsche Arbeitsfront*. In addition to these measures, Hitler outlawed all other political organizations.

The National Socialist monster it had, perhaps inadvertently, helped to create was rapidly swallowing Germany. Very soon, the press, economy and all activities of a cultural nature were placed under Nazi authority. It soon became very clear to many that one's livelihood would depend on one's political loyalty. This applied particularly to the wealthy.

There were thousands who opposed the Nazi regime and the way that it had seized power. Many of these anti-Nazis were rounded up and transported to concentration camps. No secret was made of the fate of those who opposed the Nazis – the existence of the concentration camps was widely publicised. Between 1933 and 1944, a total of 13,405 death sentences were passed in Nazi Germany, and of these 11,881 were carried out.

Soon, any sign of dissent within German society disappeared within the brutal veil of a massive propaganda campaign that hailed the destruction of democracy in Germany. At the same time, huge specially staged rallies were organised, giving the casual observer the impression that everyone supported Hitler. There were of course a great many who did support Hitler. Most of his support came from the working and middle classes, as it were they in particular who had suffered the most after Germany's defeat in the First World War, particularly as a result of the implementation of the hated Treaty of Versailles.

Hitler had taken care to ensure that he gained the support of these social and economic classes during his rise to prominence. By 1933, unemployment had reached an all-time low of thirty-five per cent. That said, things improved only very marginally for the working and middle classes, many of whom could still not afford to feed their families. The re-armament of Germany, as ordered by Hitler, far from improving things actually proved detrimental to the economic situation.

By the mid-19th century, a dense mass of tenements had been erected to the northeast and south of the central '*Mitte*' district of the city of Berlin. Known as the '*Mietskasernen*' (rent barracks), these buildings were the homes of the working-class families who worked in the nearby industrial plants and factories. Aristocrats and middle-class families lived in the peripheral communities of Dahlem, Grunewald and Kopenick. The *Mietskasernen* was a typical industrial area, crammed with terraced houses and where everything appeared to be dark and forbidding. In fact, the *Mitte* district of Berlin was much like London's East End, its populace looking and going about their lives in much the same way.

It was in this *Mitte* district that Anna Dann was born on 14 January 1929 into a working class family, consisting of her mother Hanna, father Erich, and two older brothers Franz and Josef. Though Anna did not join the *Jung Madel* until 1939, by which time both school and *Jung Madel* activities were concerned primarily with the issues of war, she explains:

> I was only four years old when Hitler came to power and I can remember certain things such as my father Erich coming home from the factory which he was employed at. His face and hands were almost permanently stained black from smoke and oil and whatever else he had to work in. His health suffered greatly as a result of his work and I remember how he coughed and wheezed to the point where he almost vomited. I remember my mother and father talking about Hitler and I wondered whom this Hitler was, but had no understanding of what he was or what he was doing at that time, as few young children ever have any political understanding. To me Hitler was a kind of cartoon character back then.
>
> From looking back at those early years I cannot say that our basic living conditions improved that rapidly under the Nazis as our home was small, often dirty and frequented by rats and mice (a legacy of the nearby factories) and with very few of the amenities of a modern house in Berlin where the '*Mitte*' district borough still forms the heart of the newly unified city, along with five other central borough areas.
>
> I know that my father was impressed with Hitler's vision and of what he might offer by the way of prosperity. Everyone wanted to

have a better standard of living and my father joined his friends by going to listen to Hitler. It was a bitterly hard existence and we were often hungry and in the winter we were cold.

My mother Hanna did her best to care for us to ensure we were as clean as was possible and most of our clothing was never thrown away as it was always repaired and worn again. At that time there was no financial help that families like ours could fall back on and it was the job of the father to provide for his family, while the mother cared for the children. In fact, there were times when I did not even have shoes or socks to wear on my feet. It was only as I grew older that I became aware of my surroundings and of course the Nazis and what their plans were for Germany and its peoples.

My father was patriotic and I can remember him reading a Nazi Party publication. I do not remember so much the text but the cover. It portrayed a group of German workers with their fists raised towards the sky and they looked like my father and I would say, 'Father, this is you.' The cover caught my eye because it was so colourful and powerful in a visual sense. I suppose that looking back it was meant to provoke aggressive patriotism. It is so strange to think that I myself would later meet, though very briefly, and shake hands with this man Adolf Hitler as I too became a part of the machine.'

By the summer of 1933, Hitler was in complete control of Germany. Having made sure that existing social, economic and professional organizations had been completely absorbed into the Nazi Party, Hitler appointed party members to various key positions of authority to ensure loyalty as well as to keep an eye on the conduct of the ordinary individuals within. Even the leaders of the Protestant and Catholic churches pledged their support for the Nazis, unaware that they were in a sense supporting what was to become a slave state.

Hitler and the Nazis kept its promises to the working classes as all manner of building projects were started in an effort to defeat the scourge of unemployment. One of Hitler's successes was the creation of the German autobahns. These roads were not really created out of any particular automotive necessity, though they were strategically vital once the Nazi war machine began to roll, but it gave the working-class man, who at best could only expect to be able to perform menial tasks, a job and a wage. He could gain back his self-respect, and feed his family. Such initiatives achieved great success, and by 1938, unemployment in Germany had fallen to less than five per cent. This was in every respect a monumental achievement and went some way to convincing the sceptics that Hitler's policies could indeed create radical social change.

The *Winterhilfswerke* (WHW), or Winter Relief Fund, was established in September 1933. The WHW collected donations from businesses, institutions and wealthy individuals around Germany, donating such funds to those Germans suffering from the combined effects of poverty, unemployment and homelessness. Again, this proved to be a success. It was of huge benefit to the poor working-class families of the industrial heartland who suffered particular hardships during the past winters of the pre-Hitler years. The WHW adopted the morale-boosting slogan of 'A People Helps Itself'.

It was also in 1933 that Hitler ordered the rearmament of Germany. The rearmament programme would further aid the problem of unemployment as well as form the foundation of Nazi aggression in Europe.

Kirsten Eckermann was ten years old when the Nazis came to power in 1933:

> I remember my father's initial excitement over Hitler. My father and mother had both suffered like many German families as a consequence of the First World War. My father had lost members of his family in that war and I suppose looking back he can be forgiven in a sense because of that. We lived in the industrial village as some called it in central Berlin. The men there were all labourers but some were very skilled at their work. There were times when unemployment caused great misery and if men could not work they could not feed their families and violence in the home became frequent.
>
> My father like many men of his kind was a very strong disciplinarian with a temper. He rarely ever displayed any open affection towards me. Even as a young child he would not kiss and cuddle me very often. I always did what I was told and obeyed my parents, it was the way that girls were expected to be. I myself was never really interested in politics and often ignored the conversations that my mother and father had about Hitler and the Nazi Party. The name Hitler was mentioned many times in our house. There were days when my father would come home drunk and all he would go on about was Hitler. I dared not leave the room without my parents' permission and had to sit there and listen to him rant on and on until he had got it out of his system.

I know that there were a great many working-class Germans who blamed Jews for their predicament. That was because they had been listening to Hitler and he had exploited their fears to further himself politically, though of course there were obvious problems and maybe Jews were to blame for some of them. Many factories, workhouses and businesses in the streets were under Jewish ownership. When the men lost their jobs they obviously blamed the Jewish bosses and there was that resentment that Hitler and the Nazis exploited. My mother also once tried to find work within a Jewish-owned shop but had to leave because one of the owner's sons had tried to make sexual advances toward her. My father was furious but he could do very little about it at that time. Hitler considered Germany to be a racial sewer and he would shout and rage about how the inferior races, if tolerated, would destroy the Germanic race and its purity.

Hitler for some strange reason attracted girls and held their attention. 'Germany for Germans' he would shout at every meeting and he would do so with an immense depth of emotion. He would almost make you cry and he touched you in a way that no one else could. It really was no surprise to where this was all leading. I don't think many really considered the long-term reality of a Nazi government and the penalties that would have to be paid as a result of supporting it.

At school Nazi influence came into the classroom very rapidly. There were many Jewish children in our school but once the Nazis had gained control this soon changed. At my school, Jewish children became the subject of ridicule and over a period of time became victims of bullying from the non-Jewish children and the teachers. We dared not talk to Jewish children anymore as our teachers said it was forbidden. Groups of girls would gang up and single out a Jewish girl: they then pulled her hair and tore at her clothes and as she lay crying on the ground they would spit on her and shout '*Juden*' repeatedly.

My god, those were dreadful times and it is one of the many reasons why up until now I have refused to talk about it. For heaven's sake, all we needed was bread – it just all went too far.

As Hitler began his programmes to mobilize his workers and rearm Germany, he also began to put into effect plans to rid Germany of undesirable racial elements by introducing discriminatory laws. Jews, gypsies, Communists,

Jehovah's Witnesses and blacks were all considered as undesirables. When questioned on the issue, Hitler raged, 'Because they are independent of the German will and of German values, as an uncommitted race of criminals they can therefore contribute nothing to my Germany.'

The Jewish families who chose to remain in Germany were soon deprived of their citizenship. They were deemed unemployable and were not allowed to own even a motor vehicle. Jewish children were often expelled from public schools, while families had their valuables and property confiscated. Jews were in some cases also deprived of everyday essentials such as food and medicine. Such acts of racial extremity shocked many visiting foreigners.

Hitler had become so completely obsessed with racial purity that he had had numerous meetings with key henchmen to discuss what he referred to as the 'Jewish Problem'. While Hitler and those within his close circle discussed the Jewish Problem, violence towards Jews on the streets was becoming commonplace. Kirsten Eckermann:

> Though it was some years until *Kristallnacht* ('Night of Broken Glass') of the 9th November 1938, when Jews were murdered by Nazi mobs, violence towards Jews could be witnessed regularly on the streets of Berlin in particular. Of course, we used to have to buy goods from Jewish-owned shops and before Hitler became Chancellor we never really thought anything about it much.
>
> Once Hitler was in power he wasted little time in nurturing the resentment, which existed between working–class Germans and the rich Jewish families who owned businesses. It had been there for a while and was like dynamite waiting to be lit. The Nazis had gone to great lengths to prevent Germans from using Jewish-owned shops. Often it was the job of the SA/Brownshirts or *Sturmabteilung* (Storm Troopers) as they were known to us, to do this work. They would paint the Star of David on the front of the shop and add things such as '*Juden*' or '*Achtung Juden!*' (Beware Jews!) to make sure you knew not to buy goods from there.
>
> I often went with my mother to buy the few goods and there were to be many occasions where we could not help but witness violence. A group of SA men were gathered outside a shop that had just received its Star of David symbol; they had also painted a skull and cross bones onto the front window. 'Don't buy from Jewish shops,' they cried as people walked by, 'Buy from German shops only', 'Keep away from these dogs!' and things like that. The

owner of the shop had tried desperately in vain to reason with the SA, but in return they turned on the man and began to beat him in front of his wife and children. Other SA members began to smash the windows of the shop while the man was on the ground being beaten. My mother took me by the hand and quickly walked away from the scene. We had to push through a large crowd who had come to watch and as we pushed our way through, I remember the screams of that man's family, hysterical screams of the man's wife and the children. I looked up at my mother and asked '*mutter*, why are they doing that?' And 'why can't we buy food from there anymore?' I understood the scrawl that the SA men had painted upon the shop windows but still did not fully understand why they had to do that to those people.

In school, they began to teach '*Mein Kampf*' and they told us that if we did not destroy the Jews within our society then they would destroy us. When I joined and became a member of the *Jung Madel* (Young Maidens) and *Bund Deutscher Madel* (League of German Maidens), I began to understand the situation more, though I still could not fully grasp the politics. I can say with all honesty that I was not anti-Jewish, and that I would not have physically harmed anyone regardless of their race, etc. We were told it was the rightful way for us as German girls, and we had certain obligations to fulfil for our country and must obey the new German order in the name of Adolf Hitler our Führer.

The Nazis also wanted to create within its Third Reich a new culture, and on 10 May 1933, a parade of students arrived at the University of Berlin where a huge pile of books were set on fire. The books burned were all those concerned with traditional German thought, society and home, and in fact any material that referred to the German people and what was now regarded by many as 'the bastard culture' of the old Germany.

The Reich Chamber of Culture was created, under the direction of Dr Joseph Goebbels. Any individual or body engaged in fine arts, music or theatre, radio, etc, were all required to join their respective chambers. Anyone failing to comply with the strict legislation was given a jail term. Of all the chambers, the music one fared best, as music was the least political. That said, music written by Jewish composers and playwrights, such as Mendelssohn and Reinhardt, were forbidden. Jewish musicians were also removed from orchestras and opera.

The press and radio in Nazi Germany were also subject to the new culture laws. Everything was scrutinized, and journalists were told what to write and how to write it. Often editors of newspapers had to be Nazi sympathizers who had to be both politically and racially clean. Those newspapers that had been under Jewish ownership were closed down and their equipment confiscated, along with any funds. Radio suffered in exactly the same way by being totally under state control. Radio was by far the most important propaganda tool the Nazis had. As a result, the broadcasts were unexciting and monotonous in content, so few Germans listened to the radio. The film industry also suffered. German films generally attracted very small audiences at first. Most would spend their time watching B-class Hollywood movies instead. Most of the German films produced at the time were of such poor quality, that even the lower classes of German society found them boring. A former bomber crewman with the Luftwaffe, Horst Frank, commented during the writing of this work:

> The German films were dreadful, and were constantly interrupted with propaganda and it is probably just as well that we paid little attention to them. We were much more interested in our girlfriends to actually watch those awful films. We only went to those places so as we could get into the warm and away from our parents' homes and things. Most of the time we went to the *Haus Vaterland* (House of the Fatherland) – this was a very popular amusement centre in the Saarlandstrasse. We would get together and put our money together and that is where we would take our girlfriends. It was a popular place with young people back then. At home, girls were often chaperoned by their mothers and fathers and you dared not touch them or kiss them in their parents' presence, not even on the cheek or anything.

With the dictatorial control of the Third Reich in place, even children became victims of Nazi propaganda, culture and ideology. The Hitler *Jugend* for boys had been in existence since 1926, under the direction of Kurt Gruber, who on 19 and 20 August 1927, led 300 Hitler Youths in a march at the Nuremberg Rally, earning himself a special commendation from Hitler. It was, however, not until Hitler gained power in the mid-1930s that the female equivalent to the male Hitler Youth – the *Bund Deutscher Madel* would come into existence. The only other country that could boast a strong and regimented fascist youth movement at the time was Germany's ally, Italy.

The Italian equivalent to the Hitler Youth and BDM was the *Opera Nazionale Balilla* Organization (ONB). It is interesting to note that Italy's fascist youth organization chose not to educate its children, particularly females, to the levels of political awareness that existed within the Hitler Youth. Italian society would also have never tolerated the militarization of its children and young people. The Italian fascist youth organization was more symbolic of Italy's support for Nazi Germany than an active or aggressive political force.

The uniform worn by girls of the German BDM and the Italian ONB were of a similar pattern, which does reaffirm to some extent that Italian fascist dictator Benito Mussolini created the ONB purely out of fascist uniformity, and not through any political or social necessity. That said, there was, however, in fascist Italy at the time, substantial acts of violence aimed at minority groups such as blacks and gypsies. The hatred of anything Jewish was encouraged and endorsed by Mussolini.

In reality, though, fascism and war had no place in the hearts of the Italian people, so Italy's subsequent costly alliance with Nazi Germany was to be short lived. Mussolini was later executed and his body strung up at an Esso petrol station in the Piazzale Loreto in Milan, where mobs of people kicked and punched his corpse. It was a violent and undignified end for the man many German girls referred to as 'Hitler's Clown'.

The German youth of the 1930s already had a strong identity of its own, much like the modern youth society of today. Yet, owing to the strict family values of the day, German youth, particularly girls, were both very confined and repressed. Hitler understood the vital role that youth plays within a society, and his Third Reich would be no exception. He also understood, more than most, that the ethic in which the youth form the foundation of every society, both old and modern, allows each society to define the role of its youth via its own individual sets of rules and its cultural teachings.

The youth, especially of the feminine gender, were to prove an important factor within the social fabric of Hitler's new Germany. It was the female that would bear the biological burden of the Nazi Aryan-race philosophy, though in the beginning much of what Hitler was offering girls and young women in Germany appeared attractive.

Young girls were soon to find themselves under pressure to ensure that they became, in every sense, the embodiment of Aryan culture. That said, one must also note that the issue of male supremacy and domination over females in Hitler's Third Reich was very clear, and therefore the standing of young males and men as masters within the Third Reich was never questionable.

Hitler was obsessed with young girls and women, yet the thought of women working as equals with males in politics he found unacceptable. This is reflected in the fact that, before the Nazis came to power, women had the vote and there were thirty female MPs. When the Nazis came to power in 1933, they threw out all of the women MPs. They were also removed from clinical practices, positions within the civil service and the teaching profession. They were also banned from law courts as judges, lawyers and even jurors.

Hitler was of the opinion that women were unable to think logically or reason objectively, since they allowed themselves to be ruled only by their emotions. Yet for most women, particularly young girls, it can be said that the Nazis had particularly sinister intentions in the way that they were to form at least one half of the gene pool of the Aryan Race – they were to be Hitler's biological Nazis.

Married women were supposed to fulfil their role as child-bearers and wives, and not have jobs. Childless women were labelled traitors, while mothers of large families were given certain financial benefits and presented with a variety of awards. A German woman giving birth to her sixth child could earn herself tea and cakes with Hitler himself, as a reward for procurement of children for the state.

Upon reflection, it is strange to think that, even after all the prejudice orchestrated by Hitler and the Nazis towards their womenfolk, they would remain loyal. By the time Hitler's life finally reached its insane conclusion, many young girls and women would be lying dead or wounded in the ruins of such cities as Aachen and Berlin, after fighting in a vain bid to save the Third Reich, whose leaders looked upon them as no more than second-class citizens who were only fit for motherhood.

In creating his youth movement, Hitler viewed himself as the architect of a new generation of German boys and girls, from the very young to those in their teens. During the mid-1930s, Hitler defiantly crowed to the outside world the pride that he had for his Hitler Youth generation: 'The youth who graduate from my academies will terrify the world.'

In later years, those very words would receive their prophetic justification.

Chapter Two

Mitte Girls and the Jung Madel

It is early morning in the *Mitte* borough of Berlin, the only sounds being those emanating from the nearby factories and workhouses. A member of the local district *Nationalsozialistische Deutsche Arbeiterpartei*, or National Socialist German Workers Party (NSDAP) is busy walking the streets, pausing every so often to paste posters at suitable vantage points along the way. By the time the children leave their homes for the short walk to school, the *Mitte* is bustling with life. Men cycling home from their 'graveyard' shifts, while others mill around the streets, smoking and talking amongst themselves, before disappearing inside their homes.

On the way to school, a group of girls, aged from nine to eleven, stop to look at one of the brightly coloured posters pasted on a board at the end of their street. The poster depicts a broadly smiling girl in uniform, and the poster is emblazoned with the words: 'All ten-year-olds join the Hitler Youth!' For some, the allure of the image of the smiling girl on the poster is just too much. The girls gather around and gaze at the poster. They talk about becoming Hitler Youths in the twin organizations of the league of German girls. Not wishing to receive a tongue-lashing for being late for school, they reluctantly walk away and continue their journey. The poster and its contents, however, would be on their minds for the remainder of the day. On their way home, they would look at it again, absorbing the image of the smiling girl. For some, she personified everything that they could never imagine themselves being.

The *Mitte* girls did not have popstar icons with which to identify or create an identity for themselves. Instead, via his propaganda, Dr Goebbels offered them a chance to become servants of the Reich and Hitler. In turn, they would be offered a nice uniform to wear, trips to summer camp, and the chance to become a part of what was the new prosperity of German society.

The *Mitte* girls had seen the posters many times before when they had first appeared on the streets in the mid to late 1930s, after the female Hitler youth organization first came into existence in its lesser form, the Hitler Youth for boys having been founded earlier in 1926. Now, however, the girls had come of age. They had done so on a tidal wave of national euphoria, so had begun to question their own individual identities and status within their predominantly male-dominated community. As a ten-year-old, Anita Von Schoener remembers the attraction which the *Jung Madel* had on young German girls:

> It's like when girls these days reach the ages of between nine and ten years old, all that they want to do is listen to their favourite pop stars and their music. They also become aware of their bodies and begin to show an interest in boys. We did not have pop stars or pop music, although I learned to play the piano, and as for boys, we were never allowed to really mix with boys in the way that girls do today.
>
> Girls were expected to take on the responsibilities of housewives at an early age and Nazi-sympathising parents expected that of us. Time was divided between going to school, coming home and helping our mothers; if we had time we would play with our friends.
>
> My parents supported Hitler and the reforms that the Nazi Party began to implement in 1933. I had seen the propaganda posters that called for all ten-year-old girls to join the Hitler Youth. They were designed to appear attractive, even to those who had no political understanding or loyalty. I had no problems joining the *Jung Madel*, though I had to firstly fill in a kind of application form. I was required to give details on my family history such as names of my parents, grandparents and great grandparents, also stating their religious beliefs. The form was then handed to the authorities who contacted me some two to three weeks later, if I remember correctly. My parents were not at all apprehensive about it and told me it was my duty, and that it would do me some good, so they did not mind. There were many benefits with joining, one of which was the sense of pride in belonging and being representative of a nation where massive changes were taking place, and a nation that was restoring its sense of pride, which had been taken away by those who had beaten Germany in World War One. The nice uniform that we were given was only very slightly different from the traditional one worn by schoolgirls at the time. We could go out into the countryside and forests on camp, which is one of the main reasons I joined, I wanted to have fun, have adventure in life. Of course, there were certain sets of rules and criteria governing who could join, and Jewish girls were excluded. Every pure German girl was expected to join and if you didn't, then questions would be asked as to why.

The *Deutsche Jung Madel* was an organization for girls between the ages of ten to fourteen. Many, however, would already have been indoctrinated into the Hitler Youth membership system via the organization called the *Jungvolk*, or Young People. The *Jungvolk* catered for the very young child, from the age of six up.

Both the *Jung Madel,* and its senior equivalent, the *Bund Deutscher Madel* (The League of German Girls) for girls aged fourteen to eighteen, can trace their origins to 1930 when both organizations were founded. Although, in theory, these organizations were not compulsory in the early years, by December 1936, the Hitler Youth law made it compulsory for both males and females to join their respective youth organization. From the age of ten, they would remain with their organization until aged eighteen, when they would be called on to perform compulsory labour service for up to twelve months with the *Reichsarbeitsdienst der weiblichen Jugend* RADwfJ, the female youth branch of the Reich Labour Service.

For this critical period of study, the leaders of the German youth organizations for girls and young women included Baldur von Schirach, Artur Axmann (Schirach's successor), and Gertrud Scholtz-Klink.

Gertrud Scholtz-Klink was appointed Reich Women's Leader in 1933. Her first itinerary was to promote male superiority and dominance over the female and the importance of child bearing. Like Hitler, she was a highly gifted orator. As the wife of a high-ranking SS officer, she was feared by many of the young girls whom she often addressed. Once away from the spotlight, she was described as arrogant and spiteful. She once confided to one senior BDM girl leader – who requested that her name not be revealed – during a debate on male bullying and domineering, 'What woman could possibly object or not want to be forcibly taken by her man. If she is honest then every woman enjoys that.'

In one of her speeches she said 'The mission of the woman is to minister in the home and in her profession to the needs of life from the first to last moment of man's existence.'

Later in July 1934, she was promoted as head of the women's bureau in the *Deutsche Arbeitsfront,* or German Labour Front. Her responsibility was to persuade women to work for the good of the Nazi government. In another one of her speeches in 1938, she argued that 'The German woman must work and work, physically and mentally, and she must renounce all luxury and pleasure.' Klink was as politically insane a monster as Hitler. She would later achieve notoriety for being the driving force behind the organizing of young girls and women into home militia or localized combat units, which would see action during the closing stages of the Second World War, particularly against Russian forces.

Baldur von Schirach was a loyal and fanatical Nazi who had first joined the NSDAP in 1925 at the age of eighteen, when it was just a mere fledgling movement. Von Schirach held various appointments within Nazi youth organizations. By June 1933, with Hitler's government in power, he was appointed Reich Youth leader, a position he held until 1940, when he was appointed Reich Governor (*Reichsstatthalter*) of the *Reichsgau Wien* (administrative division of Vienna). Artur Axmann took over his position as Hitler Youth leader.

Von Schirach had already been appointed Nazi youth leader on 30 October 1931, and had gained immense experience in the skills required to influence and convince Germany's youth in the Nazi ideology. In doing so, he was responsible for the converting of students to National Socialism. He must therefore bear a major portion of the blame for the crimes committed in the Second World War by elements of the German armed forces. In this task, he showed an unbending loyalty and enthusiasm.

Under von Schirach's direction, the *Jung Madel* flourished, further fuelled by Goebbels's clever propaganda. There were very few girls who could escape the appeal of the *Jung Madel*. Further pressure was applied through the education system, where even teachers encouraged girls to join. Kirsten Eckermann explains:

There were certain teachers at our school who suddenly disappeared over night, being replaced by new teachers. The old teachers and some with Jewish ancestry who we had come to like and respect in our everyday lives had gone because they did not agree with the Nazis, and as a result they were basically driven out of their professions and many had to leave Germany, though some of them returned after the war. The new teachers would describe the old ones as 'treacherous old leeches not fit to teach pigs!' Hitler wanted no connections at all with what he termed as the 'old Germany' and its defeatist attitudes so many of our schools had new teachers. The new teachers, as we called them, were Nazis and went to great lengths to inform us of what the Nazis and the Hitler Youth could offer us as young Germans. What we were told seemed too good to be true as children of the *Mitte* borough who had very little. We were told that we could go on summer camp and that we would have a nice uniform to wear on important Nazi Party days and that we would learn many things which would be beneficial to us as adults.

We were shown pictures of the *Jung Madel* girls and their activities, we were taught a little on how to march and we were also told that special awards would be given to those who worked hard. Everything in the classroom began to change when Hitler gained power, even the way that we greeted our teachers upon arriving at school each morning. We were told that from now on we must greet all of our teachers by raising our right arm and saying 'Heil Hitler'.

A huge red flag with a Swastika in its centre section hung at the side of the room behind the teacher's desk. This seemed rather funny to most of us and we did not really understand what it was all about. Though I can remember going home one afternoon with the other girls eager to become members of the Hitler Youth for young girls, I very much wanted to become a *Jung Madel*. We asked ourselves all of the usual questions like, 'what will our parents think about it?' We were very excited by it all and the need to feel like an adult that came with being a Hitler Youth was something I still find difficult to describe.

Excitedly, Kirsten and her friends made their way home from school to ask their parents about joining the Hitler Youth. The reaction from their parents would be mixed. Kirsten Eckermann:

When I arrived home my mother was always there to greet me and on this one particular afternoon I stood up straight as if coming to attention, clicked my feet together, thrust up my right arm and shouted 'Heil Hitler!' My mother, visibly shocked, grabbed my arm and bundled me inside the house and began to ask me questions.

'Did you have to do that at school today?' And then when I explained she said 'oh' and then remained very quiet for the rest of the afternoon, in fact she seemed troubled which was unusual. Nazism had entered the classroom and she may have thought that all of that saluting was not really necessary or perhaps too political for a young girl – I don't really know.

As for my joining the Hitler Youth, my mother then said that it must be discussed with Father. The father always made the decisions in the household and that was the way things were. When my father arrived home much later and Mother gave him his dinner, she mentioned what I had asked her earlier about joining the Hitler Youth. My father, though supportive of the National Socialists, did not believe that young girls should be so politically motivated. Father told me to leave the room while he and mother talked. But I think he knew deep down what was coming, besides those parents who forbade their children membership into the Hitler Youth were looked upon as non-conformists or Anti-Nazi, and many had been visited by Nazi Party officials. These officials often threatened non-conforming parents of the consequences of their offspring not joining the Hitler Youth. So, in the preceding days my membership was submitted, but as a *Mitte* girl this was more or less expected though clearly some of the other girls had problems particularly with their fathers. We all possessed a great respect for our fathers and never dared argue or question their decisions; we only spoke when spoken to at times. I know girls who were beaten badly by their strict fathers. You had to be very careful not to adopt too much attitude upon becoming a *Jung Madel*, as in the privacy of the house Hitler did not rule, our fathers did and this was made perfectly clear to me by my father. Of course there were some girls who threatened to tell the authorities of their parents. The whole system encouraged you to inform on non-compliance.

For those girls entering the ranks of the *Jung Madel*, there were certain important preconditions of membership. The first and most important condition was that the female in question had to be a 'pure German'. Those of Jewish and other ethnic origin were classed as wholly unsuitable for the Hitler Youth and were condemned to their own 'racial sewer'. This was made clear within the classroom, and of course through much of the Nazi youth-propaganda material of the time. Vetting procedures were impossible to avoid. The applicants' family records were carefully scrutinized by the local Nazi authority who ensured that any German girl, or boy, with any non-pure (mixed race) or Jewish ancestry, was quickly eliminated from the membership programme. Birth certificates and family records of the applicant's grandparents and other relatives were also carefully checked.

The paramount importance of mental and physical health to the Third Reich meant that a programme of very thorough medical and physical inspection had to be devised to ensure that only the finest physical and mental specimens emerged as students for the *Jung Madel*. Anita von Schoener recalls her thorough medical inspection and inception into the *Jung Madel*:

An application had to be submitted and you could not hope to join the *Jung Madel* until the local authorities had verified all of the relevant information. The papers contained names and dates of birth of all family members, the authorities wanted to ensure that only German girls joined the Hitler Youth. Our family records going back for two generations were examined closely by officials of the local NSDAP authority. It was strange, as only a short period of time later I was notified to attend a medical examination to ascertain my fitness for the Hitler Youth. It was not a very pleasant experience at all and I have not ever mentioned it in a book or publication before. The medical inspection lasted some time and a doctor who wore one of those white surgical masks and his nurse gave me a very detailed examination.

When I entered the examination room, the first part of the inspection was concerned with eyes, hair, teeth and ears. Notes were made of my hair and eye colour and condition of teeth. I also noticed that my birth records were also present and the doctor had obviously been examining these documents. The doctor then asked me to remove my clothing. I did not feel comfortable at all about this and was embarrassed to take my clothing off in front of a man, but the nurse reassured me in quite a firm manner that everything would be all right, and that it was just an examination and I should not be afraid. The nurse carefully took my clothing and folded it neatly and placed it on a chair. Once I had removed all of my clothing including underwear the real examination began.

I was firstly asked to stand up as straight as I could with my chin up so as the doctor could take a measurement of my height. He then measured my chest, shoulders, neck, head, waist and thighs, all the time dictating notes to the nurse who scribbled the information down onto a form attached to a clipboard. The doctor also examined very carefully my skin and looked for such blemishes as birthmarks and moles and any signs of scar tissue.

After that he said 'very good' and then asked me to assume different gymnastic positions, some on the floor and some standing up. He then asked me to get up onto the examination table where I had to lie down. The doctor leaned over me and looked deep into my eyes with an instrument that looked like a pen that shone light into my eyes as he examined them. After returning the instrument to its box he then began to examine my breasts with both of his hands, which made me flinch and feel very uncomfortable – again the nurse firmly asked me to lie still and co-operate with the doctor. The doctor examined my breasts in great detail even though there was very little to examine, as I was only just ten years of age. The nurse then said to me, 'Anita, you must now raise your legs up so the doctor can examine you down below as this is very important. Please do not worry and lie still; all of the girls will be having the same'.

As she said those words the doctor was putting on some of those tight-fitting surgical-type gloves. My heart started to pound in my chest and I think both the doctor and nurse could sense how uncomfortable I felt. As instructed, I raised my knees and the nurse gently parted my legs so I was laying with my legs open while the doctor examined my private parts. I could feel the doctor insert a gloved finger, he then pushed his finger in deeper and it started to hurt, and I cried out. He then stopped and walked over to a basin where he removed and disposed of the gloves and rinsed his hands.

He then picked up the clipboard and wrote down further notes. Then the doctor slipped on another pair of those horrible rubberized gloves and I wondered what he was going to do to me next. The nurse instructed me again to open my legs and pushed them apart at the knees with her hands.

'What are you doing?' I asked.

The nurse replied, 'Please do as we ask and the examination will be over very quickly'.

The doctor inserted a finger into my back passage and began feeling around. I complained again that he was hurting me and the nurse got angry with me. When he finished he again removed the gloves and said, 'Very good, you are perfect and very healthy.'

While he was writing down the notes, the nurse checked my hands and feet and then told me I could now dress again. Once dressed the doctor said to me, 'Miss von Schoener, you are physically fine and have passed my medical inspection. A report of the medical inspection will be retained on file for the authorities' reference'.

He then smiled and said, 'You are a special child, but do you understand why? Well, you can go now, I am sure you will be a very good German maiden and have lots of German children as our Führer requires of you.'

It struck me as being strange, as I had not even thought about the future or what I had wanted to achieve in life; children especially was something I had never considered as I had only just begun to register certain changes of a physical nature, and certainly did not wish to exploit them at that time.

Outside of the makeshift examination room there was a long line of girls who were standing talking excitedly amongst themselves. As I came out they asked me what it was like and what would happen in there. I must have looked a little pale and they guessed it was not going to be just a straightforward 'flea check'. It occurred to me much later why the doctor called me a special child: I was tall, blonde, and blue-eyed, with milk-white skin – I was a good example of the Aryan female. I later discovered that so called doctor was on the payroll of the SS; that was what I was later told. He and his nurse were both SS and to this day I still have no understanding of what they did that day or why.

It is certainly evident in many cases that sometimes painful gynaecological examinations were carried out on pre-pubescent young girls prior to their entry into the *Jung Madel*, especially young, blonde girls with blue eyes. The concept of the Aryan race was already something that the Third Reich had begun to realistically consider. There is reason to believe in some cases that these examinations were also conducted on one in four of the pre-pubescent subjects, in a kind of quality-control approach, as not all received the genital examination, where in many cases fingers were inserted into their vaginas and rectal passages. Anita von Schoener was convinced that the doctor who had examined her had been someone connected with the SS, and that the purpose behind the vaginal examination, in particular, was to ensure that her hymen was intact and to compare her results with the girls of non-Aryan origin.

Anita viewed the gynaecological examination as one that had been totally unnecessary:

I was only just ten years old for God's sake and it would have been totally absurd in every respect for that doctor to have reasoned that I may have lost my virginity in any way. These of course were all post-war theories given to me by American and British physicians who asked me personally about the membership process and the medical examinations performed. Looking back though, it is now quite easy to see why the vaginal examinations were conducted as we were to form the basis of Hitler's breeding experiments and the mothers of his 'Master Race' dream. We later learned much about the *Lebensborn* or Fountain of Life project, and it was very obvious that we Aryan girls were the chosen subjects for this programme. Whether we liked it or not the state was going to choose for us the German men who were going to make us pregnant in order to preserve and continue the very finest of the German race. Really, we had no future if you think about it and we were just to be used to produce offspring.

For the girls who had been cleared to join and had passed their medical examination and were fit for enrolment within the *Jung Madel*, the ordeal was not over. At school a simple enrolment ceremony would be conducted. The student wearing the traditional German school uniform would stand next to the flag bearing the Swastika and swear an oath to Adolf Hitler. Usually the student repeated the words after her teacher read them out, all the time with her right arm raised in the Nazi salute. Once the enrolment ceremony had been conducted, the student was then given her uniform that consisted of a white blouse with black tie, navy-blue skirt and brown jacket, and a Hitler Youth membership badge. The badge was a small metal, diamond-shaped pin with a silver-backed, central, black-Swastika emblem on a red and white enamelled background. The badge could be worn either on the girl's blouse or jacket lapel. Girls had to wear shoes or sandals with white socks, though a pair of black, leather, military-style boots was also supplied. The student would have to keep her uniform and footwear in good condition at all times, and wear her uniform at all important Nazi Party events.

For the girls who joined the *Jung Madel*, there lay ahead a strict regime of hard physical exercise and political commitment which served to hone them to Nazified perfection. This would set them aside from the youth of other countries and cultures around the world. To emphasize the physical prowess and sheer perfection of the young female Hitler Youths, the *Jung Madel*, like its sister organization the BDM, had squads of young girl athletes who competed in many sporting tournaments all over the world during the years before the outbreak of the Second World War. At the Youth Olympiad held in Tokyo in July 1939, a young girl named Hanna Butthinghaus won the *ballwurfwettkampf* (medicine-ball throwing event) for Germany. Miss

Butthinghaus, a Berlin schoolgirl, was pretty, with dark hair and large brown eyes. The German photographer Schirner photographed her at the event holding a medicine ball, her white sports vest emblazoned with the Swastika.

The young girls' school education would be greatly supplemented by the teachings of the *Jung Madel*. The young girls had to study Hitler's *Mein Kampf.* They were frequently expected to recall passages and to explain their interpretations of the content.

Much emphasis was placed on Nazi ideology, culture and ethos, and, of course, the role of the female in Third Reich society. The teachers would go to great lengths to ensure that their pupils fully understood what they were being taught. To further enhance the appeal of the *Jung Madel*, students were treated to camping excursions, the most popular of which were based in Grunewald Forest with its adjacent lakes and sandy beaches. Along with the usual exercise routines that were often the prelude to the daily events, the girls were taken on hiking trips into the woods, where they carried their banners and sang patriotic songs. They also learned to do many things that only boys had previously been allowed to do. In a sense, the *Jung Madel* was giving its female students a taste of equality, while at the same time a sense of comradeship, in much the same way as a military regiment.

Girls were given detailed instruction on how to cook and prepare different kinds of foods. They were expected to find and cut wood for their fires, and take turns cooking on their camping trips. Anita von Schoener:

> I remember the first time I ever went to one of the summer camps at Grunewald Forest as a *Jung Madel*. It was the first time that I had ever been away from home and my mother and father. It was also the first time that I had ever journeyed on a train and I was just so overwhelmed by it all. So many emotions tore through me, I was crying with sadness and yet was overcome with happiness too. My mother and father could never have taken me to the countryside, as we just did not have the money or the means to do those things. Later, however, the Nazi Party ensured that even poor families received financial subsidies so as they could have proper holidays.
>
> I think every one of the '*Mitte*' girls felt exactly the same way. The journey on the train was spectacular to me as all of the different scenery lazily passed by with the gentle rocking of the train. We girls spent most of our time hanging out of the windows flailing our arms in the warm wind and shouting out to people we saw on the way. 'Heil Hitler!' we would cry and the people would wave

back at us. We felt like different girls in our crisp uniforms and polished boots, and I found the countryside landscape breathtaking as the factories with their tall, blackened chimney stacks slowly disappeared, giving way to open fields, rivers and woodland. The train stopped at a station and we were surrounded by woodland. We all disembarked from the train and lined up as we had been taught. Two *Jung Madel* leaders or *Jungmadelgruppenführerin* as they were known, then took a roll call to ensure all of the girls were present and that no one had been left on the train. Once they were satisfied that we were all there we moved off on the short hike to the summer camp, which was around a mile from where the train station was. Upon arrival at the camp, we formed into a line in front of a flagpole and the leaders raised a flag bearing the Swastika. This was one of the first things we had to do upon arrival at camp.

Afterwards our tents had to be arranged and a fire was lit and a meal prepared. The meal nearly always consisted of German sausages that we loved. We girls could talk amongst ourselves until we had to retire to our tents, or billet, as the English people call them and prepare for bed. We were not permitted to be up late into the evenings and often had to be in bed by 8.00pm, our teachers and leaders insisting that sleep was vital for mental sharpness.

On the first morning we were awoken at between 7.00 and 8.00 am by the leaders, and after washing and changing into our gym kit we had to exercise outside the tents for half-an-hour, sometimes a little longer. Afterwards we were taken down to a small river where the water was fairly shallow. We removed our clothing and jumped in, splashing one another and messing around; it was wonderful even if a little chilly during the early dawn. After being instructed to leave the water we dried ourselves and often only put clothes on again once back at camp. Once at camp, we dressed into our proper uniforms and did our hair – usually we did this amongst ourselves.

Once ready, we had breakfast that usually came fresh from the local farms in the area, as we often collected our own supplies as part of the activities. When the day began, it was a mixture of basic survival skills, like how to make a fire and how to shelter from bad weather and things, and also what foods were available in the woods. We also did climbing and orienteering, which was very enjoyable to us. In fact we learned many new skills that put us on equal terms with the boys, and we were then able to apply the new skills we learned back home into our everyday lives. One thing I did find unpleasant was when a rabbit had been snared in one of our wire traps that we had been taught to make. Our group leader grabbed the rabbit quickly by its back legs and it began to shriek, and then she delivered it a heavy blow with a short club to the base of its neck. I had never before seen a wild rabbit in the flesh, let alone seen one trapped and killed. It was a pretty little thing and I didn't like it at all what was happening. After a few convulsing spasms and some passing of urine the rabbit was still. Katharina, our group leader, laid it down onto the ground and we could see the fleas coming out of the dead rabbit's earthy-brown fur, and one of the girls said, 'Errr, I think I am going to be sick.'

I was amazed at it and couldn't help stroking it, but the teacher ordered us to move away quickly as the fleas might jump onto us.

'You must always wait until the rabbit is cold before you can handle it,' were her words of wisdom.

From a short distance she then showed us how to skin and prepare the rabbit for cooking, tossing its entrails into nearby bushes. We all stood watching in disbelief with our hands over our mouths, we all felt sick. The rabbit, along with others that had been snared that day, were later cooked with some vegetables in a kind of a stew. When it was served, many of us just poked at it, afraid to eat the rabbit, though some stern words from our leader soon made us try it. I have to admit it was a meal that I enjoyed thoroughly, and we had bread with it too. In fact, I had not eaten that well in a long time, and I felt so much fitter and stronger on my return home to the *Mitte*.

To many of the girls, the *Jung Madel* became a kind of family. It was an organization specifically designed to function in much the same way as a large family. The Nazis were anxious, as with the boys, to detach the young girls as much as possible from their parents and elders. The Nazis held the view that their elders still retained much of the predominantly old and worthless German attitudes, which could not be tolerated within Germany's Hitler Youth. There was a kind of pecking order that all the girls would respect and adhere to at all times.

A system of rank was devised, which operated in much the same way as Germany's military forces. Under von Schirach's direction, the *Jung Madel* was arranged into squads, platoons and companies. Each company was within a territorial formation based upon a system referred to as the *gau*. The *gau* was a term used for the territorial and administrative divisions of Germany for the purposes of the Nazi Party. There were two *gau*: the *untergau* and the *obergau*, lower and upper respectively. All were organized into the *Gauverband* (Association of *Gau*) and were subject to the authority of the *Reichsjugendführung* (Reich Youth Leadership). All affairs relating to the BDM fell under the scrutiny of the *Reichsreferentin*-BDM or official in charge of the BDM, and *Jung Madel-Untergauführerin* respectively. Within the embrace of the *Jung Madel* individuals were encouraged to strive toward proficiency within the organization and earn medallions and awards along the way. The *Jung Madel* rank system was as follows:

Jungmadel
Jungmadelschaftsführerin
JM-*Scharführerin*
JM-*Gruppenführerin*
JM-*Ringführerin*
JM-*Untergauführerin*

The *Jung Madel* motto was much the same as that adopted by the *Bund Deutscher Madel*: 'Be faithful, be pure, be German'.

Baldur von Schirach quoted to the girls in one of his patriotic speeches: 'We do not need intellectual leaders who create new ideas, because the superimposing leader of all desires of youth is Adolf Hitler'.

Dora Brunninghausen, another ten-year-old who joined the *Jung Madel* in 1933, admits that she came to value the *Jung Madel* more than her own family as time went by:

> Having come from a *'Mitte'* family, I viewed the Hitler Youth as a kind of deliverance if you like. In our house the standing of females was pretty much clear. I loved yet resented my older brother who had joined the Hitler Youth (for boys) before me. He was always treated differently, especially by our father. Mother and me were bullied to a certain extent and I was made to feel worthless at times as if I had no role. I grew tired and resentful of my father and felt intimidated around him. Fathers back then were sometimes very hard on their daughters and my father was very strict. If I did anything wrong most times it was the father who did the hitting. I used to get hit with a leather belt and that would really hurt. I could not wait for the times when I went away with the *Jung Madel*.

Things were different with them, and we girls respected and had a common bond with one another, something which lacked severely in our home lives. I still had a love for my father but it was not a deep love, not like it should have been.

In 1933, Germany was still six years away from another world war. The years prior to the outbreak of war in 1939 were considered by many German girls as some of the best years of their lives. For the *Jung Madels*, their entry into the world of Adolf Hitler and his politics was just the beginning of what was to be a fantastic rollercoaster ride of summer camps, better nutrition, new friendships, and the chance to parade before the world in some of the biggest political rallies ever staged. At the same time, their attitudes were being altered to the ways of Nazism and they began to view the world around themselves very differently. The *Mitte* girls had come of age, and, through the dark world that was now absorbing them, they sought their place in Hitler's Third Reich. Here, for once, they could escape from their dull and almost Georgian lifestyles and be made to feel a part of something worthwhile and special. Many, however, were just too young and a little too naïve to see the danger signs.

Chapter Three

Sugar on the Dog Shit

The education formulae devised for ten to fourteen-year-old girls in Nazi Germany, was in total contrast to that of the pre-Hitler era. Huge changes had taken place within the entire education system. Hitler's ever-present suspicion and paranoia of the old generation led him to rid Germany's schools of many of the old and established teachers, whom he considered as unfit to teach his new Hitler Youth generation.

There were very few actual textbooks in German schools, and the Nazi schools did not use textbooks at all. In fact, the only real textbook that many young Germans girls and boys owned was Adolf Hitler's *Mein Kampf.* There was an official teachers' handbook titled *Education and Instruction, Official Publication of the Reich and Prussian Ministry of Knowledge, Education, and National Culture.* This manual was the work of Dr Bernard Rust. It outlined a schedule emphasizing primarily physical education, including only those of an academic nature that were viewed as an important factor in the creation of a 'good Nazi'.

The Nazi education curriculum included Nazi versions of German history, ideology, art and eugenics. A proportion of the mathematical subjects taught had military applications. For example, some mathematical problems involved the calculation of bomb-fall, and munitions trajectory and delivery.

As mentioned in the previous chapter, many of the old teachers had been replaced by those who were fanatical Nazis, and therefore familiar with the doctrine, and its principles and ideals, especially where the youth were concerned. When war broke out in later years, the changing situation of both social and geographical natures that came with it were also absorbed into the education system. For example, firstly Russia was regarded as an enemy of the German nation, and then an ally when Hitler and Stalin entered into a non-aggression pact early in the war. This was in reality a ploy devised to stall possible Russian intervention while Hitler achieved his early territorial objectives in Western Europe. This precariously short peace was soon shattered by Hitler's attack on Russia when Operation Barbarossa was launched in 1941. Russia was then once again defined as the enemy.

Where ten-year-old *Jung Madel* girls were concerned, it was made clear as to what the Nazi regime expected of them. Girls were not permitted to wear any nail varnish on their fingernails or makeup on their faces. They were expected to grow their hair long when it would then be put into plaits or a bun. Girls were educated within a single-sex environment, under the motto 'Church, Children and Cooking'.

The seeking of normal interaction or contact with members of the opposite sex, other than the playing of games if parents permitted it in the streets where young boys joined in, was spurned. This is something that affected their sexual attitudes later in their adolescence, especially where relationships with males were concerned.

Foreign languages were no longer taught in schools, though English was a unique exception in the early years of the Nazi education curriculum, as being perhaps the only 'foreign language' allowed to be taught in schools in Germany. Later, English too was omitted in favour of a total commitment to only German being spoken in the Reich.

Sadly, many of the subjects taught, including that of science, was selective. For example, only science that could be applied to both cooking and childcare was considered acceptable to be taught to girls. The subjects of primary importance to the Nazis where young girls were concerned, were those of physical fitness, health and the ability to produce children. Cleanliness was also a vitally important subject, with great emphasis placed upon the personal hygiene of the individual. These would be the only necessary attributes required for German girls in Hitler's Third Reich, and consequently, their education deviated very little from that required by the state.

Tremendous efforts were put into the physical-exercise programmes that encompassed nearly every conceivable form of physical activity, including naked dancing. Regular health checks were conducted, and parents were warned that their daughters must have the absolute minimum of eight hours' sleep each night. The German maiden had to be beautiful, supple, radiant and strong, yet at the same time athletically graceful.

Perhaps the saddest thing of all was the government-teacher conspiracy that ensured a degree of illiteracy was maintained within the female population, in an attempt to prevent the girls from having any forms of serious career opportunity later in life. As a result of this abuse of the education system, many girls could only ever hope to perform menial tasks, until required to leave work to marry and produce children. Thankfully, after the war the implementation of the Allied re-education programme saved many young German girls, who then pursued careers as doctors, scientists, politicians and schoolteachers.

Jung Madel meeting sessions were held on weekday evenings and weekends – the schedule deliberately prevented many of the young girls from completing homework set by their schools. Important Nazis were often present at these meetings to give lectures on National Socialism and answer questions on Hitler, who, in every case, was spoken of as some kind of hero of the German people. Education for young girls in Hitler's Germany was deliberately narrow and directionless. Hitler often made comments that highlighted his general loathing for female success. On one occasion, Hitler said, 'The female should be beautiful, caring, sweet and very, very stupid.'

Dora Brunninghausen reflects upon her education as a ten-year-old in Nazi Germany:

Of course we had been introduced to politics at an earlier age, as Hitler's name was everywhere, especially during the years just prior to his seizure of power in Germany. In Berlin you couldn't escape Hitler because he was everywhere you looked, on posters, in school and sometimes at home. At school all of our concepts and thoughts that we had all become accustomed to had to be adjusted. We had not been born as Nazis, so the Nazis had to convert us within school via its new education system. Making the transition was not that difficult at all, as it never is with young children. Children are more ready and able to deal with changes than are adults.

I remember vividly how in class we talked about what was termed the 'Jewish Problem' and how it would be solved by forcing the Jews out of Germany. The teachers reasoned that Jews were not permissible to German society as they did not contribute to its social fabric, besides the teachers, especially the ones who taught science, referred to Jews as a vastly impure, greedy and unworthy race; 'a race of vermin' one called them.

The hatred Hitler possessed for anything Jewish was reflected directly into the classroom. In 1933 there were no books by Jewish authors in school and Jewish art was also excluded. Germany was becoming a dangerous place for Jews, and Jews were always ridiculed in the classroom. The teachers often abused them and paid little to no attention to them or their work, and certainly did not attempt to help them in any way. It was clear that they were not wanted. While one by one the Jewish girls were ostracized, the education became predominantly more racist in its content. There was frequent violence in the playground and German girls were encouraged to fight the Jewish girls. Many would leave school battered and bruised, until their parents withdrew them altogether. We were also taught about the menace of Slavs and Gypsies. We also had to study Hitler's '*Mein Kampf*' in and outside of school. We would be questioned by our teachers and expected to answer and put forward our explanations.

As ten-year-olds, we also had to study what they call Home Economics these days. This subject dealt with needlecraft, cooking and keeping the home. It was a most important subject second to that of physical education. I remember that our physical exercise often took place inside in the gymnasium, as there was a great deal of equipment in there for us to develop our bodily strength. The usual kit consisted of a pair of black shorts, a white sports vest, and we often had to go bare footed. We would firstly have to warm our muscles and perform stretching routines, and the teacher would come around us all one by one to ensure we had done this properly. I did not really like the physical exercise, but we were told this was important for us, as we had to develop and strengthen our bodies in preparation for motherhood and for bearing healthy children. When we were outside on the sports field, we participated in many strength-developing team games that involved medicine balls and throwing. As a ten-year-old though, the thought of having babies horrified me. I did not want to have any babies, in fact I was not sure what I wanted to do in life. But everything came down to preparing for children and cooking and housekeeping and things, it was something we were constantly reminded of.

Helga Stroh, another young girl who joined the *Jung Madel*, remembers the stories that they were told both at school and with the *Jung Madel*, stories which seemed to promote and glorify warfare. She recalls one particular story:

They used to read us stories, many of which it seemed were preparing us for war. One such story still remains very clear in my mind. A group of soldiers are advancing into enemy held territory. The path they are taking leads them through a swamp. It is nighttime, pitch black and everyone has been ordered to remain completely silent.

Suddenly one of the soldiers falls and is in danger of drowning. None of his comrades notice his predicament. Rather than shout for help and put his comrades' lives in danger, he buries his face in the water and slowly drowns himself. It was a reflection of the kind of loyalty that the Third Reich required of everyone, even small girls.

Anita von Schoener has some relatively happy memories from her school days:

I grew up and associated with most of the girls at my school, many became members of the *Jung Madel*. When we were at normal school all we talked about was the next *Jung Madel* meeting, and I always looked forward to putting on my uniform and going to the meetings that took place after normal school twice a week.

I didn't care too much about my home studies or homework if you like, and I don't remember ever being told off for not doing it. Though my parents tried hard to ensure I did homework, the teachers at school were not too strict about it, I suppose now we understand why that was.

Most of us eagerly absorbed what we were being taught and we were sometimes shown films about Adolf Hitler's life and how he had saved our nation from total economic collapse. We believed in everything we were taught passionately and looked upon Hitler as a kind of god, as we knew our parents had suffered hardships like not being able to work at times. Such things were blamed entirely on the old regime through Hitler's 'new history' that blamed everything else for Germany's troubles. In school, much of the truth was cleverly avoided or disguised. Much emphasis was placed upon the failings of the old government in our everyday lessons. We were told that we must be proud of ourselves as Germans as the German race would one day inherit the whole world. Can you imagine how that felt for a ten-year-old?

I remember that many important political figures in Hitler's government often visited our schools and *Jung Madel* meetings, and gave lectures – people like Baldur von Schirach, Heinrich Himmler and Joseph Goebbels. All stressed the reasons for not tolerating Jews anymore and the changes being made in Germany by the Nazis that would be of great benefit to us all. They would say that Germany was becoming strong again on its foundation of a loyal breed of German girls and boys who would serve their Führer and inherit his ideology and thinking, and apply it to all future generations. They also stressed that Germany would take back everything that it was robbed of by the Versailles Treaty, though they did not make particular references as to how this would be achieved.

I of course knew some girls who were Jews and it was very sad in the way that I could no longer talk to them or have any association with them at all. It was forbidden and was the one thing that I could not fully grasp, why do the Nazis hate Jews so much? What had they ever done to me personally? Was it true what the Nazis were saying? I had no answers to those questions, yet had to fall in line with everyone else and do as I was told to do. As a youngster I did not possess sufficient maturity or knowledge to challenge what I was being taught, yet I understood perfectly the differences between right and wrong, but school and the *Jung Madel* were saying things to the contrary and were adjusting our moral sense. It became very confusing in the end, besides, those who refused to conform, faced social isolation. Look what happened to Sophie Scholl, she was a BDM who began to challenge the Nazis and disagree with what they were doing, and they killed her by cutting off her head, yet she was German, a German citizen. Gypsies and Slavs were treated with even more contempt, and were termed as a separate sub-human species.

Anna Dann says of her education in fifth grade:

I found it very difficult to maintain my concentration for long periods of time. I had very little understanding of National Socialist politics and what it was all about. It was not the fact that I was not interested or anything, as we were all interested in being a part of what was happening in Germany at the time in a kind of sub-conscious manner. But I found that there were many subjects that I found boring. I didn't like music and was not particularly good at art either, and as for the politics, well, I once fell asleep during a talk only to be caught by the teacher, Frau Mohnicke. She had a vicious temper and roared like a lion when she shouted. She dragged me to the front of the class, and although she did not hit me, I was forced to remain standing throughout the whole of the lesson, she would not even let me sit down to do my writing, yes, it could be very strict for those who failed to conform to the exact expectations of the new teachers. My friend Kristina helped me with my work, she was a very clever girl and could recite whole passages of *Mein Kampf*. Kristina spent much time with me helping me to read and understand what Hitler was about, and with time I was able to contribute more in political discussions in class, though you were ill advised to ever criticize Nazi policy. My father did not like the political teaching, as he believed that a woman's place was in the home and not the political stage, but he approved of me learning to cook and do first aid and childcare and things. I liked doing those things at school and my results were pretty good in all. Many of the girls enjoyed art as a subject very much, but even art had become Nazified and we had to draw upon Nazi influences for the creation of our work, and were not really allowed any freedom of self-expression. We had to conform to the Nazi ethic and interpretations of art, which is why I did not like it, we could not use our imaginations and paint or draw what we wanted.

Certainly art did figure quite highly in the Nazi school curriculum, as art had been Hitler's great passion, along with architecture, and would remain so until his death. German artists glorified the German citizens, soldiers and Hitler's ideals, and Hitler, in particular, was always painted in a people's hero-like status. He was always portrayed as a kind of a visionary figure and the core element for the cure of all of Germany's ills. Germany's people were portrayed in a way that made them appear as one huge united community with no class divides. The artists of the Third Reich went to great pains to portray the Jew as an inhuman and inferior subject. The artists often used grotesquely distorted facial images that had claw-like hands and wore dirty, long black coats.

Anna Dann:

Yes, the Jews, Slavs and Gypsies in particular were always painted to appear as the classic 'Bogeyman' style characters. The images that appeared on much of the propaganda material of the time clearly illustrate the fact. When we were shown these kinds of images for the first time it scared us to death. We were shown this kind of material in normal schooling and within the Hitler Youth also. We were told as youngsters that the Jew was a kind of monster that would destroy us if we did not force him from our homeland. The films, posters and our basic education within school and the Hitler Youth claimed that Jews were more or less running the world of finance, and that their greed was affecting the financial stability of our nation and the world. The propaganda films shown in school contained much the same content, but were very graphic in detail. The Jews selected for the films were deliberately chosen for their unattractive and sometimes sinister appearance.

Girls also studied a whole range of anti-Semitic writings in books other than Hitler's *Mein Kampf*. There were those women who did challenge the Nazi's education and attitude to women. One such female author was Irmgard Keun, a German novelist who had all of her work banned by the Nazis after she criticized and challenged their defamation of German womanhood. She was very lucky not to have been murdered by the Nazis.

Kirsten Eckermann:

I remember the most strenuous physical activities that we had to perform. We had to move like ballet dancers in perfect synchronization with each other. Everything we seemed to do had to evolve around moving in large formations, and much of our physical routines depended on strength, balance and precision movement. It was important for us to look good at public events staged by the Nazis and we had to work very hard for hours on perfecting our routines. It was important to appear as visually impressive as was possible. Aryan physicality was in my opinion the most important part of our education from the view of those in power. Though even the not-so athletic girls could find a role to play within our exercise routines.

So, fitness and strength and beauty became obsessive qualities with Hitler and were things that were put before anything else education-wise. Hitler wanted his females to stun the crowds at his rallies and other events, always with our athleticism and precision. We were also taught how to march like soldiers in perfect unison, like soldiers without guns. Some of the very good-looking girls would be selected to perform tasks on their own with hoops and things, where they would catch the eyes of visiting press and photographers. There was also a great deal of sports-style training conducted in school time as a result of the Nazi's obsession with young females.

Biology for the ten-year-old girls had also been completely reformatted by the Nazi education system. The subject had become under Hitler's guidance a 'racial science', which is perfectly illustrated in the biology textbook for fifth graders at the time.

Lebenskunde fur Mittelschulen, (Biology for the Middle School) by Hermann Schroeder Verlag, which had been published in 1942, had been thoroughly reviewed by the Nazis prior to its publication, during which Hitler insisted that quotations from his two *Mein Kampf* volumes were included in the text. By modern standards of biology, and its accessibility and ease of understanding to young people, Schroeder Verlag's work can only be best described as drivel. The book examined the principles of genetics, spring, summer, fall and winter in the forest, and the human body. The idea of using the principle of plant reproduction and then applying it to human beings was a Nazi means of avoiding certain acts considered to have been unclean in their nature.

The various types of *Mein Kampf* quotations selected for inclusion in the book included: 'He who wants to live must fight, and he who does not want to fight in this world of perpetual struggle does not deserve to live' (page 317). The book avoids even the most basic references to human male and female sexuality, emotion and reproduction, as if it were a shameful act. It is well known that many of the top-ranking Nazis enjoyed almost every available form of sexual excess, yet they could not even face up to the responsibility of educating their females into what were subjects of fundamental importance to their everyday lives. Young girls were basically taught nothing on the facts of human sexuality and reproduction. Many ten-year-olds were often only taught the very basic rudiments of the 'facts of life'.

After joining the BDM at fourteen, some of the older BDM girls would discuss sex when together during summer camp, but only when out of the earshot of their teachers and leaders. The older girls were taught that sexual activity was something one only engaged in with a male specifically for the production of offspring. The Nazis taught the BDM that sex was indeed shameful and dirty and belonged only in the realm of the Jew, and was not something to be used for the pursuit of pleasure. Yet many leading Nazis who were supposedly happily married, were in fact often sleeping with other women – such as propaganda minister Goebbels – until Hitler, fearful of scandal, intervened and stopped them.

Dora Brunninghausen agrees that the biology textbook was a waste of time:

> It puzzled me, and I can remember trying to work out in my mind just how the reproductive cycle began, what caused it between a man and a woman? And how exactly were babies made? All the rubbish about plants and forests and things only confused the reality. They just did not want to explain sex and reproduction in the human sense, and so tried I think in an unsuccessful way to apply it via nature, to make it read more cleaner and less lustful to us young girls. Anything to do with lust was considered in the realm of the Jew, Slav and the gypsy and was a dirty subject. Sex was not spoken about at school, in the *Jung Madel* or at home. It was a completely taboo subject, and that is perfectly reflected in the biology textbook of the day. There were no diagrams showing how a man fertilized the woman or anything, and if we questioned in class they always did their best to avoid any directness. I only learned about having sex when a BDM girl told me what her brother had been doing with his girlfriend. We were very inquisitive and we laughed about it an awful lot. I remember the girl drawing a picture of a woman's vagina and she then drew a penis going inside of it.
>
> I was shocked and said, 'Does that thing really have to go in there?'
>
> 'Of course it does silly, how else are you going to have a baby. The one hole is to pee through, the other is for *schiesse*, and the most important one is for having babies,' she replied, and we laughed.
>
> The thought of it really shocked me at first, but how we laughed. I learned more about sex in the BDM than anywhere else in those days. The older girls also educated me as to what periods were; mothers were quite embarrassed to have to explain this to their daughters. Why the Nazis did not teach this in school I don't know, they were insane not to have done so.

There were other distractions to a girl's education beside that provided by the Hitler Youth outside of school hours. Girls in 1930s Germany were expected to help their mothers around the home. Many even had to take time off from school to help their mothers with such mundane tasks as doing the family washing and laundry. This was deemed as acceptable, as girls had to be taught from an early age as to where their place was in the home. Anita Von Schoener:

> I hated washing day, it was very hard work and I was expected to help my mother with this weekly task. It was not just a case of throwing all of the washing into a tub then hanging it out on a line to dry. Washing our family's clothes and things was a job that could take up to three days to complete. My mother would soon tire and then I would have to take over from her. The combination of the hot water and the coarse soap made your hands very sore and tender indeed. In winter it was a cold and miserable task that still had to be done. My mother would check all of the clothes for any leftover dirt. Eventually she would hang them out to dry. If it was raining the clothes would have to be hung up in the kitchen where the heat from the stove would dry them. I didn't like doing it, but it was something we had to do, we had no choice. It was very difficult to catch up with schoolwork and attend the Hitler Youth meetings in the twice-weekly evening sessions, though I tried very hard to do both. I can remember many times staying up quite late and reading books by the light of the moon. My parents would never have allowed me to stay up late, even to catch up on my studies – back then it was not the done thing, especially for girls. It did seem unfair to me even then that boys appeared to have more freedom and more time at school, and as a result they received a better education than we girls. Parents those days were not like the ones of the current generation. They could be very hard and strict and this was why so many girls joined the Hitler Youth. It was a means of escaping from and rebelling against their elders in some cases, and also a means of gaining some degree of equality. There were just so many barriers being placed before us as girls and when you get older you begin to question and examine these things more closely, then you realize, I know I realized after a few years, I thought to myself, what future do I have?

Our education was built around five menial principles: physical exercise, cooking, washing, cleaning and babies, though they never told you anything directly about sexual intercourse. Yes, it was a joke really and it does make me angry. I remember one of our teachers lecturing us one morning on the virtues of womanhood. She started to go on about how our bodies were receptacles of moral importance to the Third Reich, that we were divine and had no equals, and that lust should not define our thinking or soil our wombs in any way whatsoever. As youngsters we trusted these people, and we believed and we followed, and did our best to absorb what we were being taught.

Though we had so little creative freedom and that is something all children should not be denied. Everything within us as individuals had to evolve around either Hitler or Nazism or both. Friction often developed in the home as a result of this, as our loyalties became divided between the *Jung Madel* and our parents; fathers in particular did not like their daughters to have attitudes of their own. There were many arguments in our home and I frequently received a beating for being disrespectful to my father. Even now I deeply resent the way that he hit me for silly things and I could never find it in my heart to forgive him. Though my disrespect was never honestly intended, it was something that came about from events that were happening around me and the environment with its increasing tensions. A girl's life back then was hard and it saddens me a great deal when I look back over those years. One BDM girl later summed it up very perfectly by saying that we girls were no more than 'the sugar on the dog shit'.

From the previous testimonies, we can see very clearly how narrow the Nazi education system had become for the young girls, especially when compared to that of the old system, which offered the student much more both socially and creatively. The old system had been completely replaced, as perfectly reflected in one of Hitler's many quotations on the subject of Third Reich youth education:

My theory of education is harsh. All weakness must be hammered out. The youth who grow up in my academies will terrify the world. I want a youth who is violent, masterful, intrepid, cruel and they must endure pain.

In another one of his famous rants, Hitler boasted, 'No boy and girl must leave school without having been led to an ultimate realisation of the necessity and essence of blood purity.'

The issue of 'blood purity' was of prime importance to Hitler, especially as applied to girls. German girls had the responsibility to understand just how important racial purity was to the Nazis and Hitler, so much so that it became the burden of girls to ensure that they would make the right choices later in life.

While the same 'racial purity' regulations were made clear to young males, it appears that they did not suffer too greatly from the severe restrictions that had been placed upon the womenfolk. There are accounts of young German males, well after Hitler came to power (especially within conquered territories), having sexual relationships with girls of non-Germanic origin, including Jews, and in some rare cases gypsies. Though a good many were able to get away with such 'crimes', if caught they could face the death penalty.

Kirsten Eckermann recalls:

Racial purification we were told could only be achieved when the weaker races of Slavs, Jews and gypsies had been destroyed. Hitler had said that much damage had been done to the German race as a direct result of breeding between the races. For example, Jewish and gypsy sperm was referred to as a venom and a poison, which created weakness and mongolism, which in turn led to ineptitude, greed and self-destruction. Through propaganda, the message was soon spread to every individual. Girls in particular had come to accept certain male role models as the ideal man. Usually these role models came from the ranks of the SS and girls were told that they should strive to marry an SS soldier and have babies of racially pure Aryan origin, who in turn would go on and reproduce.

To be honest, at that time I did not know what the word 'Aryan' meant. Our education evolved around those biological and domestic theories of home and husband keeping and baby rearing. These days it would be a lot like a farm of prized cattle, where no foreign beasts would be allowed, even if they were perfect in every sense. Our education became a kind of human cattle market designed to meet one particular need – we were to be birth machines and vessels for sexual gratification where life became a kind of impasse. As we grew older and perhaps a little wiser, some of us became aware of this, and I do say some of us. Many of us were mesmerized by Hitler and were captivated by what the Hitler Youth offered us, and obeisance seemed to be the only price and we did exactly as we were told in every way. I don't think that many knew, myself included, just what was going to happen in the future. We may have had our own suspicions but at the age of ten you question very little and tend to put your hand in the honey pot and just go with the flow – that is what made the Hitler Youth and the educational format set out for its students such a successful organization.

Nazi education for the *Jung Madels* was clearly based upon the propaganda and beliefs of their country's leaders, and was therefore designed to poison the minds of youth against the better judgement of both their own consciousness and that of their parents. It was designed to create a kind of 'pit-bull' individual that, through an instilled intelligence and almost insane belief, would be prepared to suffer intolerable hardship in the pursuit of the creation of their preferred ideological society. A 'factory education', it was perhaps one of the greatest exercises in mass-mind poisoning ever devised, and would create many problems that would extend far beyond the years preceding the end of the Second World War in Europe.

Chapter Four

An Audience with the Devil

Perhaps the most well-known of the Nazi pageants was the *Nürnberger Parteitag* (Nuremberg Party Day). This huge rally, the first of which was held in Nuremberg, Bavaria, in September of 1923, was the primary propaganda tool of the Hitler regime. Carefully staged, the rally encompassed society and the armed forces together in a huge exhibition of Germany's political, military and social muscle. The quaint medieval setting of Nuremberg was ideal, providing a powerful backdrop for the nationalistic pageantry. Set against a fairytale landscape of ancient buildings and castles, it created a unique atmosphere.

Planning, as usual, was of immense importance. Preparations were set in motion well before the event to ensure that everything and everyone would be ready. Nuremberg possessed an almost religious atmosphere during the party days, attracting hordes of visitors from all over the world, all eager to experience the atmosphere, and to get a glimpse of Hitler and other leading figures within his government.

Nuremberg became the standard against which all future Nazi Party rallies would attempt to emulate. It became a constant headache for the organizers, who had to ensure that the townsfolk lived up to Hitler's expectations. It became compulsory that flags bearing the Swastika be hung from every possible building, along with portraits of Adolf Hitler and various other forms of Nazi Party insignia and iconography. Flower arches and other decorative floral schemes were created to blend in with the flags and insignia to make the whole event as colourful as was possible.

The local Nazi Party officials prepared speeches while the Hitler Youth practised their part in the rally. Again, the girls featured prominently in the rally, their gymnastic displays breathtaking in skill and precision. Helena Vogel reflects on Nuremberg in 1934, a year by the end of which the Hitler Youth – boys and girls – would boast a combined membership of 1,500,000.

I came from a fairly wealthy upper-class family and was born and raised in Nuremberg. My father owned a share of a small but productive metal-working business making fittings such as nuts, bolts and bits for furniture and things. My father, being a businessman, became a member of the Nazi Party, but only because he was under pressure to do so by other companies and local Nazi Party officials. Though he generally supported the Nazi Party because it had rejuvenated the economy and he felt Hitler was doing a very good job.

I joined the *Jung Madel* at the age of thirteen for one year before joining the *Bund Deutscher Madel*. The big rallies held at Nuremberg were really quite something to all of the youngsters who lived there, and the girls Hitler Youth were always considered an important element of the rallies. I can only describe the events at Nuremberg as I remember them, a little like a national celebration day in England I suppose, but lasting several days to a week. I had always liked gymnastics and sports at school and my abilities were recognized by the teachers there. The best girl athletes were selected to perform special routines and our best routine was the Swastika formation. We would practice as a group for hours until we had honed our routine to perfection; only then would we focus on the days of the rally itself. I remember the colours and the soldiers in their beautiful uniforms, and the masses and masses of people who came to watch. It was good for Nuremberg in many ways as the foreign visitors brought much needed revenue with them. Of course it was a political event in reality, but to us it was one great happy time. We practised doing our Swastika formation some weeks before the event and it was something which required much discipline to get right.

On the actual day, we would be a little nervous, but very eager to do our bit. The gymnastic displays were held at sporting arenas or Zeppelin fields, so as the crowds could see us properly. We would file out into the arena flanked by two girls carrying flags. The girls with the flags, who would sometimes wear a Nordic style traditional dress, would peel away from us and leave the arena and we formed up into a line and began to move around into a circle. We had to keep perfect timing as we moved and at the critical moment we would very mechanically form into a Swastika. Some girls would stop while others formed up to make the Swastika shape. Once this was completed, we moved around in a circle and the crowds would roar with delight.

After completing our routine, we would again form up into a line and the girls with the flags would return and escort us out of the arena. As we moved off, other *Jung Madels* were preparing to come out for their routines. We often watched them and cheered them on, as they were our friends and comrades. It was amazing some of the things we did without apparatus, things like human pyramids. The human pyramid was something which took extreme concentration and sometimes faith. We performed this routine at the same rally two days later. The strongest girls formed the base of the pyramid while the not so strong ones climbed and formed the top. There were many times when a girl lost her balance or slipped and we all ended up in a large giggling heap on the floor.

I remember seeing Hitler for the first time at the Nuremberg rally giving a speech and the reaction of the crowds to his words were wild. Other members of the Nazi Party took to the stage to address the people including Goebbels the propaganda minister. The most exciting parts of the rally for us were the marches. We watched the soldiers of the *Wehrmacht* goose step followed by tanks and big guns. We would cheer at them and wave these little Swastika flags in the air.

Afterwards, sometimes Hitler would mingle with the crowds and come and talk to us. Very often when he came to talk to us, it would be at special presentations and the press would be there taking photographs of him shaking our hands, and it would be broadcast on the radio also. Hitler's speeches often captured the imagination and we listened to him intently. 'The Jews,' he would tell us, 'are your enemies,' and that the Jews threatened the stability of Germany. Racial purification was also of great importance to the Nazis. I was one of the girls that Hitler spoke with at Nuremberg in 1934, and he said to me something about 'making a fine German wife for a fine young German man,' which struck me as a little odd, as I was only very young and was not sure what I really wanted from my life at that stage. Hitler congratulated me and the other girls for our 'breathtaking efforts' and he told us that he was honoured and proud to have seen us again. I remember discussing the events with my mother and father at the time, and it was made clear to me by both of my parents that when I come of age I should find a suitable man and settle down and get married. Even as a thirteen-year-old, I often lay awake thinking to myself 'is this what life is and what it is all about?'

I felt for the Jews in Germany at that time; they were being very cruelly treated everywhere and Hitler made clear at Nuremberg that they would not be tolerated. They just did not fit into his thinking at all. I can remember talking or trying to talk to my parents about Hitler's verbal attacks on the Jews. In the end my mother and father forbade any of us to talk about or even mention Jews in their presence. My father said to me that 'the Jews were the responsibility of the politicians and I should not concern myself with such politics.' Fearing the wrath of my parents, I never mentioned the word 'Jew' again in our household. The lives of children, particularly females, evolved around absolute obeisance and that is the way it was and we accepted it.

Though quite a long way from Berlin, many Berliners travelled to Nuremberg to take part in the celebrations staged usually in August or September. Nazi Party officials and members and their families travelled all over Germany to attend rallies, and as the economic situation improved, many working-class Germans were also able to travel, at least by train, to other parts of the country. As a result, Germans from all over the Reich territory attended Nuremberg, along with the other Nazi pageants held over the years. Melissa Schroeder and her family travelled from München (Munich) to experience and enjoy Nuremberg.

Even by steam train it seemed to take a long time to get to Nuremberg. When we arrived, we got a taste of things to come. The place was packed with people from all over the world and there was an atmosphere of hustle and bustle. I travelled to Nuremberg with my mother, father, three sisters and one brother. We had packed our clothes into small suitcases and I had my Hitler Youth uniform with me, which I wanted to wear when we went out. My brother had also brought his uniform with him as it was required of us to wear uniform on all party occasions. My father, being a member of the Nazi Party, was able to get us rooms in a lovely hotel near the centre of Nuremberg. It was a beautiful place and very gothic, looking just like in the picture books of knights in armour.

The street celebrations had already begun and there was a kind of party atmosphere and the weather was pleasantly warm even during the evening. My three sisters and myself shared two single beds in our own room which had this balcony. When our parents put us to bed in the evening and turned out the lights, we could lie and watch the stars and listen to the people outside singing and dancing. Every so often, our door would open as my father had instructed one of the maids to keep an eye on us. We were soon fast asleep, exhausted by our journey, even though we were all excited about what we would see and do over the following days.

We awoke at 8.00am and washed ourselves in the bathroom before joining our parents in the dining room for breakfast. It was very lavish in that hotel and I often wondered how my father managed to get us in such a place, as he was not exactly rolling in money as you say.

We went out into the town and all sorts of things were going on and we wore our uniforms. We watched a huge parade of soldiers and although it was very difficult to see, we got a glimpse of Hitler as he drove past in a huge black car flanked by members of his staff. People went hysterical when Hitler came along, and women fainted and had to be carried away. I thought it was quite funny and wondered what all the fuss was about really. We saw Hitler again the day before we left for the journey back to München, as a group of press photographers wanted to photograph Hitler with members of his Hitler *Jugend*. I was there by pure chance and my father pushed me forward to join the handful of boys and girls who were to stand with Hitler for the photograph. We gathered around Hitler and he put his arms around our shoulders and smiled very broadly at the camera. I remember looking around at him and smiling and his eyes looking into mine. The pressman shouted something, then with a flash of silvery light, the photograph was taken. The bodyguards quickly moved back to Hitler's side and I could see clearly their collar tabs with the two SS runes on. These soldiers were the crack SS troops we had learned about at school and *Jung Madel*. Hitler talked briefly to us and asked if we were enjoying ourselves at Nuremberg, and he patted our heads in a gesture of affection. There were no strong sentiments like those delivered in his speeches, and this surprised me. He came across as being very warm, caring and quite normal, though his eyes were different in a way I cannot explain. I asked him for his autograph and he obliged with a broad smile, and I was the envy of all my friends because I had got the Führer's autograph. I had it for many years but it was lost many years ago along with other possessions.

On Sunday, 14 September 1936, the ceremony of the Hitler Youth was held at Nuremberg stadium. This was an important event for the whole of Germany's Hitler Youth. Thousands came from all over the Reich to attend what was clearly one of the pinnacle youth gatherings for many years in Germany.

Starting from the early hours of the morning, huge columns of Hitler Youth marched into the stadium. It was an awesome spectacle, as each respective youth organization marched in like soldiers. The *Jung Volk*, *Jung Madel*, *Bund Deutscher Madel* and boys Hitler Youth filed into the arena with military precision. It was a warm day and the girls wore their easily recognizable uniform of white blouse, black tie and navy-blue skirt. Each regiment wore the cloth arm patch of its particular borough of origin, stating the town or city. Standard bearers carried their regimental pennants. It was a marvellous sight for the German and foreign press photographers, who greatly admired the sheer discipline and strength of the Hitler Youth organization. One photographer commented:

> It was easily one of the most memorable things I had ever witnessed at that time during my career as a photographer. The girls in particular looked beautiful in their white blouses and dark skirts marching like soldiers. There was something about them which set them aside from the boys' regiments, perhaps because they were an unusual organization. Nowhere else in Europe could boast of creating such an admirable institution. My main job on that Sunday was to photograph the girls; everyone wanted pictures of the girls.

Other high-ranking Nazis who would be joining Hitler on the platform that day were Max Amann, Martin Bormann, Dr Ley, Dr Dietrich, and the leaders of the individual Hitler Youth regiments. Military representatives were also present in the form of Hermann Goering, the commander of the Luftwaffe, General Fritsch of the *Wehrmacht*, and Admiral Raeder of the *Kriegsmarine*. There were, however, a great many army, navy and Luftwaffe officers present, along with numerous other and lesser-known Nazi Party leaders and officials of the state and diplomatic corps. These people were seated behind the Reich ministers. Standing proudly just in front of the Hitler Youth leaders was the easily recognizable, pug-faced form of Heinrich Himmler, the *Reichsführer* of the SS (*Schutzstaffel*), and the SA's (*Sturmabteilung*) Viktor Lutze.

By 9.30 am, the whole stadium awaits the arrival of Adolf Hitler with the usual anticipation. Girls of the *Jung Madel* and *Bund Deutscher Madel* stand and quietly swap words with one another. Just before the strike of ten, a command booms out across the stadium. There is an instant silence and the regiments of the army, navy, Luftwaffe and Hitler Youth stiffen to attention. The silence was then broken by a sea of cheering men, women and children as Adolf Hitler arrives, surrounded by his guard. Hitler walks slowly through the lines of the SS with Reich minister Rudolf Hess at his side, pausing every so often to raise his right hand in acknowledgement of the crowd's cheers. He makes his way up the flight of steps onto the platform, and the roar of the crowd dies down.

The Reich Youth leader steps forward to the microphone to introduce the Führer. He then steps back as Hitler walks towards the microphone. Hitler stands silent for what seems like an eternity to the boys and girls who eagerly await his words. He gazes around expressionless, his eyes as black as coal, building the air of anxiety and excitement before delivering his greeting: 'Heil, my youth.' There is a momentary roar as the thousands of girls and boys return their greeting to their beloved Führer. Many have waited a very long time for this moment, but the sight of their Führer gazing down upon them is too much for some – already girls are fainting. Groups of the SS quickly lend assistance and take them to receive first-aid treatment.

Trumpets from the towers, which flank the stadium, announce the beginning of the ceremony. A band under the direction of *Bannführer* (band leader) Spitta begins the song aptly titled, '*The Freedom Song of the Youth*'. The youth of Germany are as familiar with the lyrics as British children were with the words of the 'Lord's Prayer'.

As the song fades, there is an atmosphere of building emotion, which reaches out and touches everyone. The press and hordes of photographers try desperately to capture the uniqueness of the moment. A song titled '*A Young People Rises Up*' is the next hymn to be sung, and as the crowds of boys and girls sing, the field banners of the Hitler Youth and their bearers enter the arena as the crowds roar their welcome. Some of these bearers, it is reported, have marched across Germany for weeks with these flags of faith in Adolf Hitler, their Führer. They came from all corners of the Reich, from the mining towns, the industrial *Mitte*, from coastal towns, and from where the mountains puncture the skies. The idea of such a march was to reaffirm the love, obedience, and loyalty to the Führer. The flags are special in the way that they were sanctified upon the very tomb of Frederick the Great. A Hitler Youth also carries the bloodied flag of

Herbert Norkus, the fifteen-year-old martyr and member of the Hitler Youth who had been murdered by German Communists on 24 January 1932. The flags were carried across the country, through rain, sun and snow, and it is with great pride that these flags arrive at the stadium. Hitler steps forward to make a closing speech – he pauses, adding to the building tensions of his audience. When he delivers this last speech, he does so with venom and with anger. His words, in hindsight, reflect a little of what was to come:

> We are used to battle, for out of it we came. We will plant our feet firmly in our earth, and no attack will move us. You will stand with me, should such a time come! You will stand before me, at my side, and behind me, holding our flags high! Let our old enemies attempt to rise up once more! They may wave their Soviet flags before us – but our flag will win the battle.

With that closing statement, Hitler steps back and salutes as the masses shout Sieg Heil!

A barely audible command is called, and the columns line up once again in perfect precision as the presentation march sounds out. At that moment a roar seems to fill the entire arena, only this roar is not that of the crowds, but of the German Luftwaffe. Everyone gazes skyward as waves of Messerschmitt 109s, Heinkels and Dorniers pass over in an aerial salute of magnificent proportions.

Hitler, along with Schirach and Hess, walks slowly down the columns of the Hitler Youth boys and girls. He stops and gazes at them every few paces, visibly proud of his new generation and their discipline. He shows particular interest in the *Jung Madel* and *Bund Deutscher Madel* girls, spending many minutes talking to them and shaking their hands. For the girls this is a moment they will never forget in their lives. Some of them have a total adoration for their Führer, others have brought him flowers. There are more and more scenes of genuine emotional outpourings for the Führer. One girl kisses Hitler's hands with tears streaming down her face. Hitler cups the girl's face with his hands and smiles broadly at her. Other girls seem to fall under the same spell and burst into tears. Hitler's SS guards, following close behind, are visibly bemused by the spectacle of all these young girls kissing Hitler's hands and uttering words of love and devotion. Some are so overcome by the experience that the guards have to hold them back. Helga Bassler was one of the girls who received an audience with the Devil. She recalls the experience:

My knees began to shake and I had butterflies in my stomach as I watched Hitler slowly make his way down the row of girls towards me. I watched how girls cried and reached out to him and how some had brought flowers especially for him. When he came and looked at me I instinctively held out my hands, but quickly remembered I had not saluted him, so I pulled back my right hand very quickly and thrust it in the air and gave a loud 'Heil Hitler.' I think this impressed him and he thanked me very much for being there to honour him that day, and he told me that he had hoped that he had expressed his honour and respect for us on this special day for us. I nodded my head as I could not speak I was so happy. His eyes seemed to smile and he was radiant, and as he walked on along the row I could not take my eyes off him, I was transfixed. From that day on I looked upon Hitler as a saviour, a personal saviour. It was a little bit like how modern girls look up to their favourite pop stars; many of us became infatuated after meeting him, and we were in a way in love with him, even though few of us really understood our own emotions, we were too young.

There can be no doubting the importance of the ceremony of the Hitler Youth on that warm Sunday in September 1933. It was the Nazi way of cowing the young masses support. There were many other important occasions in which the Hitler Youth and the Nazi regime would honour itself, other than Nuremberg.

Another day of extreme importance, particularly to Hitler, was 12 August, as this was the date of his mother Klara's birthday. This date was declared a public holiday, and although solemn in some ways, the masses were again urged to celebrate the memory of the dictator's mother. On this day, Hitler would award the Cross of Honour of the German Mother (*Mutterehrenkreuz*) to all fertile mothers. A woman who has borne four children would receive a bronze cross, while the one with six would receive one in silver. The highest class of this award was in gold, which was awarded to all women who had eight children. The awards themselves had no particular value other than the fact that Hitler usually presented them to the women in person. Hitler totally adored his mother, so declaring this day to her was his way of keeping her memory alive. He never got over the death of his mother, something that would haunt him until his suicide in 1945.

On 8 November, there was also the commemoration of the Beer Hall Putsch, Hitler's failed attempt to overthrow the German government in 1923. This commemoration was to honour the Hitler supporters who were killed by the authorities on that fateful day. Flags were draped across the tombs of those who were killed, as they were reconfirmed as heroes of the cause of National Socialism.

The Berlin Olympics of 1936, where German athletes competed in a magnificent multi-national event, winning the majority of the gold medals, was described as one of the most atmospheric events to have taken place in Europe for many years. However, even this spectacular event was soured with both hatred and racism.

Chapter Five

Young Women, Sex and the Führer

Adolf Hitler's emotional and sexual attitudes towards young females are worth exploring, as these attitudes – though maybe inadvertently – essentially influenced his ideas on the role that young girls and women were to fulfil in his Third Reich. A great deal of myth surrounds Hitler, his sexuality, and his sexual encounters with women. Hitler's sexuality became the subject of much private talk, especially during the early years of the Nazi Party, where many homosexuals found positions of authority within its ranks.

Ernst Röhm was said to have been homosexual, possessing sexual preferences for young boys, though Röhm's sister has always denied that her brother was a homosexual, contending that this accusation was orchestrated by Nazis who wanted him eliminated as leader of the SA. Rudolf Hess, the one-time deputy Führer, was also believed to have been homosexual or possessing homosexual preferences, being nicknamed 'Fraulein Anna' by members of the Nazi Party. Martin Bormann gained a reputation for having an eye for anything wearing a skirt. It was Bormann who asked his wife's permission to keep a mistress. She later suggested that they alternate in childbearing so that one of them would always be available to him for sexual intercourse. SS chief Heinrich Himmler and propaganda minister Joseph Goebbels also had a history of sexual deviance, also taking mistresses.

In later years, Hitler was forced to purge the Nazi Party of its undesirable elements, which inevitably led to the murder of people like Ernst Röhm, who had served Hitler well over the early years and had been indispensable. It was all very hypocritical and contradictory, as Hitler had previously insisted that the private lives of members of his party were of no concern to him at all. His general attitude had been 'do what you like, but don't get caught doing it'.

Over the years, it has become very difficult to separate fact from fiction when dealing with the subject of Hitler and his sexuality. There is a great deal of evidence to suggest that at least some of his generals disapproved of many of the antics that went on. The conservative General Hermann Rauschning commented:

There is a reeking miasma of furtive sexuality that fills and fouls the whole atmosphere around what I can only describe as an evil emanation. There are so many secret lusts and relationships that nothing in this man's surroundings is genuine, and nothing has the openness of a natural instinct.

Some of the fiction attached to Hitler and his sex life can trace its origins from the obscene propaganda material derived from the wartime psychological profiles on the Führer. Much of the obscene propaganda material came from the British Special Operations Executive, SOE. Some of the material was considered so obscene, that at first even British prime minister Churchill questioned the morality of it all.

The material came in a variety of forms, ranging from cartoon-type caricatures of Hitler, through to specially touched-up photographs, including one showing Hitler holding his erect penis in his hand! There were, of course, the radio broadcasts, which were so cleverly orchestrated, that many German listeners were convinced that the transmissions were coming from inside Germany, when in reality they were emanating from Britain. The radio broadcasts were primarily aimed at the German soldiers who were known to tune into that particular radio band. The programmes revealed many invented sexual perversions in which prominent members of the Third Reich had been involved, Hitler included. There were stories of sadomasochistic orgies involving Hitler's generals, homosexuality and bestiality. Hitler himself was accused of having a fondness for wearing women's knickers, a subject to which there is a degree of truth attached.

As a propaganda tool, such things were worth their weight in gold, perhaps even if in a time of war they did go a little too far. There is, however, a very good degree of truth surrounding Hitler and his staff, and their personal conduct once out of the limelight of public adoration. Homosexuality was said to have been rife within the SA and Hitler Youth. There are those who will testify to the fact that there probably existed as big a paedophile ring within both ranks as would not be out of place in our modern society.

Young boys and young girls were easily bribed, and there were those within the Hitler Youth who kept silent and allowed themselves to be abused by their elders. Some of the girls will here attest to the fact that there were many sexual encounters between BDM girls and their leaders, and indeed between each other. One of the primary causes of lesbianism within the BDM was the fact that girls were very rarely allowed to mix with boys in any natural context. As a result, lesbianism became a natural resulting regression amongst some of the girls.

Girls had always been taught that it was considered unclean to have any form of sexual thoughts or feelings towards members of the opposite sex, or indeed their own. Sexual intercourse was primarily for the purpose of producing offspring, and not something that one would partake in for the purpose of pleasure and fulfilment. That was the basic Third Reich sexual doctrine as taught to the Hitler Youth, particularly the girls. It was completely hypocritical when one compares it with the sexual conduct of both Hitler and some of his most high-ranking staff.

Women, who made up the major part of the electorate in Germany, were viewed by Hitler as being more influenced by image, profile and the general superficialities of their leaders, and not necessarily by their political qualities and abilities. Both young and old women alike found that Hitler possessed a strange allure, finding themselves strangely attracted to him sexually.

Hitler became aware of his 'magnetism' early on in his political career, something that is strongly reflected in later years in his relationship with and attitude towards his mistress, Eva Braun. Hitler was by no means an attractive man, yet girls often admitted to have become sexually aroused in his presence. These girls, in reality, were aroused on a subconscious level more by the immense power he had over them and the rest of Germany, rather than by his own physical being. He had over the years become a domineering bully where women were concerned. He dominated them socially, mentally and sexually, in a way that he had to be in total control at all times.

During the First World War, Hitler's comrades in the trenches often thought him odd. Whenever they had the chance to get some much-needed respite away from the frontlines, they usually found comfort with prostitutes, but Corporal Hitler never once went with them. He much preferred his own company. This led some of his comrades to assume that Hitler was homosexual, though none of them ever approached him directly with such an accusation.

When it came to relationships, Hitler chose young, naïve and often vulnerable women. It was women with these characteristics that he discovered were easily dominated, thus posing no threat to him. Hitler had sexual encounters with many young girls, one being a certain Maria Reiter. Hitler met Maria Reiter while they were both walking their dogs in a Munich park in 1924. Reiter was only sixteen at the time, while Hitler was thirty-six, yet he became totally smitten with the young girl. During their relationship, she often complained that Hitler was overbearing, suffering from extreme bouts of jealousy and a frightful temper. Reiter desperately wanted Hitler to marry her, but these plans were scuppered by him in favour of his political ambitions. After a period of some two years, their relationship ended. Reiter, like so many girls that would fall under the Hitler spell, attempted suicide, but was saved in the nick of time by her brother. She never talked openly about her sex life with Hitler, but she commented that he was very passionate when it came to the sexual act itself.

It was also during the 1920s that Hitler began a relationship with Winifred Wagner, the daughter of an English father and German mother. Wagner became obsessed with Hitler and although she may have denied it, their relationship was undoubtedly sexual. Wagner never once showed any regret for her relationship with Hitler, even during the years after the Second World War, when the horrors perpetrated by Hitler and the Nazis had been fully exposed.

Film actress Renate Müller also caught the attentions of Hitler. As their relationship progressed to a sexual level, Hitler's behaviour became increasingly strange. He became infatuated with her, but his sadomasochistic demands in the bedroom greatly upset her. She confided in her director, telling him of Hitler's demands during a night spent with him in the Chancellery. The relationship ended in very suspicious circumstances when Müller was found dead, having fallen forty feet to her death from her hotel room. It is widely accepted now that Hitler certainly did have something to do with the young woman's death. It is believed that SS assassins, under Hitler's direction, were responsible for the murder, though suicide was the given verdict. Müller's sister, Gabrielle, insisted that she did not commit suicide, but had died from complications following a leg operation at a clinic in the Augsburger Strasse. This is an unlikely scenario, considering the circumstances in which her sister was found. Perhaps Müller had intended to reveal Hitler's sexual perversions or some other personal oddity. When Renate confided in her director, she mentioned that Hitler was perverted. He had expected her to do unnatural things to him, including acts where he had to be beaten, and urinated and defecated on. There are even some reports, which suggest that Hitler had insisted the woman, after kicking and beating him, straddle his face and defecate into his mouth.

Perhaps the most well-known example of Hitler's sexual domineering is that which he had perpetrated upon his young half-niece, the twenty-year-old Angela 'Geli' Raubal.

It was in 1928 that he fell madly in love with Raubal, when she had spent time with him at his summer retreat in the Bavarian Alps, along with her two daughters Friedl and Geli. Hitler had a schoolboy infatuation with Raubal. The two soon moved into an apartment in Munich and began what many believed to have been an intense and very bizarre sexual relationship. Hitler spent a great deal of time drawing pencil portraits of Raubal, and painting her in the nude. Hitler's domineering personality inevitably led to very heated rows as Hitler attempted to control her every move.

Raubal had expressed an interest in opera, having dreams of becoming an opera singer. She had planned to travel to Vienna in pursuit of her dream, but this led to another violent row with Hitler who forbade her to enter what he called 'that Babylon of races'. Events came to their inevitable conclusion on 18 September 1931, when the young Raubal was found dead in their Munich apartment, apparently from a self-inflicted gunshot wound to the chest. She had, by all accounts, shot herself with Hitler's personal sidearm, a pistol that he had kept in a set of drawers in their apartment. Hitler never recovered from Raubal's loss, to the extent that in the years following her death, just the mere mention of her name was enough to reduce him to tears.

Over the years, there have been many theories as to what had happened to Raubal. Some historians and theorists believe that Hitler had ordered her murder, and that this had been carried out by members of the SS. This is a feasible theory, especially when one considers what had happened to Renata Müller. The circumstances of the two women's deaths are very similar, but the truth of what had really happened to Geli Raubal went with her to her grave.

Hitler's relationship with this pretty young girl is well documented. In all respects, she must have suffered terribly as her uncle's fascination in her increased. Raubal was forbade the company of any male other than Hitler himself. There can be no doubt that Raubal enjoyed her uncle's company, as she could take liberties that few other women would dare. Raubal often ridiculed Hitler in front of his guests, but she would get away with it like a playful kitten. It was only when Hitler's possessiveness intensified that her attitude towards him began to change. She could see what kind of a man he was, and that she would have little future in any long-term relationship with him. She also became aware of what little respect he really had for womenfolk in general, yet she still loved him.

Of the sexual encounters that were alleged to have taken place between Raubal and Hitler, perhaps the most perverse was when, during one bout of intercourse, Hitler insisted that she kick him while he curled up on the floor, naked in the foetal position. He then demanded that she either urinate or defecate on him so that he could become aroused enough for intercourse to take place. There were also rumours that Hitler enjoyed wearing Raubal's underwear; a pair of her knickers were once found amongst his personal clothing.

There are many accounts, which state that Hitler enjoyed young women urinating upon him, claiming that he found great difficulty becoming sexually aroused during normal sexual activity. This would not be too surprising as Hitler was at that time a borderline psychopath. Many criminal psychologists will endorse the fact that large numbers of psychopaths enjoy wearing female underwear and partaking in bizarre, masochistic sexual behavior, where they often endeavour to become the victim. Hitler, however, only felt secure in becoming the victim behind the closed doors of private apartments. At any other time, grovelling, particularly to a female, was something that certainly did not fit into the Hitler persona. It appears that his perversions were most certainly some form of fantasy.

Raubal, through no real fault of her own, must have been thoroughly horrified and ashamed of her uncle's increasingly bizarre sexual requests. Like so many others, however, she was powerless to resist that fatal charm. Hitler often boasted openly, 'There was no greater pleasure than that of sexually educating and deflowering a young girl.' He tended to ignore relationships with older women, possibly viewing them as 'mother figures', who could not be so easily manipulated.

There were a great many other intimate relationships that Hitler had with various women, but the most well-known of his women was Eva Braun.

Born in Munich on the morning of 7 February 1912, Eva Anna Paula Braun first met Adolf Hitler in 1929. A relationship began soon afterwards. At first Braun's father could not understand his daughter's infatuation for someone he at first described as 'an ogre'.

As the Hitler and Braun relationship progressed, her parents and Braun's equally attractive sisters spent much of their time enjoying the Führer's hospitality at the Berghof, Hitler's retreat near Berchtesgaden in the Bavarian Alps. This helped to ensure her family's consent to the relationship.

Braun was a very desirable and attractive young blonde with an athletic figure. She had a bright, bubbly and very playful personality, but like Hitler, she was prone to mood swings, Hitler's personal guards sometimes described her as being 'grumpy'. Some also commented, cruelly, that Braun possessed a bird-like mind, and that she was very childlike in many of her ways. Either way, Eva Braun became the most envied woman in the Third Reich when she moved into the Reich Chancellery with Hitler on 16 December 1939, but here she led a secret and melancholy existence out of the Hitler limelight.

While Hitler was away from the Berghof, Braun spent much of her time exercising, swimming, and practising her gymnastics. She became deeply unhappy and irritated as Hitler would never take her on any of his personal engagements, and when guests came to the Berghof, she was often kept out of the way. Some of Hitler's guards immediately sensed Braun's unhappiness and felt deeply sorry for her. However, they dared not talk about her, even amongst themselves, for fear of being betrayed by a comrade. Dieter Frischmann, at the time a member of the SS, once visited the Berghof with an adjutant in 1943.

We travelled up the winding track to Hitler's mountainside retreat. It was the first time that I had been there on official business to deliver maps and various other papers to Hitler. It was a pleasant sunny and warm day and when we arrived at the Berghof we were warmly greeted by senior SS officers including Himmler. Hitler collected the set of brown envelopes and asked Himmler and the other officers to follow him. They disappeared inside while I waited outside admiring the view with the other soldiers.

While I was gazing around at the scenery, I noticed this woman staring out of one of the large bay windows. She had her arms folded and paced back and forth, occasionally glancing our way. She wore a white and red checkered kind of dress and clearly she had a lovely figure. 'Eva Braun, I thought to myself, there you are,' as it was the first time I had seen her in the flesh. None of us dared acknowledge her or anything, as she was the Führer's woman. Though I remember thinking to myself back then, as would any normal red-blooded male, that I would not have minded ravishing her myself, she was much prettier than most people gave her credit for, photographs and news films do not capture her very well. She was like a ghost, walking back and forth and one could sense her sadness and that Hitler paid her little attention. After the war I heard from other SS comrades that some had fallen for Eva and could not bear to see the way that Hitler treated her. One had hurled himself from the Kehlstein [a rocky outcrop that rises above the Obersalzberg near the town of Berchtesgaden] as he had fallen in love with her and could not be with her. One it was believed had hoped to persuade Eva to run away with him, but she would not agree to it, saying she also loved Hitler. It was very sad and what a terrible waste of a young girl when you look back. She did not really have much of a life, did she?

The last sentence of Dieter Frischmann is very poignant when one reflects on Eva Braun's life. The old question arises time and again: why did this young girl, who already had everything that she needed to live a happy life, commit herself to such a selfish and manipulative ogre as Hitler? Again, one possible answer is the attraction of power. Eva Braun was not interested in personal gain. She was genuinely in love with Hitler, to the extent that she tolerated his unreasonable behaviour and rejection, and increasingly weird sexual demands. Eva Braun was Hitler's ultimate plaything, epitomizing everything that the pure Aryan woman should be physically. Her interests lay solely in physical fitness and gymnastics, plus she was there for whenever Hitler wanted her.

The intimate details of the Hitler and Braun relationship are not exactly clear, but one would imagine that Hitler would have retained his sadomasochistic traits even where the lovely Eva Braun was concerned.

Hitler had affairs with at least two other women during his relationship with Braun. Most of these rendezvous took place at midnight, the girls leaving during the early hours of the morning. One of these, as already mentioned, was Renata Müller. The other was filmmaker, photographer, actress, dancer, and ostensible propagandist, Helene 'Leni' Riefenstahl, who continued to visit Hitler at the Reich Chancellery until the outbreak of war in 1939.

As the war progressed, the situation turned increasingly against Germany's favour, through a mixture of poor decision-making and interference from Hitler himself. The dictator had no real understanding of military matters, and behind the scenes, he began to consume huge amounts of drugs that had the inevitable negative effect on his libido. Some who were close to both Braun and Hitler insist that he was never able to fully satisfy the young woman who always had boundless energy. This was almost certainly the case late in the war, as Hitler became a severe manic–depressive, addicted to thirty different kinds of prescription drug, while suffering from chronic insomnia. As Hitler's mental and emotional state became increasingly more bipolar, he was physically incapable of performing any sexual activity. One of those who witnessed his behavioural changes in later years, including the last days in the Führer's bunker, commented:

> We heard many funny stories, but dared not ever repeat them, even to our close friends or family. I once heard that Eva Braun could

not even rouse Hitler's desire with her hands [masturbation] or mouth [oral sex]. He became totally and utterly impotent, yet that gorgeous young woman still stayed with him. There were many men close to Hitler who secretly lusted after Eva, though it was foolish to even think of taking things any further, if one valued one's own life and family. The truth about Hitler's sexuality lies with those who were closest to Hitler himself, his personal adjutants [photographer Heinrich] Hoffmann and [Julius] Schaub, who were the kind of men Hitler trusted to keep things quiet. Even after the war, few of them, apart from Gerhard Boldt [*Rittmeister der Reserve* Boldt, seconded to the bunker] have ever talked, and he had never really mentioned anything of a sexual nature that I know of.

Only when their whole world was collapsing did Hitler begin to pay any attention to Braun, the ultimate insult was the offering of his hand in marriage, something that he had always denied her. His offer of marriage to Braun was a meaningless gesture, a kind of last act, and maybe one both symbolizing and acknowledging his personal failings and defeat. By that time, the Hitler that Eva had met and fallen in love with all those years ago, was a broken old man, who spent his last hours either sleeping, eating cake, rambling to himself, or cursing his staff for their failings. The Hitler-Braun marriage was a prerequisite to suicide, ratifying the end. Only when Hitler had lost everything else, would he finally marry Eva Braun.

Even the act of wreaking vengeance on those who had conspired and failed to assassinate Hitler in the briefcase bomb plot on 20 July 1944 had mildly sexual overtones, indicating a degree of perverseness.

Well before those deemed responsible for the plot were put on trial, Hitler had decided the inevitable outcome that fate would determine for the eight men. Hitler wanted them strung up from piano wire on meat hooks, just like slaughtered cattle. He wanted them to die as slowly as possible, insisting that the whole execution be filmed.

The men were brought into a special execution cell where, and one-by-one, they were stripped to the waist before being hoisted up into the air on piano-wire nooses wrapped tightly around meat hooks suspended from the ceiling. The meat hooks had been specially brought to the prison cell from a local butcher. It was a horrific spectacle, the men making dreadful gagging noises as they slowly died, twitching and convulsing violently. After the execution, the film was handed over to Hitler who was most eager to watch it. During the course of the showing of the film, Hitler found it particularly enjoyable when the dying men's trousers slid down to their ankles, leaving them completely naked as they gagged and writhed on the wire. One of the men who had witnessed Hitler's reaction to the film commented:

> It seemed as if he had at one stage become almost sexually aroused by the spectacle of the dying men, especially when their trousers came off during their execution. He sat through it with a smile on his face; it was a vile and disgusting picture, which even Joseph Goebbels could not sit through in its entirety. Hitler watched it frequently while taking tea and eating cakes until he eventually became bored with it.

It is also widely believed that Hitler enjoyed pornography. There is mention that his personal photographer, Heinrich Hoffmann, prepared many lewd movies especially for Hitler, which he could watch in his private theatre by himself.

Hitler, it was said, had never expressed concern over the preoccupation of manhood size, as the personality cult that had become his hallmark attraction far outweighed such issues. Besides, Hitler once argued privately in a rare moment that 'it were not just the Luftwaffe that were the Third Reich's greatest phallic symbol, but the new generation of virile and aggressive young Germans'.

Although the sexual exploits of the Führer were largely unknown to the ordinary German people, the sexual excesses of other leaders within the various organizations reached out like a cancer. In some cases, older girls of the *Jung Madel* and the BDM became affected by the improper behaviour of certain individuals within their ranks.

Lesbianism, however, was not exactly rife within the *Jung Madel*, as the girls were of a much younger age group than that of the senior *Bund Deutscher Madel*, and were therefore less inclined to having any feelings of a sexual nature. The problem mainly concerned certain individuals placed in charge of the girls; individuals who would sometimes exploit their positions of authority over the young girls. This was something not unique to the *Jung Madel*, BDM or indeed any other youth organization anywhere else in the world at the time. There will always be those deviants who will exploit certain situations to their own advantage.

Kirsten Eckermann:

There was one woman whose name is known to me even now, and I will not mention it as she may still have living family or relatives somewhere. She held the rank of a senior leader and was often present when the girls were washing, changing and showering and things. She just always seemed to be around and was always keen to give advice on personal matters and things which we felt we could not discuss with our parents. Her interests in some of the girls stretched beyond that of a purely platonic level. She was irritating sometimes and she annoyed me when she once put a towel around me so tight that I could not move and kissed me on the lips and touched me down below. I was very angry as I knew what she was doing was wrong, but had I reported her it would have been my word against hers, wouldn't it? Some of the other girls said that she had touched them also and I told them she had tried to kiss me, but dared not say that she actually did. I was thirteen at the time and it was my last year with the young maidens. I certainly did not have any sexual feelings at that age, girls tended to come of age much later back then than they do now. When things like that went on you just had to keep quiet.

German society at the time did not permit its women to express their sexuality. Young girls and women were told, quite explicitly, that that was for common prostitutes and those of the lesser races such as Jews, gypsies, Communists and blacks.

When girls were considered old enough to take a male partner, they often attended church hall dances. The dances were much like those that young people attended in England at the time, where the girls' parents were always present to make sure that there was no chance of anything happening between the opposite sexes. Girls were not even allowed to hold hands with their male companions and kissing was absolutely out of the question. In fact, there were few real chances for girls and boys to meet on their own. There were a few exceptions to the rule, as will be looked at later.

In all, the Third Reich did not need its women to express their sexuality as this was achieved through the showcasing of their strength, power and aggression. Some photographs taken of *Jung Madel* and BDM girls, however, even now seem to hold a degree of sex appeal, and would not be out of place on some modern-day advertising boards. The press often photographed the girls after their performances at Nazi Party rallies, when they could be photographed in a way to best capture their physical prowess. There are many photographs that show girls posing proudly in their white swastika-adorned vests and black shorts. Often, the photographers asked the girls to kick off their sports shoes to reveal their white socks to further enhance the clean gymnastic lines of the subject. More likely, though, it was to enhance the sexuality of the image. Even now, when one looks at some of the many hundreds of photographs taken of the *Jung Madel* and BDM, there are those that may be deemed sexually provocative in the context that they were originally taken. The press did not want photographs of big-boned or 'butch' girls – the pretty, petite and cute-looking girls were naturally preferred. The cute image of Nazism was much easier to sell to the non-fascist outside world.

The Third Reich was also awash with sex appeal for visiting foreigners attending the big party rallies. There were really no other countries at that time that boasted a generation of uniformed girls and boys who appeared to have been sculpted from bronze, and who marched like soldiers, showing the kind of discipline, order, and self-belief that became the envy of the world. Certainly, as reporter Bud Hanna wrote in his diary in 1934:

> Third Reich Germany is unique and its new culture is unique. It has an army of girls and boys who obey their leaders every command. They are totally awe-inspiring, and when the girls march it seems that they would follow their leaders over cliff tops if necessary and never show any sign of breaking rank or formation. They exude absolute confidence and natural ability and have absolutely no fear whatsoever. German women and girls in particular are the Third Reich's greatest investment in its future.

Bud Hanna's entry would, like those of so many others, become prophetic words in the not-too-distant future, as Hitler's regime steadily inched towards its goal of world domination.

During the course of the author's research, many of the contributors to this work have mentioned unwelcome sexual and rude remarks being made to them, mainly by boys of the Hitler Youth and young soldiers.

Kirsten Eckermann, Anita Von Schoener and Anna 'Tiny' Dann – as she became known to her friends – had all been the victims of some very unpleasant name-calling and sexual banter. Most of the remarks were predictable in their content. The girls were asked things like 'can we give you babies?' or 'are you at our service?' While not exactly as vulgar as what one would have expected, the boys often followed the girls around until the girls threatened to tell a superior, which often had the desired effect. The BDM were also given nicknames designed to ridicule them. These will be examined in the next chapter.

Such things did not help the girls. They began to feel, in some cases, like second-class citizens in a society dominated by males. Anna 'Tiny' Dann recalls:

> I was a BDM at the age of fourteen years in 1943. Because of the war I didn't go out much, but the male attitude towards us by then had also changed. Our role was slowly shifting away from that traditionally planned for us by our elders and leaders. Women were by this time becoming involved directly in the war effort.
>
> Though one time some older Hitler Youth boys once followed me and asked me if I would have their babies and that they would all like to 'do me' as they put it. This did not happen all of the time, but certain members of the male Hitler Youth had a pig-headed attitude and it hurt when they said these things to you. I once reported some boys to a *Jung Madel* leader who caught one of them by his ear and slapped him very hard around the head. She also reported him to his own group superior who then made him give the names of the other boys. They should have been disciplined, but I found out that their group leaders thought it was funny and that I had misunderstood what they had said to me. They said I had told a lie to attract attention, and horrible things like that. Yes, it's true, things like that did go on back then, even in a totalitarian society.

Chapter Six

The Bund Deutscher Madel

U nlike the Hitler Youth for males, the *Bund Deutscher Madel* (BDM), or League of German Girls, had never officially been intended to become a military arm. It was largely due to the catastrophic changes in Germany's military fortunes by the middle of the Second World War, which dictated the necessary transition that had to take place within the organization. At the same time, this would completely redefine the role of German female society as a whole.

There is no doubt that both the *Jung Madel* and BDM operated in many ways the same as Girl Scouts organizations did in other countries. It has to be said, however, that the *Jung Madel* and BDM were radically different in the way that both had been created with far more sinister political and physical intentions in mind, which will become even clearer during the course of this book.

The basic philosophy of the BDM followed in much the same vein as its precursor, the *Jung Madel*. Being older, the roles of the girls in the BDM were different in many ways. Other more important expectations were placed on the girls' shoulders, particularly where political matters were concerned. BDM girls were certainly more politically active than their younger *Jung Madel* counterparts.

The system of joining the BDM was much the same as that of the *Jung Madel*. There was one exception, however, and that was the physical fitness test that all prospective BDM girls had to undergo. If any girl failed to pass the physical test, they could not join the BDM.

This physical prerequisite of enrolment required that each girl had to complete a series of punishing physical tasks. The recruit had to be able to run 60m in fourteen seconds, throw a heavy medicine ball 12m, complete a two-hour march, swim 100m, and finally, she had to know how to make a bed.

Most of the girls were already quite strong, athletic and fit individuals, with the result that surprisingly few ever failed to complete the gruelling test. Upon completion of the test, all that was left was a simple enrolment ceremony, at which the student had to take the stage, stand beside a flag bearing the Swastika, and swear an oath of absolute obedience, allegiance and purity to Adolf Hitler and the German Reich. Usually the student repeated the words read out to her either by her BDM *Gruppenführer*, who was always present to watch over the enrolment ceremony, or the girl's school headmistress.

It has to be said that, owing to the immense emphasis placed on physical fitness and well-being, German girls of that particular period under Nazi rule tended to be fitter and stronger than their modern-day counterparts. Physical strength, agility, and finesse were an essential part of the Hitler Youth and BDM.

At first, Hitler's plans for the BDM girls revolved around a very specific biological aim. Subsequently, they were educated on the principle that they were to be mothers and housewives of his future Reich. Their education would have to centre on this chosen role and purpose. Particular career goals and the achievements of individual girls were not encouraged or considered, being deemed unnecessary. In fact, many of the Nazified teachers would successfully dissuade the girls from studying hard and aiming toward university education, often against the wishes of their parents.

Hitler is quoted as once having told a class of BDM girls 'that the German girl is better employed as a wife and producer of children, rather than a wasted university graduate'. As a result the Nazi school education criteria for females was somewhat minimal.

The boys did not fare much better. They were being raised to be warriors and conquerors, but they received considerably more variety of attention and basic tuition than did the girls.

The BDM education system was tailored to the needs of the Reich as determined by Hitler himself. It therefore became like everything else in the nation: an industry geared to the factory-rearing of the most extreme Nazi ideology, which most girls found they had a duty to respect and assimilate. Yet there were also those who found it narrow, boring and uninteresting.

There were, however, many exceptions to the general thinking that young German females lacked interest in Nazi political matters. Many BDM girls became greatly interested in the Nazi geopolitical goal and would excel in their political theory. For such girls, the rewards could be impressive. The Reich designed a series of attractive proficiency awards especially for the BDM girls. Perhaps the most notable of these awards was the BDM *Leistungsabzeichen* or proficiency clasp. This award was officially instituted around 1936, and came in the form of a clasp consisting of medal ribbon of red, white, and red horizontal bands enclosed in a metal frame and beneath the three letters BDM. The clasp was issued in bronze or silver, depending on the age of the individual. The reverse of the clasp carried an individually stamped number of issue.

To qualify for the award, the BDM girl had to pass rigorous tests in first aid, nursing, home craft, physical exercise, knowledge of geography and Nazi political theory. All tests had to be completed and passed within a period of twelve months. Upon earning the award, there would be a small presentation ceremony, when the award would be pinned to the left breast of the BDM uniform jacket. Such awards carried with them an overwhelming sense of achievement and personal pride, therefore it is little wonder that so many girls strived for that sense of personal excellence within their respective BDM groups.

BDM girls were taught the Nazi curriculum throughout the state-operated Nazi girls' schools. Select subjects such as biology, geography, physical education, political theory and dancing were considered to be subjects of immense importance to German girls and women.

Biology was, without doubt, the subject of prime importance to the girls. As already mentioned, a great emphasis was placed upon the issue of physical and mental well-being, and the maintenance of blood purity and the creation of racially pure offspring.

The blood purity issue was one that had been raised on an almost daily basis in the BDM education system. Hitler was fanatical about the blood purity of his new generation, which should not allow itself to be soiled by the poison of mixed-race breeding. The anti-Semitic language of the Third Reich education system, together with Hitler's loathing of Communists, Slavs, Jews, gypsies and blacks, did not have to necessarily be attractively packaged in order to make it as appealing as possible to his new generation. Years of brainwashing had already instilled much of the party politics where race and creed were concerned. German girls were taught that relationships with men other than those of pure German origin would only serve to contribute to the racial sewer that Germany was in serious danger of becoming throughout the early 1930s.

For girls of the BDM, schooling was to form the nucleus of the new generation. It was therefore imperative that girls be educated separately from the boys, as both had to perform different roles within the new community. Boys were educated to become soldiers and upholders of the Reich, and were taught that they were superior to the girls. Girls, on the other hand, were to remain at home as servants to their men, fulfilling a passive role as childbearers and house *frauen*. The girls were frequently reminded that this should be their sole commitment in life.

In order to hammer this message home to the girls, only the most dedicated and hardline of Nazis were given the authority to teach the girls, while those unsympathetic to the Nazi cause, as explained earlier, were forced from their professions. The Nazis chose to try and erode certain basic principles of morality from the thinking of their females. Many were taught, using principles adapted from nature that one should not feel any form of guilt from the repression and disposal of those considered as being weak and or racially inferior within their communities and the new German society. It was instilled through teaching that it was their duty to remain strong by eliminating the weaklings amongst them, just as the same principle is applied in the kingdom of nature. They were taught that the inferior races and those considered as being biologically weak could only remain on this earth through evolving within their own incestuous communities. Such communities, it was said, were poisonous, immoral and unfit. They were abhorrent to nature and must therefore either be prevented from breeding or destroyed.

As the new German Reich was to operate as one singular social mechanism, there was no need and no room for individual communities anyway. The girls were also taught that, in the interest of producing perfect offspring, commitment to a single German male should be their goal. Any girl committing the offence of adultery risked creating a whirlpool of mixed genes that may become incestuous. Yet it is interesting to note that in later years and in contradiction, German women and BDM girls were encouraged to sleep with as many German males out of wedlock as they chose and produce as many illegitimate children as they desired. Many girls displayed a fierce pride for such squalid actions, which they regarded as a biological service to the Reich and their Führer, attacking all those who dared to protest at their immorality, parents included.

The reality was that the girls were being exploited. Not only were they being used by those males who slept with them, but also by the state itself for allowing such exploitation of its supposedly most valuable resource.

It is unclear just how young many of these girls were, but there is reason to believe from my own research that some were not of a suitable age to partake in any form of sexual activity. The ages of BDM girls engaged in this desperate Reich policy range from as shockingly young as fourteen, to nineteen years of age. One can only imagine the nightmare effect this would also have had on the girls' families.

In the Third Reich, the morality of the German girl and boy was adjusted to suit. There are many hypocritical contradictions to be found in many of the quotes and speeches made to the Reich's generation of young people by various Nazi leaders, including Joseph Goebbels and Heinrich Himmler. A quote from one witness of the time perfectly emphasizes the fact:

> All children are defenceless receptacles, waiting to be filled with wisdom or venom by their parents and educators. We who were born into Nazism never had a chance unless our parents were brave enough to resist the tide and transmit their opposition to their children.

Parents who opposed their daughter's involvement with the BDM not only risked the wrath of the Reich authorities, but also of being socially ostracized. So as a result, many were forced to conform and allow their offspring to absorb the views of their Nazi teachers. Kirsten Eckermann can verify perfectly the effect that the BDM had on both her and her family:

> Upon joining the BDM aged fourteen in 1937, I eagerly attended the weekly BDM meetings. There were few differences in reality to the *Jung Madel*, though we did become involved in more activities. It was not without its shortcomings though and after a while I found that I was becoming ever more distant from my parents. Of course I cared for them both, but what I had been taught over the last five years led me to challenge much of what they themselves had been taught and believed in and what they had taught me. While my father and mother generally supported Hitler during the early years, they came to resent his power, which he had even over us children. My parents felt as if they were no longer in charge or formed a part of my destiny as their child anymore. This inevitably led to tension within the home environment.
>
> The BDM further endorsed the idea of challenging the ideals of our elders, and some viewed it as a means of rebelling. I had a relatively trouble-free upbringing until my inception into the Hitler Youth system. It was good fun at first especially in the *Jung Madel*, but the BDM was much more disciplined and less tolerant, and forced us to challenge everything which opposed what we had been taught over the years by the Nazi system. You could not just switch off when your parents told you to and that is when problems, and in

many situations violence, began in the home for many young girls. Though many young girls lived in fear of their fathers in particular anyway.

The BDM was packaged in a way that made it appeal to us as young people. We yearned for adventure and escape from the city and the BDM continued to provide those things, in return of course for the absorption of certain political realities where we would then be rewarded with attractive little medals. I earned my bronze *Leistungsabzeichen* well within my first year with the BDM.

The Nazis even challenged the subject of German history, changing much of it to suit the new Nazi ethos. Much of the history the Nazis taught was based around the philosophy of the ancient Greeks and their gods and goddesses. Hitler also had great admiration for the Nordic tribes and their culture and aggressiveness. An adaptation of the Nordic-race culture was visibly emulated in certain ways by the BDM. For example, regardless of whether a girl had black, brown or blonde hair, it had to be worn like the Nordic tribeswomen – long and in two ponytails.

Certain traditional dress styles adopted for women in the BDM also had a similarity to those worn by the Nordic races. This is perfectly reflected in some of the photographs of BDM parades, where the students are wearing their BDM uniform, while flag-bearers walking at their sides are wearing the Nordic-style dress of Viking women. From these such subjects emanated Hitler's realization of the Aryan race ideology. Hitler had plans of creating an Aryan race from his new generation of Hitler Youth girls and boys, who would generally serve as the experimental material for this sinister endeavour. It was accepted that it would take two full generations before a true Aryan race would consistently emerge from the Nazi gene pool.

Geography taught to the girls of the BDM in school revolved around the dispute over territory taken from Germany after the First World War. Girls were given detailed explanations of how losing the war, and the implications of the French- and British-brokered Treaty of Versailles affected parents and grandparents of the pre-Hitler era. Such topics were not just confined to school, but were also discussed at the weekly BDM meetings. When war broke out again in 1939, the geography of Germany then centred on the territorial gains made by the *Wehrmacht* and Luftwaffe. After the war, when the Allied re-education programme began, the geography of German territory changed yet again, to a position worse than that just after 1918.

BDM girls were also expected to take childcare classes, as having children was to be their primary role whether they liked it or not. Groups of girls were taken to maternity units, usually in local hospitals, where they would meet new and old mothers alike, and discuss childcare subjects. The visits also served to give the girls some firsthand experience of holding a real baby. Though many of the girls already came from quite large families where there were infants present, and as the girls had to help their mothers with everyday chores, the maternal-care subject was nothing out of the ordinary for them.

The Nazis created new laws to protect the hereditary health of the German nation. Two such laws were the Marriage Health Law and the Law for the Prevention of Hereditarily Diseased Offspring. It was made clear to the girls that they were to have no sexual association whatsoever with those males considered to be weak or inferior racially, physically or mentally. It was continually stressed to the girls 'to be healthy and to remain healthy is not our private concern, but our duty'.

Heidi Koch remembers a visit from her BDM group leader, or *Gauleiter*, who addressed the importance of the issue of avoiding mixed-race and incestuous breeding, particularly with the mentally unfit, and gypsy peoples and those of Jewish origin:

> The *Gauleiter* explained his theories to us and was becoming quite agitated as he talked. His talk came to a climax which would have made Hitler look boring, when he glared at us and shouted, 'If any of you here dare to sleep with Jews and gypsies, then you are poisoning not only yourselves but the very soil of your homeland. You will be condemning everything that you are, and you are Germans, and as Germans only German men will lie at your sides in your beds.'
>
> Most of us looked at one another in slight embarrassment, but the message was made quite clear, and one of the older girls of our group later said as we left the library where the talk had taken place, 'Why couldn't he just not say "girls, please don't fuck Jews and gypsies!"' We laughed about it and went on our way.

Health hygiene and nourishment all came under the scrutiny of the state. Parents were told that their girls should take care of their skin, hair, teeth and nails. The use of cosmetics to enhance their natural beauty was forbidden. The girls had to have at least ten hours sleep a night in a well-ventilated room. Much emphasis was placed on ensuring that they ate well, and received meals that would give them the right balance of vitamins, minerals and protein. Families received special subsidies to ensure that their offspring could eat the correct foods and remain healthy. It was a form of science in itself, and the girls of the BDM became like prized cattle, subject to regular health and fitness checkups.

The BDM uniform had to be worn on all important days, including all special family and school festivals. The uniform had to be washed and ironed properly and had to be worn with pride. No jewellery was permitted to be worn, either with the BDM uniform, or without it – only the small Hitler Youth membership badge was allowed.

The Nazis wanted simplicity and uniformity at all times. This had to be strictly obeyed by all of the girls. Their own uniforms were usually received within one to two weeks of joining the BDM. They were then fully responsible for its care and maintenance.

There was also a BDM knife issued by the authorities. This was identical to the type issued to the boys of the Hitler Youth, but was much lighter and carried no inscriptions or manufacturer's markings. This weapon was an unofficial accessory, offered to girls as an 'optional' private purchase. As it was considered at the time unladylike for girls or women to wear or carry weapons, very few of these knives were actually issued, and as a result today they are rare.

The subject of sex education within the BDM was virtually non-existent, as sex was seen as a biological function performed only in the interests of reproduction. Talking about sex was something completely alien to the Nazi regime and its so-called 'new morality'. The fact that very few girls received adequate information on the subject of sex and intercourse inevitably led to problems later on. There were many unplanned pregnancies amongst BDM girls, particularly in the American Occupation Zone after the war. This had occurred due to the lack of basic sexual knowledge.

Many girls found that there would be certain young men waiting to take advantage of them especially during their work placements in the early years with the RADwf, where during the early years, they mixed frequently with young males during the course of their work. There certainly were, however, an adventurous few who did find out all about the birds and the bees, and began to exploit such 'forbidden' knowledge. This will be looked at later.

Religious education went more or less unchanged, not that many of the girls ever took it as seriously as their elders. As far as most girls were concerned, the only bible that really meant anything to them was Adolf Hitler's

Mein Kampf. Through religious debate, the teachers taught them that the destruction of the Jew within German society was an intended course of history. It was God's will, and a logical conclusion to the amputation of a diseased portion of the evolutionary mechanism of the human race. Nazi religion challenged that it was one of the reasons that God had appointed Hitler to save Germany, and that the Germanic Aryan race would one day inherit the earth.

The BDM were also expected to attend regular seminars given by such prominent Nazis as SS chief Heinrich Himmler. Himmler, a former Bavarian chicken farmer, would become the architect for the annihilation of Jews, Slavs and gypsies in Europe. He would give hour-long seminars on the subject of the Jew, and in particular why the Jew could no longer be tolerated within German society. Himmler was cold and calculated. He had no scruples whatsoever as to how he would achieve his aim. As a chicken farmer, he had planned to dispose of Europe's Jewish, Slav and gypsy populations in much the same way as he did his chickens: keeping them in communal huts surrounded by wire, before slaughtering them with ruthless efficiency. Many of the girls listened intently to Himmler, and many believed and accepted without question his theory on race and eugenics. By the time most girls had joined the BDM, they had already been poisoned against Jews, Slavs and gypsies, accepting that the decisions made by their leaders were correct. There were, however, a good number who secretly began to question the ethics of the BDM, and Hitler Youth in general.

One such brave German girl was Sophie Scholl. Along with her brother Hans, she became involved with the White Rose student resistance movement at Munich University. This body began to oppose Nazi ideology and the education of Germany's youth through the publication of various anti-Nazi leaflets and handbills. Sophie Scholl and her important role and stance in opposing the Nazi regime will be examined later.

Girls who had no involvement with the BDM came under immense pressure to join, mainly from their friends. In an effort to determine their loyalty, the authorities also began to scrutinize those who resisted. Neighbours were often asked to act as informers. If parental interference was to blame for a child not volunteering for the BDM, then a visit with sinister intentions was certain. In the end, fear proved to be the major motivating factor, resulting in the parents of most girls not objecting to their joining the BDM.

Prior to 1939, it had, in some cases, been possible to buy oneself out of the Hitler Youth and BDM by agreeing to pay a subscription fee. Under the new compulsory laws, however, this was soon scrapped. It soon became obvious to most parents that their own sets of values had either been distorted or replaced by those of the Nazis. Girls joining the BDM became the property of the state, and over a period of time, parents lost almost complete control over their daughters. Theresa Moelle explains:

My adoptive parents Walter and Greta Moelle adopted me on 12 November 1933 when I was five years old and I was brought up within their strict Christian community. The Moelles already had three other natural children, and while my relationship with them was reasonable, I was always a difficult and sometimes aggressive girl. We lived on the outskirts of Berlin in a very comfortable environment. My problems inevitably arose from the fact that I came from an orphanage, and my adoptive parents never tried to disguise this fact from me. Though I have never to this day discovered who my real parents were, I certainly don't want to know. Walter Moelle was very strict and if I stepped out of line he would take a stick to me, just like his other children. Well, he did until I got older when I once hit him back. Walter Moelle did not agree with everything which the Nazis were doing to change Germany from 1933, but generally benefited from certain things they did. People used to say 'Don't worry about Hitler and the National Socialists, they are good for German business.'

He did not like the idea of the BDM, as he believed, unlike many fathers, that it was a deviant organization. He also felt that young girls should not become a part of any political circus or anything, and that their role was in the home. He didn't believe in all the big parades and rallies and things either and did not like the fact that we marched and wore uniforms. I suppose he felt it went a bit too far and it must have made him feel insecure in some way.

By 1937, the whole Hitler Youth thing had become compulsory and you had to join, it was really very simple. *Jungvolk* and *Jung Madel* prepared us for inception into the BDM, though the BDM was different in many ways. It was certainly more political and encouraged us to think politically, especially where Jews, blacks, Slavs and gypsies were concerned. Biology and eugenics were also studied in detail and these subjects were very interesting, though their principles were much different back then in the mid- to late-1930s.

Aryanism was also studied and served as a kind of role model, what we as a race should strive to become. I joined the BDM in April of 1942, and I suppose my adoptive parents did not really approve of it, except for the above given reasons, but the BDM took me away from home and I was able to enjoy doing things that I could never have otherwise done. We did many of the normal feminine things such as making things for old ladies and kindergartens, but we also did many things that only boys used to do. When we went camping we made rope swings attached to trees and swung across streams on them and things, those were things that girls did not do normally.

The BDM also taught us the rudiments of first aid, along with home economics and childcare, though the latter certainly did not interest me very much. I found babies quite messy and unpleasant things as a fourteen-year-old. The BDM changed my attitude to myself completely and after only a short period I started to think about how I wanted to change my life in some way and do something really positive. Maybe the BDM made me feel like a part of something big, which had happened and was continuing to build in Germany.

I began to question my adoptive father's discipline in certain ways and wanted more freedom, and that spelled much trouble. Walter Moelle hated violence and did not want me to be a part of an organization which endorsed the use of hate and destruction in any form. This led to inevitable rows in the Moelle household. My language could be appalling at times and after one particular row with my father over the BDM I shouted, 'Well, are you going to go out there and tell the fucking *Gauleiter* and the Nazis, that you don't want me to be a part of them? Why don't you do that and get us all arrested and shot?'

Poor Walter Moelle reacted in the only way that he could and he actually slapped me hard across the face. He had never done that before. I remember screaming that 'I hated him and would one day shoot him dead for hitting me if the BDM didn't do it first.' Everyone had changed under Hitler and it was done in a very clever way where young girls and women were concerned. We were manipulated away from the good senses of our homes, upbringings and parents, and led to follow a very dangerous political and military course of action. Though our activities would become very limited by 1943, this mainly due to the constant threat of bombing, this only helped the Nazis to reaffirm our belief that the world was indeed not our friend but our enemy.

As the property of the Reich, the girls had to be prepared to work hard in the interests of the national community. All individuality was therefore rendered as an unimportant factor. In fact, individuality was viewed as the path chosen by the traitor.

Life became a sterile beehive of conformity, where all girls were bound to the same grey ideology and social process. It was a process carefully manipulated by the hierarchy to make the girls believe that they were the driving forces behind their own personal destiny, and were indeed acting upon their own sets of initiative. The reality of the situation was, in fact, the exact opposite.

Faith and honour were traits created through the strict BDM discipline, and hard physical exercise routines, which conveyed the sense of national responsibility that was the code by which all of the girls would live. They had sworn an oath to serve and honour their Führer. They would even die for him if called upon to do so.

In order to promote the idea of a unified body, soul and spirit, in 1934 national youth leader and head of the Hitler Youth from 1931 to 1940, Baldur von Schirach, introduced an achievement badge for physical prowess. The award was similar to the BDM *Leistungsabzeichen*. Of course, von Schirach had absolutely no real interest in the competitiveness aspect as such, but this was an easy way of ensuring that the girls always performed physically to the very best of their ability. In turn, this would ensure a healthy breeding stock of young females. It was a very simple philosophy. The award of pretty metal badges and 'tinnies' created a great sense of personal pride in the girls, who therefore worked very hard to earn them. Such proficiency awards were the only items that a BDM girl could wear on her uniform. It was also one of the reasons that so many sporting festivals were held in towns and villages all over Germany, through which a framework of achievement could be easily seen and then turned into yet more racial and biological propaganda for the BDM.

Many in German male society also secretly scoffed at the BDM. It also found itself the target of some particularly unwelcome and vulgar jokes and remarks from the male population, particularly boys of the Hitler Youth, members of the SS, and young soldiers of the *Wehrmacht*. The initials BDM were given improper substitutes such as '*Bubi Drück Mich*' (squeeze me laddie); '*Bedarfsartikel Deutscher Manner*' (requisite for German males); '*Brauch Deutsche Madel*' (make use of German girls); '*Bald Deutscher Mutter*' (German mothers to be); and '*Bund Deutscher Milchkuhe*' (League of German Milk Cows).

BDM girl Heidi Koch recalls:

> We were at times the target of ridicule and name-calling from the boys and young men. A gang of local Hitler Youth boys were always making unpleasant remarks to me, while also mocking my name. They would say to me, 'Heidi, hide my cock' and things like that. I also remember the same boys discussing out loud about the origins for the design of the steel helmet as worn by our soldiers. They said that the idea came from the shape of the end of the male sexual organ. Girls like myself were often far too embarrassed to report such incidents.

Under the Hitler influence, the general attitude towards girls and young women in Nazi Germany had begun to change radically – it became something of a slowly tightening noose.

Dora Brunninghausen:

> Our lives more or less began to revolve around five particular things. These were school, our two hours each week with the BDM [*Heimabend* meetings], helping our mothers with home chores, church and Adolf Hitler. School was all right as I mixed with my friends and we were able to talk amongst ourselves, often about things we shouldn't. The two hours a week with the BDM was divided between ideological tuition, the role and work of the BDM organization, and German history and culture.
>
> In fact, anything that was happening at the time was open for discussion, but only in a limited and very controlled sense, and although we always contributed with our opinions, our opinions evolved from the poison of what we had been taught. Most of the themes revolved around the subjects of loyalty and honour, particularly towards our men folk and our personal courage and conviction to serve males. After the serious work was done, we could sit and talk with the other girls and BDM leaders, and we often knitted or sewed and did handicrafts. Sometimes we were treated to a magic or puppet-theatre-type show. These were often terribly amateurish but they made us laugh.
>
> Before we went home, we all stood to attention and sang a patriotic song. It was designed to not only educate us but also ensure we understood just how important it was for us to love our

fatherland and to understand what it was that Hitler was saying to us all in his speeches. The BDM was special to me at that time. We were a community of our own, and each of the other girls was like a sister to me, that's how close we became to each other.

There were also a number of important publications that were produced mainly for BDM leaders, the most well-known of these being *Die Madelschaft*. This was a form of guidebook for the BDM leader, containing information on activities, training and the basic teaching themes. All manner of topics were thrown in. These ranged from subjects relating to the First World War, to political figures, and so on. The issue produced in November 1938 dealt with the National Socialist Party and its early years of struggle, painting its members, such as Horst Wessel and Herbert Norkus, as heroes and martyrs. In April 1939, the publication dealt with the issue of the struggle against Bolshevism and Germany's role as a kind of bulkhead against the spread of Communism. The text included sections on how Bolshevism destroyed the structure of normal marriage and family life. Everything that the BDM leader absorbed was directed like a hypodermic needle into the minds of the other girls, as the leader often became the potential BDM teacher.

The summer camps, which the BDM girls enjoyed, were also saturated with Nazi politics and ethos. However, many did not mind the lecturing and the strict drill, as they enjoyed the escape from their everyday surroundings and the monotony of the inner city. The camps were centred on very strict discipline that had to be observed at all times.

Girls could be fined for leaving anything lying around, such as personal items or pieces of clothing, etc. The particular item would be returned to the girl only after the fine was paid. Sometimes, the fine would be replaced by certain duties such as extra washing and cooking.

Life on the eight to ten-day summer camps adhered to a very regimented timetable. Flag-raising, meals and training all had specific time allocations, so girls had to be punctual to ensure that the timetable was kept.

The day normally began early when the girls were roused by their leaders. They then washed, had breakfast, combed their hair and brushed their teeth. The agenda for each day differed. Sometimes the girls began their day with a song, while on others they went on a march or a swim in lakes and rivers.

The main reason behind the summer camp was to study contemporary political events occurring in Germany at the time away from their parents' eye.

A BDM leader would give a lecture on the current political events, done in a way that the girls could easily understand. Of huge importance were subjects that dealt with the Treaty of Versailles, and the shame that it had brought upon Germany during the slump into economic depression and anarchy after 1918.

Adolf Hitler's foreign policy and the need for *Lebensraum*, or living space, were also discussed in detail. The whole of summer camp was designed for a single specific educational objective. The activities in which the girls took part, such as hiking, dancing, swimming and play, were merely sweeteners to make the whole thing more attractive.

BDM household schools were also built, the first of which came into existence in 1936. Here too, the whole idea of these schools was to train girls in domestic management and childcare. The schools ran intensive home economics-style classes for the girls, covering everything from cooking, gardening, needlework and nutrition, to caring for infants, the elderly and the sick. Theory lessons were also devised where the individual could be tested for sound knowledge of the subject. Racial science was included, as was the understanding of the national economy and sports. It was an extension of the 'human-factory' principle.

For girls who came from small families, where there were no infant brothers or sisters, a compulsory placement scheme was implemented, where the girl would be placed with a woman who had four or more children. This way she would learn firsthand all the necessary skills required for her future motherhood. Girls could also be placed to work with farmer's wives, which was something most girls who lived in the cities did not mind. The authorities were keen for the city, and *Mitte* girls in particular, to experience life in a rural community. In a broader sense, it would also help them to feel closer to their homeland.

Kirsten Eckermann:

> By the end of my first year with the BDM, I found that I was so much more confident and perhaps, rather foolishly, independent, at least that is how I felt. I felt that I had learned and accomplished quite a lot of new skills and also understood our country's stance on the world stage at that time. To me it was all made justifiable through political necessity and maybe divine will.
>
> I found that my parents were very wary of me in certain ways. For example, if I argued with my father, something I would not have dared to have done before the BDM, he would not discipline

me in the manner he used to. He used to take his belt from his trousers and hit us with that. As a BDM I became the property of the state, and if any girl was beaten and the schoolteachers or those at the BDM meetings became aware of it, often the police were informed. The father could be arrested and imprisoned. This put an immense strain upon certain parents and there were many times when my father and I just could not talk to each other. The Nazis had created a kind of generation gap and we were of differing generations and had been taught different things, and as a result we had this mutual fear and misunderstanding of each other, and talking to Father became awkward. My father's generation wanted a decent economy and wage so as they could feed their families. This the Nazis gave them to a degree, but the BDM regime taught us to hate Jews and not to accept the old submissive ways of our parents. My parents were not stupid, they understood what was going on and they lived with it as best as they could. I know that after several years there were times when perhaps both they and I wished that Hitler was dead.

Another young girl who joined the BDM in the 1930s was Ursula Sabel.

Sabel was a pretty schoolgirl who lived in Duisburg, Wedau, with her mother and father and brother. Her parents, like many, embraced the National Socialist cause at first, but later their views were to change very drastically. Now living in fulltime residence in the beautiful town of Heidelberg in Germany, she reflects on some of her memories with the BDM:

Throughout all of my school years, there was an evening of every week where we attended the Hitler Youth for girls [the *Bund Deutscher Madel*]. I had a great desire to become involved in music when I was older. The Hitler Youth supplied all of the girls with a uniform; it consisted of a dark blue skirt, a buttoned-in white blouse, a so-called travel cloth, and a black tie was also worn.

My parents were loyal to the National Socialist cause, though rather sceptically. From the messages broadcast over the radio, one experienced only what was accordingly censored for the population, and none of the broadcasted material was therefore of a critical nature. So one also had to be content with discovering news from word of mouth. My parents suspected bad things, my father, being a civil servant, had guessed that the Nazi Party would inevitably happen. It took quite some time for me to get my uniform and decorations, though I was still allowed to go to the weekly meetings. When I received my complete uniform I had my picture taken wearing it, and I still possess it today.

In the summer of 1939, I travelled with my BDM group from Duisburg up the Rhine on a steamer boat. Our small unit then rode along to Mannheim, and then we moved along the beautiful Neckar. We stayed overnight in youth hostels, a wonderful experience for me. The high point of the trip was the attendance at the realm festivals in the brightly illuminated Heidelberger lock.

From my early years with the BDM, two particular things are very memorable to me. After I had participated a long time in the weekly Hitler Youth meetings held in evenings and afternoons, and without finding the politics of it all too noticeably unpleasant, I was entrusted, after agreement with my parents, with a group of younger girls, who I would be in charge of at the weekly meetings of the BDM. I assumed the role with great joy, but the fun of independence did not last for too long, the reason being my mother. I had no more time for the school, and had to give it up.

Another experience fresh in my mind was when I went to the Mülheimer forest. We moved as a group from Wedau about two hours walking distance into the forest, which belonged to the Mülheim Ruhr. An important man from the top management of the steel industry, Mr Kierdorf lived there in a mansion (though we did not get to see it). He celebrated a special birthday on the day we arrived, and because the *industriebosse* for Hitler was so important, both Hitler's and our attendance had more or less been assured. We girls with our small uniforms sat in the grass at a roadside for what seemed like a long time. With several hours of delay the first automobile came, then gradually behind it other vehicles began to appear, and we immediately stood up to see who were in the cars. We were surprised to see in the first vehicle Rudolf Hess the deputy Führer. It was an open car and we could see him very clearly. Other cars drove past then and in the last open car was Adolf Hitler. He looked full of pride for his youth and greeted us with a raised right arm; we children returned the salute by raising our right arms and calling 'Welfare, welfare!' The cars were soon gone, but the waiting had been worthwhile itself, we had seen Hitler and Hess, a great experience was had by us all.

Former BDM girl Helena W. Wessel best tells some of the lesser-known incidents, regarding in particular the issue of 'moral conduct' expected within the BDM.

It is quite an amusing little story, which I will have to tell to you. It was an incident which occurred at one of the church hall dances in a town near Essen. There was this young woman and man, both aged around sixteen years. The pair had shared a romantic dance but their chaperone, a big old lady named Frau Ebner, certainly would not let this couple out of her sight. The couple somehow managed to sneak outside through a door after some friends created a diversion by knocking over some coffee pots and cups, distracting Frau Ebner's attention. The women were busy cleaning the mess up and did not notice Albert and the town *Burgermeister's* niece disappear. They were gone for around eight to ten minutes and were able to get back in through the same door.

During one of the summer camps three weeks later, we girls gathered around and she told us what she and Albert had done. We giggled like mad things as she told us in great detail how she had given Albert what would be known as 'hand relief' nowadays. God knows how risky that must have been, and what would have happened had they got caught or found out.

Some of the BDM girls got away with sheer murder, and it was not uncommon for one or two of the older girls to play around a little. It was one way of learning about real sex, and some of the girls found out about it from their older brothers who brought their girlfriends home sometimes. One girl told us that she had seen her brother on top of his girlfriend 'pumping away', as she put it. We roared with laughter as she asked, 'Well, do you know how it is done?', then proceeding to explain in great detail.

There were always certain characters who could be relied upon to tell us all the details, and as we were comrades, we kept it all to ourselves and did not betray each other to the superiors. It was a kind of rule we had amongst our closest girlfriends, and helped to keep us informed of what was really happening outside of the BDM and in the real world. Subsequently we could not write such things in our diaries or notebooks for fear of it being discovered either by parents or BDM seniors, though I did manage to keep a diary for quite some time.

The BDM in a way was really nothing special; it was just another example of how Hitler's influence permeated everyday society. The BDM was created to bring young girls and women under control of the state, so as the state could do what it wanted with them and manipulate them accordingly. Hitler wanted us to be good Nazis and produce good Nazi offspring, who in turn would be poisoned with the same shit. That I believe was the principal idea of the BDM – it was a means of creating an Aryan race stereotype.

Heidi Koch remembers the total change in attitude of the elders of her small community when she had become a member of the BDM.

One afternoon I was very anxious to visit the *Süßwarengeschäft* [sweet shop], to buy my favourite treat of liquorice, and after my mother gave me a small amount of money off I went. I always looked forward to buying some sweets because we were not often allowed to have them. Anyway, I chose what sweets I wanted and gave the shopkeeper's wife my money. She handed me my small brown paper bag and I said '*Danke*' [thank you], and I turned away and began to walk out of the door when she called out to me, 'Heidi, have you not forgotten something girl?'

I stopped, turned around and I was embarrassed and puzzled for a moment, as everyone in the shop stopped and glared at me like I was a thief or something, and I could not think what she could possibly mean. As I stood looking at her puzzled, she deliberately pulled up a part of her apron and began to polish the badge she wore on her breast with it. The badge had the Swastika on it and was one worn by all those who were closely associated with the Nazi Party. I quickly apologized saying, 'Sorry Frau Mühlbauer,' and quickly thrust up my right arm and gave her a loud 'Heil Hitler!'

I could not believe that she had scalded me for not saluting, but that is exactly how much things were changing. It would be 'Heil Hitler' this and 'Heil Hitler' that, and before long it was used in place of the usual greetings such as those we used to say, like 'Good morning' or 'Goodbye', or even 'Thank you'. As a BDM girl it was very important that you remember your 'Heil Hitler' salute at all times.

The BDM was obsessive where physical prowess was concerned. Some girls possessed a natural ability with sports and physical exercise classes, whilst others did not. Those who were obviously talented at sports were encouraged to train in order to master a multiplicity of sporting disciplines. The training was of a very high standard, but hard, aggressive, and sometimes a little too excessive, even for the most gifted of BDM students.

For girls, the standard sporting outfit consisted of a pair of plimsolls or dancing shoes, a pair of black shorts, and a white vest with the triangular Hitler Youth badge bearing the swastika emblem in its centre.

BDM girl athletes competed at numerous high and low-profile sporting tournaments around the world before and up to the outbreak of war in 1939. It was clear that many of these girls, having been raised in such a totalitarian regime as that of Nazi Germany, where fitness, health and strength were requisite female virtues, were incredibly gifted athletes, who could sometimes outperform their adult sporting counterparts. One particular BDM girl who notched up an impressive record of awards was Doris Schriber.

Schriber was born on August 1924, in the town of Villingen in southwest Germany. The author was able to obtain copies of Schriber's sporting-award certificates gained while a member of the BDM. The first award dates from March 1939, when she was fifteen years old. She had won first prize in the Gau Baden figure-skating championships of that year and awarded the prized golden oak leaf. Other awards soon followed, including:

March 1940: Second prize in the Gau Baden figure-skating championships, and awarded the silver oak leaf.

June 1940: First prize in the Hitler *Jugend* District 407 in the triathlon discipline.

11 January 1941: Awarded the Fourth Class figure-skating qualification certificate.

July 1941: Hitler *Jugend* swimming certificate and covering letter from the Villingen BDM leader. For some reason, Doris had not bothered to collect some previous awards from the BDM office.

Dates unknown: First prize in the Hitler *Jugend* District 407, 4 x 100 m relay race. Second prize in the Hitler *Jugend* District 733 in the high-jump discipline.

1941: Second prize certificate for Hitler *Jugend* District 407 national sports contest, Villingen team. Second prize certificates for the Hitler *Jugend* District 407 in javelin throwing, the pentathlon event and the long-jump event.

17 January 1943: First prize in the Hitler *Jugend* District 407 awarded in an unknown sporting event. This was her last recorded sporting event at the age of nineteen years.

During work on the manuscript for this book, I attempted to make contact with Doris through the Villingen-Schwenningen *Rathaus* (city hall) to talk about her experiences in the BDM and Second World War Germany, but she declined to be interviewed.

Chapter Seven

A White Rose Remembered

It was during the writing of this work and while talking with Kirsten Eckermann and her husband in a teashop in Dover in July 2000, that she asked the author if he had ever heard of Sophie Scholl. Her name was not familiar, and upon being asked who she was, Kirsten replied, 'You must include something about Sophie Scholl in your work, as she, along with her brother Hans, were two heroes of the student resistance against Nazism in Germany.'

The obvious concern with which Kirsten spoke and the fact that the author had not heard of Sophie Scholl and her brother Hans, prompted him to research and write this chapter.

There is, even today, a general misconception present in much of the military history taught to young people, particularly in school, that there were few attempts by the German people at resisting Adolf Hitler's Nazi dictatorship. The general belief is that the populace, especially Germany's youth, largely gave their full support to the political and social changes being made by the Nazi regime. There were, of course, those who were silently sceptical, but bound to conformity. Then there were those who, with time, began to analyze their political and social surroundings under Hitler and the Nazis.

Though the primary objective of this work was to concentrate purely on the female issues of the Third Reich, one has to examine in detail the important activities of Sophie Scholl and her family in resisting the Nazi regime. The Scholl children, particularly Sophie and Hans, due to the strong and committed Christian influence of their parents, became the driving force behind the student anti-Nazi movement at Munich University. Both brother and sister, and their accomplices, would meet the same fate under the so-called Nazi people's law system.

Sophie Scholl was born to Robert and Magdalene Scholl on 9 May 1921. The fourth of five children, she was born in Forchtenberg-am-Kocher, a riverside town east of Heilbronn, Germany, where her father was mayor of the town. The little town was a little isolated from the rest of Germany. Its only real connection to the outside world was a small, yellow-coloured post coach that ran back and forth to the nearby railway station.

Robert Scholl, recognizing that Forchtenberg lacked in certain basic travel amenities, was able to get the rail track extended to the town. He also had a community and sports centre erected, which was greatly appreciated by the children of the town. Not everyone supported Robert Scholl's ideas of expansion for the town, however, and he was voted out of office in 1930.

Sophie and her brothers Hans and Werner and two sisters Ingeborg and Elisabeth were raised in the Christian faith. At the age of seven, she entered grade school, where she learned easily. She was a likeable child and so had a carefree childhood. Known for her bubbly and happy personality, Sophie made friends very easily and got on with everyone. In Sophie's eyes, race and religion was no barrier to friendship.

In 1930, after Robert Scholl was voted from his mayoral office, the Scholl family moved to Ludwigsburg. And then two years later they moved to Ulm, where her father had acquired a business and tax-consulting office. Scholl had the habit of living a little beyond his means, and had rented a huge apartment for his family on the cathedral square. Ulm lacked the lush countryside of Forchtenberg, but Sophie and her siblings played in the large palace park nearby, which was some slight consolation to the energetic Scholl children.

Sophie, it was said, possessed her mother's quiet sensitivity, but her father's strong personality. Sophie and her brother Hans strongly believed in human rights, and like the rest of the Scholl children, this was a quality inherited from their father Robert.

At the age of eleven in 1932, Sophie began her secondary education at a school for girls. The following year, Adolf Hitler stormed to power with his Nazi Party. He immediately began to implement completely new reforms within the education system, urging both girls and boys to join the Hitler Youth.

Ingeborg Scholl recalls the response of the German press and radio on 30 January 1933: 'The newspapers and radio were full of the news that Hitler had come to power.'

'Now everything will be better in Germany. Hitler is at the tiller', the headline news proclaimed.

Ingeborg, who was sixteen at the time, says:

> There was much talk of the fatherland and of comradeship and the union of the Germanic peoples. Of course, it impressed us, and we listened positively. We loved our homeland and everywhere we heard that Hitler wanted to help Germany rebuild itself back to

greatness, happiness and prosperity. He wanted everyone to have employment and to have enough to eat. He promised every German citizen that he would not rest until they enjoyed independence, freedom and happiness.

At the age of twelve, along with her brothers and sisters, classmates and friends, Sophie joined the Hitler Youth for girls (JM/BDM). Sophie's father was under no illusions as to the game Hitler was playing, asking his children, 'Have you considered how he's going to manage all that he has promised? He is expanding the armaments industry and building barracks. Do you know where that's all going to end?'

The Scholl children argued that Hitler would solve much of Germany's problems, including unemployment, by the building of the new autobahns across the land.

Sophie was initially enthusiastic about the Hitler Youth movement, but she soon began to question many of the organization's ethics. She became very concerned by the Nazi attitude towards her Jewish school friends, who were not permitted to join the Hitler Youth. While her brothers and sisters became group leaders within their respective organizations, Sophie became increasingly sceptical. She became aware of the dissenting political views of her father, friends, and of some of her teachers. During this time, Hans was not on speaking terms with his father.

Robert Scholl came to despise the Hitler Youth and all that it stood for, and could no longer understand his son's eager participation. However, Hans soon changed his whole outlook of the Nazi regime when he was given the honour of bearer of the flag of Ulm at the Nuremberg party rally in 1935. He became extremely despondent with the constant drilling, hate-filled oration, and stupid conversation and vulgar jokes about silly things. He, like Sophie and their father, now understood more clearly than ever before what Nazism really meant. To make matters worse, bad stories were beginning to filter back into Germany as to what was happening to Jews in German concentration camps.

The political attitude now became an essential criterion in Sophie's choice of friends. She found that she could no longer integrate with those who supported the Nazi ideal, naturally seeking the company of those who shared the same opinions and felt the same way as she did.

The arrest of her brother and some of his friends in November 1937, for their membership of an outlawed youth group banned by the Nazis and known as the 'dj.1.11' (taken from the date of its founding, 1 Nov 1929), left a very strong impression on Sophie. She greatly admired their courage and conviction to stand by their personal beliefs.

After their arrests, the Scholl household was searched by the Gestapo. Nothing was found, however, as Frau Scholl, with great presence of mind, had managed to cleverly dispose of any incriminating material, on the pretence that she had to visit the bakery. The Gestapo let her go after she had managed to get to the attic room to hide the illicit documents for which the state secret police had been searching. She had placed it under a cover in her basket, then leaving the Gestapo to search the house.

Ingeborg and Werner Scholl were taken to Stuttgart where the authorities detained them for a week before releasing them. Hans Scholl was held for five weeks and was only saved further interrogation by a conscription order. A sympathetic German army officer had him released upon the context that he was now a serving soldier and was therefore under army jurisdiction.

Non-conformity was a very dangerous path to choose to take at that time in Germany, and few young people would ever dare to deviate from the path of such institutionalized conformity.

Sophie had a great talent for drawing and painting, enjoying anything to do with art. Her drawings of Peter Pan – each with a certain aura about them – are excellent examples of Sophie's creative skill. Many wonder why such a promising young artist chose to study biology and philosophy instead of art at university. It was through her love for painting and drawing that she first came into contact with what the Nazis termed as 'degenerate artists' – those artists who refused to embrace the Nazi perception and terminology of art as seen by Hitler.

Sophie was a compulsive reader, developing a growing interest in philosophy and theology. Engrossing herself in such books became her way of escaping from the world of National Socialism and its preoccupation with hate and violence. She also enjoyed reading the poetical works of Heinrich Heine, the 19th century German poet who was of Jewish origin. At one particular BDM meeting, the teacher asked the girls to suggest some suitable literature for home reading. Sophie, quite innocently replied that Heine was an excellent choice of reading. The BDM teacher and some of the other girls were appalled by Sophie's improper choice of selecting the work of a Jew. Sophie remained defiant, saying, 'The person who doesn't know Heine doesn't know German literature.'

Aged nineteen in the spring of 1940, and with the Second World War still in its infancy, Sophie graduated from secondary school. The subject of her essay was titled *The Hand that Moved the Cradle, Moved the World*.

She was very fond of children and she became a Kindergarten teacher at the Frobel Institute in Ulm-Soflingen. Sophie had chosen this position as she had hoped that the authorities would recognize it as an alternative service to *Reichsarbeitsdienst* (National Labour Service), which was compulsory for all females, and a prerequisite to any university education. This was an error in judgement. From the spring of 1941 onwards, she had to enrol for six months' auxiliary war service as a nursery teacher in Blumberg. The military-like regime of the Labour Service, or RADwf as it was known, only made her more determined to practise passive resistance and non-conformity. Her six months of service soon passed without any serious incident caused by her non-conformist attitude, though this had not gone unnoticed by the authorities and leaders of the RADwf.

In May 1942, at the age of twenty-one, Sophie eventually enrolled at the University of Munich to study for a degree in biology and philosophy. Her brother Hans was also at the university, studying medicine. It was here that he introduced her to his group of friends. This group later became more known for their political activities, though they had been drawn together initially by a shared love of art, music, literature, philosophy and theology. Sophie also enjoyed skiing in the snow-covered mountain ranges around Germany, and was also a fine swimmer. With her new group of university friends, she attended concerts, plays and lectures.

It was during her time in Munich that Sophie met artists, writers and philosophers. People like German publisher and writer Carl Muth and writer and cultural critic Theodor Haecker became important links to her concerns about the Christian faith. The one thing that became of prime importance to Sophie was the issue of how one should act under the rule of dictatorship.

During her summer vacation in 1942, Sophie had to do war service in a metallurgic plant in Ulm. The work was dirty and oily, involving basic manual duties on hand-operated, metal-pressing machines, as well as other laborious and monotonous tasks producing minor parts for military applications.

During that same period, Sophie's father was serving a sentence in prison for a critical remark about Hitler he had made to one of his employees. This generally indicates how very easy it was to become the victim of betrayal, and mirrors the events that would lead Sophie to pay the ultimate price for her beliefs.

During the early summer of 1942, Sophie had become involved in the production and distribution of a series of political leaflets of the 'White Rose', the name given to their student resistance movement. It is also interesting to point out that the White Rose may have been the only resistance group to have mentioned the mass murder of European Jews.

Sophie, Hans, and the other students enjoyed the support of philosophy lecturer Kurt Huber in their endeavours. The resistance fighter was already under suspicion, so the Nazis had been watching him closely, trying to gauge his political activities. Huber was much older than the student group. Whilst he was unable to lead them, he gave them much moral and material guidance, editing the last two of the six leaflets and handbills produced by the students.

Sophie and her friends shunned violence as a means of protesting against government, aiming to change the way that people viewed Nazism and its militaristic ideal through non-violent, or passive, opposition. The movement was given a studio owned by an architect as a meeting place and where they could work on their leaflets. They had also managed to acquire a typewriter and a small printing machine. Sophie was not a part of the early organization, but joined and contributed in the later stages.

The first four fliers produced by the White Rose were issued in quick succession, appearing in June and July of 1942. The authors of these were mainly Hans Scholl, Alexander Schmorell and Christoph Probst. Apart from Huber, Christoph was the only member of the group who was married. The 23-year-old Huber had two young children. His wife was expecting their third when Huber was arrested and executed, so he never saw the child.

The first of the leaflets distributed by the White Rose are striking in their content, reflecting the political maturity of its young authors. The first leaflet states, 'Nothing is less worthy of a cultivated people than to allow itself to be governed by a clique of irresponsible bandits of dark ambition without resistance.' These are examples of the type of phrases used in the leaflets to address non-violent direct action such as sabotage of the weapons and ammunition industry. They are highly critical of the non-Christian nature of the war:

'We are all guilty.' 'We will not be silenced.' 'We are your bad conscience.' 'The White Rose will not leave you in peace.'

The group constantly worked in fear of betrayal or discovery by the Gestapo, but they were driven by the desire to fight National Socialism and the spectre of Adolf Hitler. Sophie also feared greatly for her family, wondering what might happen to them if her activities were discovered. Each member of the White Rose had his or her own personal fears, but the group persisted in their goal.

The White Rose temporarily scaled down its covert activities in the summer of 1942, as Hans Scholl, Willi and Alexander were ordered to the Russian Front. They returned to Munich that October.

For the first time, Hans Scholl, during his service on the Russian Front, had witnessed the ill treatment meted out to Jews and Russian prisoners of war. There was one occasion when Hans gave his tin of tobacco to an old man and his meagre army rations to a little girl. The little girl understandably threw the rations back at Hans, but he very calmly picked them up. He then picked a daisy and carefully placed it on top of the rations, before putting them at the girl's feet. She momentarily stood gazing at him with her huge brown eyes, before kneeling to pick up the rations. She carefully took the daisy and placed it in her hair. It was the moment that changed Hans's life. The scene of that little girl putting the flower in her hair haunted him afterwards, fuelling his determination to oppose what Hitler was doing, not only to his own country, but also Europe in general.

When the group returned to their fulltime mission of opposing the Nazis, they did so with an absolute vengeance. They had managed to meet with a relative of a member of the Red Orchestra, to whom they expressed a desire to make contact with the main resistance movement in the capital, Berlin. This aim, however, was never achieved.

Sophie, having listened to her brother Hans's experiences on the Russian Front, had built up even more contempt for Hitler. A school friend once confided to Sophie: 'If I had a pistol and I were to meet Hitler here in the street, I'd shoot him down. If men can't manage it, then a woman should.'

Sophie replied, 'Yes, but then he would be replaced by Himmler, and after Himmler there would be another.'

On 13 January, an interesting incident occurred at the Munich University while it was celebrating its 470th anniversary. The district Nazi *Gauleiter* of the city, Paul Giesler, gave a speech in which he insulted the girl students by telling them: 'It was better that they get on with giving the Führer a child than wasting time on books.'

He then insulted them further by even offering some of his men to oblige this cause. Several girls immediately left the assembly hall in disgust at the statement, but they were arrested at the exit. A disturbance broke out in which the Nazi student leader was dragged from his podium and beaten senseless, before being declared a hostage as he was against the release of the girls. The Nazi authorities soon telephoned the police, who arrived very quickly on the scene to break up the trouble. This was the first protest against the Nazis to have been held by students in Munich. It forced the

Gestapo to increase its efforts in tracing the whereabouts of the White Rose organization.

Sophie knew that time was running out. She became nervous, but her thinking was never far from that of resistance. She expressed a need to write anti-Nazi graffiti on walls, stating, 'You'd need to use something that was very hard to get off, something like bitumous paint.'

The next morning, Hans, Sophie and Elisabeth Scholl went to the university to attend a lecture by Huber. Near the entrance, someone had inscribed the word 'FREEDOM' in huge lettering on a wall.

One of the older students stepped forward and asked, 'What bastard did that?'

A group of Russian female labourers were given the task of cleaning the word from the wall, prompting Sophie to remark, 'They will have a hard job, that's bitumous paint.'

Hans Scholl was smiling to himself as Sophie said these words, but they had also been picked up by those students who supported the Nazis.

The turning point came in 1943, when Sophie had contributed to the writing and production, and the distribution of various fliers and handbills around Cologne, Stuttgart, Berlin and Vienna. The authorities had been alerted and they began to search for the authors of the circulated material. The Gestapo assumed that the authors of the material were from the Munich student set. One of the pieces of literature called for the National Socialist regime to establish a 'New Mental Europe'. This particular leaflet was reprinted in England and was dropped by RAF Bomber Command aircraft over Germany. Additional excerpts were read out over the BBC Sender Radio. The subversive material was becoming a serious threat.

On 18 February 1943, Sophie and her brother Hans distributed over 1,700 leaflets on their Munich University campus. This was the sixth leaflet that the White Rose movement had produced. Sophie and Hans ran inside the university at around 10.00am, spreading their latest leaflet everywhere they could until they almost ran out. As they came out of the main building, they stopped before deciding to run back in to distribute the remaining leaflets. This they managed to do just in time.

However, the Scholls had been seen – this was now the beginning of the end. The caretaker at the university, Jakob Schmidt, raced towards them. He caught them on the stairway, shouting, 'You are under arrest!' Sophie and her brother remained quiet and calm as they were taken first to the bursar, and from there to the SS *Oberführer*, Dr Walter Wrist, a lecturer in Aryan language and culture.

The Scholls were then taken in handcuffs to the Gestapo headquarters. Christoph Probst, another member of the White Rose, was arrested the following day. He faced the same charges as Sophie and Hans. Over the following days, more members of the movement were arrested.

Sophie and Hans knew that they would now have to pay a very high price for denouncing the National Socialist regime and their resistance movement's written attacks on Hitler. Shortly before her death, Sophie said, 'So many people have died for this regime that it's about time that someone died against it.'

The White Rose had certainly caused considerable embarrassment to the National Socialist regime. They had bloodied the nose of the dictatorship in a way that very few had done so far, or had ever dared to do.

There was to be no torture carried out on the Scholls. Nevertheless, over a four-day period they underwent intensive interrogation at Gestapo headquarters at Wittelsbach Palace in Munich. Otle Aicher and Traute Lafrenz broke the terrible news to the parents, Robert and Magdalene Scholl. Nothing could be done to secure their release.

It was very obvious as to what the fate of Sophie and Hans would be. The fact that the monster known as 'The Hanging Judge', Roland Freisler, was given the 'pleasure' of conducting their court trial had confirmed the fears of most.

Nazi judge Freisler was an intimidating, raging bully, who could only ever perform such over-theatrical behaviour in his court under the notion that those who appeared before him in court had no way of harming him. In every respect, Freisler represented Nazi low life in its most virulent form, which explained why Hitler had insisted that Freisler travel from Berlin to Munich especially to preside over the case against the 'criminals'. There was absolutely no way that Sophie, Hans or Christoph would receive a fair hearing. As was the case with all Nazi political trials, the proceedings were generally concluded well in advance, depending on the seriousness of the crime committed against the Reich or its Führer.

On 22 February 1943, the trial of Sophie and Hans Scholl began at 9.00am and closed at 1.00pm. Hans and Sophie's parents were not allowed to attend the trial and had not been issued with passes to enter the courtroom.

Documentation that provides information about the proceedings of the trial against Sophie, Hans and Christoph, makes one marvel at how dignified and defiant the three were. Freisler, for all his theatrical shouting and abuse, could in no way whatsoever break Sophie or the others. She stood before him and refused to denounce the 'terribly heinous crime' she had committed against the Reich. Her wit and intelligence, together with her challenging composure certainly unsettled Freisler. For once, he was facing someone who was not afraid of either him or the consequences of her beliefs. It was a strange scenario – a young German woman aged twenty-one and a hardened servant of the Hitler regime verbally sparring.

Sophie's last words to Freisler were, 'You know the war is lost, why don't you face it?'

Judge Freisler sentenced Sophie and Hans to death by guillotine, before they were taken to Stadelheim Prison. Robert and Magdalene Scholl were able to seize a precious few minutes with their children.

Robert embraced his son and said to him, 'You will go down in history. There is another justice than this.'

Roland Freisler did in fact face the truth with which Sophie had challenged him. He was killed in an Allied air raid at around the second anniversary of his murder of Sophie and Hans Scholl.

Magdalene embraced her daughter, saying, 'I will never see you come through the door again.'

Sophie replied, 'Oh, Mother, after all, it's only a few years more life I'll miss.'

It was a statement so typical of Sophie. She was proud that she and Hans had not betrayed anyone during their interrogation and trial. Sophie's mother remarked on how beautiful and radiant her daughter looked during those last few minutes that she spent with her. Sophie was very concerned what the effect of their deaths would have on their mother, but as for herself, she was completely resigned to her fate.

Sophie Scholl's short life ended at 6.00pm on 22 February 1943, when, along with her brother Hans and their friend Christoph Probst, she was executed by guillotine, only a few hours after their sentencing. This so evidenced the extent of the fear that this young girl had instilled in the Nazis, that she and the others had to be disposed of quickly and ruthlessly.

It had been noted that, as Sophie was led away from her cell to the execution chamber, she remained defiant to the end, even winning the admiration of the prison officials. The guards later mentioned how courageous she was, and how she showed no fear of dying for her cause.

Upon entering the execution cell, her hands bound behind her back, Sophie remained silently dignified, 'like Joan of Arc', as the door to the cell slammed shut. Just a few short minutes later Sophie Scholl was dead.

Sophie and Hans were both buried in Perlach Forest Cemetery on 24 February 1943. In the nearby towns, graffiti began to appear on the walls of buildings, their spirit living on in the struggle again Nazism. Most notable of all of the graffiti was that revealed at first light on 23 February – the day after the execution – emblazoned across a building in Berlin. It was short and explicitly direct: 'FUCK HITLER!'

Sophie Scholl was a remarkable human being in many respects, possessing qualities that were instantly recognizable by her personality. From her many activities, she had made many friends over the years. That was something the Nazis could never change. The Nazis could never defeat Sophie Scholl or the White Rose. On 12 October 1987, the *Weiße Rose Stiftung* or White Rose Foundation, was founded in Munich, to keep the legacy of the wartime resistance movement alive, while reminding today's youth of the importance of fighting for human rights. Today, Sophie and her brother Hans remain at rest in the peace and tranquillity of a Germany that is completely different to the one that they knew and for which they had given their lives to change.

Recently, a German magazine for teenage girls, titled *Brigitte Magazine*, held a readers' poll to find out from teenage girls in Germany today who they view as one of the most important female figures of the 20th century. Carried out amongst the million-strong readership, the person chosen was Sophie Scholl.

A contemporary German theatrical production was also staged to celebrate the short lives of Sophie and Hans Scholl and the other members of the White Rose who were executed during those dark days in the Second World War. This theatrical production enlightened and educated a whole new generation of German girls and boys, some of whom are still struggling to come to terms with the mistakes made by their predecessors.

Today's young German girls especially recognize and acknowledge Sophie Scholl's selfless bravery and sacrifice in the face of certain death, making one wonder what Sophie might have thought about it had she been alive today.

The next time that anyone says 'all of the German nation was to blame for the Nazis and their rise to power', they need to be asked if they have ever heard the story of Sophie Scholl – the White Rose remembered.

Chapter Eight

Bombs on the Reich

The first British air attack against Berlin, the capital of Adolf Hitler's Third Reich, came during the evening of Sunday, 25 August 1940, when around forty aircraft of RAF Bomber Command struck Berlin for the first time. This first attack caused limited property damage to the city. The raid was, however, to prove an immense psychological blow to the German civilian population. Luftwaffe chief Hermann Goering had repeatedly assured the German people that such an event could never happen. It was a very foolish boast. It was a promise that amounted to a public relations disaster for Goering. He now had to go out onto the streets of Berlin to talk to angry and frightened civilians, and attempt to reassure them that a solution would soon be found to prevent such an outrage from happening again.

Kirsten Eckermann:

> Goering visited the areas where the bombs had fallen, and people gathered around his car to listen to what he had to say to them. We really did believe that Berlin could not be bombed, and now that it had happened, we began to feel insecure and afraid. Goering made all kinds of stupid excuses and gestures, and I think people believed in what he told them. We did not believe at that moment that the RAF would be allowed to bomb our city again, but they did.

Whatever excuses Goering had made to those he had addressed in the days after that first RAF raid on the capital, the vulnerability of Berlin from RAF Bomber Command was made very clear during the nights of 28–29 August 1940, when the British bombers returned to Berlin for a second time. This time, people were killed in the raids, bringing the reality of war home to the people of the city. The RAF attacked Berlin again two nights later, inflicting more death and destruction upon the city.

Kirsten Eckermann:

> There had been a degree of expectation of further attacks from the English. We knew that if they were going to come then they would

come at night. I remember it was in early September during the night the air-raid siren sounded. I had never heard one of these sirens go off before. It was a horrible howling sound that sent you into a sense of panic. We all woke startled in the darkness and we quickly dressed and put on what clothing we could. We had not really practised air-raid evacuation and it was some minutes before we got out of the house and were all running down to the communal shelter that was situated right at the bottom of our street.

Other people were running along the darkened street and I vividly remember even now the searchlight beams as they clicked on and began to search the dark sky – they reminded me of fingers clawing the darkness as they looked for the enemy planes. When we arrived at the shelter, we were surprised to find that it was still half empty and that there was room for more people. Quite a few people had decided to remain inside their homes, though some had their own little shelters built in their back gardens. We huddled up together in a corner and then it was a case of waiting for whatever was going to happen. The adrenaline was flowing and although it was the middle of the night, I could not doze off to sleep.

Then I heard the first real sounds of war arrive as the flak [from the German for anti-aircraft guns, *Fliegerabwehrkanonen*] batteries around the city began to fire at the enemy planes. It must have been terrifying for those who stayed up above the ground in their homes, as the noise was tremendous. The flak guns fired continuously, it was like a continuous series of 'booms'. The flak guns must have drowned out the noise of falling bombs, as although a stick of bombs fell fairly close by, I do not recall hearing any really large explosions or whistling sounds, only the occasional flicker of the lights and some dust falling from the ceiling.

Gradually, after what seemed some considerable time, the noise seemed to slowly die down until the guns one by one stopped firing. I think it must have been one hour later when the all-clear was sounded. We came out sheepishly from the shelter not knowing what we would see. Surprisingly, everything looked normal all around us, though a blanket of mist hung in the air. We started walking back towards our street when we noticed people gathering down a neighbouring block. As we went to see what was going on, it became obvious. Bombs had hit three of the houses and we were told that the families were inside. Groups of people began helping some fire brigade and RAD workers to clear the debris.

I remember a little girl who could not have been any older than five years of age. She was picking something up out of the rubble. It was the lifeless body of a small black kitten, and the little girl picked it up and cradled it in her arms, as if she could not accept that it was no longer alive. Some boys were picking up pieces of the exploded shells and bombs, and some people watched in stunned silence. When we arrived home, we were relieved to find that the houses along our street had not been harmed. We arrived home exhausted and went to bed to try and catch up on the sleep we had lost during the night.

Hitler was beside himself with rage over the attacks on his beloved city of Berlin, and on 4 September he delivered his most aggressive speech yet to the German nation. Clearly very angry, and shaking with rage, Hitler shouted:

When the British air force drops 200-, 300-, or 400-kilograms of bombs, then we will in one night drop one-hundred-and-fifty, two-hundred-and-thirty, three-hundred, or four-hundred-thousand-kilograms. When they declare that they will increase their attacks on our cities, then we will raze their cities to the ground. We will stop the handiwork of those night air pirates, so help us God.

In Germany, civilians in all areas of the country had begun to prepare for the inevitable air attacks.

Ursula Sabel vividly remembers how the cellar beneath her home became the only place that they could seek safety when the bombers came.

In 1940, the war began to approach us quite substantially in Duisburg. It was the terrible time of air raids. The windows of our house had to be pasted over with rolls of black paper. This was to ensure that at night not a single ray of light would escape, and give any reference point to the bombers. The first attacks came at night only, and once the enemy machines had been detected, the sirens began to sound in their terrible howling tone. The siren would sound to warn of an incoming attack and then the second to sound an all-clear when the attack had gone.

Citizens were required to either go down into their cellars or make their way to another air-raid shelter. My father had spent much time reinforcing the cellar beneath our home with thick and heavy railway sleepers. The sirens often sounded when we were asleep in our beds, and we were forbidden by the authorities to use any lights, and we had to quickly dress in the dark, grab our little suitcases, and run down into our cellar. I also took my violin with me down into the cellar. Our beds were made up from wooden planks and we would remain in these for the duration of the air raid.

Not far from our neighbourhood lived the railroad men and their families. The railroad men often built small shelters in their gardens. But only those who had helped to build them were allowed inside. So we continued to use our cellar beneath our house for protection. I heard stories of how families' houses had been struck by bombs and they had been buried alive underneath. So there were times when we stayed in our bedrooms in the house trembling and scared and unable to sleep as the bombers hummed overhead.

Gradually, the attacks on our cities increased, and it became clear to us just how much danger we were in, and that perhaps our cellar could become our grave. Father decided to dig me and Mother a shelter out in our garden. He wanted it to be as comfortable and as safe as possible. So he dug a deep hole wide enough for Mother and I to sit opposite each other. The shelter entrance had been formed with a section of curved trunk shaped like a gate. The roof had been covered with thick wooden boards with soil placed on top of them. Mother and I lined the internal walls with wattle work, and two boards were placed inside to form a seat. Once inside that shelter we were safe from everything apart from maybe a direct hit, but there were sufficient targets for the bombers away from our area, so we felt relatively safe.

Even in the middle of winter, when the siren sounded we would run into the shelter in the garden. Many winter nights were freezing cold with snow and ice on the ground. I would put on an additional jacket, coat and scarf, with an old smock over the top to protect my clothes from the damp and the dirt. I also used to put an old cap on my head and an old steel helmet on top of it. The steel helmet had lay in our garden for many years. With all of the extra clothing on it was heavy and very difficult to run. I always took my suitcase and my violin with me into the shelter. You might find it very hard to believe that Mother and I often fell fast asleep in a sitting position only to be awoken by the all-clear signal, sometimes one or two hours later. In the morning, I would go to school as normal, and as if nothing had happened. Only later in 1942, when the daylight attacks began, did we receive no peace both day and night.

Heidi Koch remembers that the first air attacks only had the effect of hardening people's resolve, and maybe increasing their support for total war. She remembers the first raids made by the RAF on Berlin, and how it had affected the attitudes of both her mother and father.

Father used to say that there would be no air attacks, not against Berlin anyway. He believed, like many, that Goering was telling the truth, and that the Reich airspace was impenetrable to enemy planes. He often lost his temper when we began to question him over this, especially when the British planes carried out the first series of attacks on our city.

He would say to me, 'You ask far too many questions, girl' and 'shut up.'

Tension began to build after the first few air raids. This was brought on by the uncomfortable shelters we had to go in and the lack of sleep. I remember one night, the air-raid siren began to sound. There was panic in the house, as Mother shouted to us, 'Don't touch any lights. Get your clothes quickly and don't forget your shoes.'

We had started going to bed partly dressed so if the siren sounded in the middle of the night we had only a few remaining items of clothing to struggle with. Once we had our things together Mother would say to Father, 'Ernst, get the girls out of here straight away, and I will join you shortly.'

Mother always put us and Father first before we left the house to enter the extremely uncomfortable shelter out in our tiny back garden. Once we were all inside, Father shut the door tightly. When the flak guns started to fire we knew the enemy planes were nearby, and soon we could hear this noise like angry bees – a continuous humming sound as the enemy planes came overhead. When they dropped their bombs, you could hear them come whistling down, followed by a loud explosion as the bomb or bombs went off. I never went outside that shelter while a raid was on, and if I felt like going to the toilet, I just held it in. Father would just get up and go outside as if nothing was happening. Once he began to shout, 'Go on, knock those bastards down!' as the flak guns fired away at the planes in the dark sky above.

Theresa Moelle has a slightly different perspective of the first RAF air attacks made on of Berlin. Having been adopted by what many would consider to have been well-off parents, and living in a house on the peripheral landscape of Berlin, Theresa often witnessed the scene as the bombers attacked the city during the hours of darkness.

Shops and businesses in the city began to close early, especially during the wintertime, when it became dark early and the bombers started their attacks earlier. We Berliners living on the outskirts of the city were largely unscathed during the early years of bombing. The bombers were after industry and railway networks and gas and electricity sub stations. At first, we would all run down into the cellar where Walter Moelle used to keep all of his wines. It was very cold in there during the winter, but it was relatively dry and safe from everything but a direct hit on the house itself. It became obvious after some time that no bombs were going to fall in our area, as there was nothing there to bomb; there were only one or two farm buildings and other residences near our house.

During one of the air raids, I decided to be difficult and refused to go down into the cellar with the others. I told Walter Moelle that I was going to stay in my room and that I did not want to go into the cellar. He as usual began to shout and try to reason with me, and I gave him some silly excuse about being afraid of spiders and things like that. In the end, he stormed off and left me in the house alone.

We were not allowed to have any lights on at all, not even small candlelight was allowed. With the house in blackness, being nighttime anyway, I pulled the curtain across just enough so I could peer through. The siren was still going off and I could clearly see the searchlights switching on and begin to sweep across the sky. If it was cloudy, the lights reflected the grey undersides of the clouds, and it could be quite bright, though the bombers always seemed to hit Berlin on frosty moonlit nights. As I peered out of the window I had to frequently rub the glass with the sleeve of my bedclothes as my breath kept frosting over the glass. The siren suddenly stopped and more searchlights began to switch on over the city, which was around thirteen miles away. Still nothing happened, and I began to wonder if it had been a false alarm, but a noise in the distance soon confirmed otherwise. I could hear the faint booms of flak guns firing, as the outermost batteries began to fire.

Then another noise could be heard, a noise that you will never ever forget in your whole life, I will certainly never forget it, as it was a chilling sound, and became a death knell for all Berliners. The sound started off as a faint hum but as it drew nearer it became louder and throbbed. The only way I can possibly describe it to you is that it sounded like one of those old seaside Hovercraft vehicles as they came onto the beach.

The BDM meetings that followed were taken up with the talk of terrorism against the Reich and how innocent men, women and children had been killed. Living on the outskirts often detached you from the reality of the war at that time. Unlike those who lived in the *Mitte*, I had not yet seen the dead being pulled from the rubble of their homes, or the effects of shrapnel and fire on human bodies.

The early bombing raids on Berlin were not without cost to the RAF. Many aircraft and their crews were lost during those missions. The Germans began to deploy more and more anti-aircraft guns in and around the city to tighten the already formidable flak belt. The introduction of heavier flak guns, such as the 105mm and 128mm, proved to be very effective when used in conjunction with the small- and medium-calibre guns such as the 20mm, 37mm, and 88mm. The smaller guns would concentrate on the low-to-medium-altitude targets, while the heavy weapons dealt with the high-altitude targets. The flak guns were situated in numerous locations around Berlin, such as the main railway network and the industrial *Mitte*.

To ease the deployment of their flak defences, the guns were often mounted on a mobile chassis, enabling them to be moved around the city. The heavy guns that could not be transported by road were often mounted onto railway carriages. Soon, the RAF bomber crews came to dread missions over Berlin, which they often viewed as suicidal. Theresa Moelle recalls her first sight of the British enemy after one of the early bombing raids on the city.

One evening there was the usual commotion as the air-raid siren sounded, and the familiar drill of rushing out of bed, throwing on our clothing, and then going downstairs into the cold and damp of that wretched wine cellar. The raid lasted for quite some time, as the all-clear did not come until well over two hours later. Once we had been roused by the all-clear signal, everyone made their way back up into the house, and back to their warm beds.

At daybreak, there was quite some excitement outside. This was most unusual as it was normally very quiet around our area, especially in the morning. There were farm workers outside talking with locals about a British plane that came down during the Friday night. The plane was down in one of the nearby fields. I wanted to go and see the plane, as some parents were already on their way to take their children to see the crashed British plane. I quickly dressed, ran downstairs and put my boots on and ran out of the door.

Walter Moelle followed, shouting, 'Where are you off to?'

I shouted back, 'I am going to see the British plane.'

I ran down the lane past the groups of people on their way down to the field. Mud was splashing up my legs as I ran, and dirty water from the puddles filled my boots, which was made worse by the fact that I had no socks on. As I came to the field, I could see this plane, its tail almost upright in the ground, with its green and brown camouflaged paint and British air-force markings along its side. The frontal section was crumpled up and lying at an angle on its side. The wings had been torn off along with the engines, and these had fallen in adjoining fields. There were guards around the plane, but I climbed over the gate and ran up to have a closer look. One of the guards was a local man known to me, whose name was Klaus, and he smiled and said, 'Ah, Herr Moelle's daughter.'

He then showed me around the crumpled remains of the plane that he said was called a Wellington. The plane had holes all over it and I was told that these were made by flak splinters or *splitters* [shrapnel] as we called them.

'Where are the men who were flying the plane?' I asked.

One of the other guards pointed to a large dark-grey tarpaulin sheet around the other side of the plane. As I walked closer, I could see several pairs of black flying boots sticking out from under the large tarpaulin cover. The crew of the plane were all dead and the guards explained that the pilot had been killed by flak splinters, which had entered the front windscreen of the plane, while the remaining crew probably died in the impact as the plane crashed. Photographs were being taken of the wreckage and we were not allowed to touch any of the pieces of the plane. It was quite a sight and I can remember thinking how terrible the last minutes inside that plane must have been for the crew. But then I thought about the Berliners who had probably died as a result of that plane dropping its bombs on the city.

As I turned away to make my way back over to the gate and return home, the guard, whom I knew, called out to me 'Fraulein Moelle.'

I stopped and turned around, he walked over to me and said, 'Here, have this as a little reminder, but keep it to yourself.'

I held out my open hand and he placed a piece of clear plastic into it. It was around three inches by four inches in size and was quite thick. He said it had come from the crew cabin area of the Wellington.

'*Danke,*' I replied, before wrapping it up in my handkerchief and putting it down my skirt.

I then ran back up the lane to the house. When I arrived home, I quickly ran inside and kicked off my boots and ran up the stairs to my room. Walter Moelle, who wanted to know what I had been doing, as usual pursued me. I shut my bedroom door and slammed the chair under the handle so no one could get in. Walter Moelle began knocking and saying things like, 'What are you doing in there?' and 'open the door.'

I pulled the piece of clear plastic out of the waistband of my skirt and placed it, still wrapped up, in the handkerchief under the mattress of my bed. I went to the door, pulled the chair away, and Walter Moelle entered the room.

'What are you up to?' he repeated. 'Nothing,' I replied.

I told him I had just been to see the plane crash with the other local people. He commented on how filthy I looked with dirt all up my legs, and said I had better wash and then go and help Mother. I swilled my boots out with cold water from the well outside and then washed the dirt from my legs. At night, I often took my little souvenir out from under the mattress to look at it for a few minutes before wrapping it back up and putting it away again.

The smashed wrecks of RAF bombers became a common sight for those living in the outlying areas of the city, as RAF aircrews in trouble, wherever possible, sought open farmland where they could attempt to put down their stricken aircraft. In the city itself, the danger from shot-down bombers and their debris proved to be as equal a hazard as the bombs they were dropping.

Heidi Koch remembers that the flak gunners defending the city also scored an own goal on many occasions, when their unexploded shells fell back to the ground.

> I know one story where a large shell failed to detonate in the sky during an air raid, and it fell back down from the sky. The shell crashed through the roof of a house in the *Mitte* and exploded, killing a young child and injuring three other family members, who had foolishly stayed inside the house. The child had been in a separate room asleep when the shell came through the roof, and crashed through the ceiling before exploding.

Helena Vogel received the perfect opportunity to voice her anger during one of 'Fatty' Goering's tours of bombed streets in the German capital:

> Word spread that Luftwaffe chief Goering was visiting an area nearby to inspect damage caused by RAF bombing raids. I wanted to confront this man and ask him questions. Well, we joined the crowd, which had begun to gather in one of the neighbouring streets, and we saw Goering arrive in his smart staff car smiling and speaking to people, trying to reassure them that everything was going to be all right.
>
> Guards surrounded Goering and people began to question him about how safe it was to remain in the city. The people were mainly old folk and women with their children. They were clearly scared and some were babbling and starting to become emotional. I could see that Goering was not comfortable with this situation; the look on his face said it all. I could not get to Goering to ask him any questions, and as things were not really going in his favour, he told everyone that he now had to leave for an engagement. He would be back to talk with us again soon and to inform us of the new Reich air-defence measures which had been devised to counter the problem of the RAF bombing raids on the city.
>
> As his driver began to drive away, anger overtook my common sense and I shouted, 'You fucking idiot, you *Dummkopf*!' [Fat head]

as loud as I could. No sooner had I shouted, two men in the crowd grabbed me from behind and dragged me out of the crowd.

I shouted at them, 'Let go of me as you are hurting me.' I was taken to the police station and the two men took me into a locked room and started to ask me questions. I told them I had recently lost my man who had been serving in the Luftwaffe, and that I was angry with Goering over this and wanted to know why this was happening. The men explained to me that they were Gestapo and that I was to cause no further trouble or else! Insulting such a high officer in the Reich was treason, I was warned, and the next time there would be no conversations or warnings. Then they let me go.

Whilst having a devastating effect on the civilian population, the early bombing raids in reality did very little damage to the actual infrastructure of Berlin. Railway yards and tracks, gas, and electricity and water stations were often up and running again within just two hours of having been bombed. Such repairs were often carried out while the air raids were still in progress.

The advent of change in the RAF bombing campaign strategy came with a man named Charles Portal, a prominent member of the British air staff. He believed that entire villages, towns and cities should be bombed, with a view to breaking civilian morale in Germany. With such a theory, there could be absolutely no considerations for any resulting civilian casualties, and even to this day, one has to question whether or not Portal could ever have slept comfortably while party to what many consider to have been a war crime.

When Acting Air Marshal Arthur Harris became head of RAF Bomber Command in February 1942, he authorized what would become known as 'area bombing', where entire villages, towns and cities in Germany would be raised to the ground. To coincide with the implementation of this new phase of the bombing campaign against Germany, raids were launched against Hamburg, Cologne, Dresden, Essen and many other urban areas in Germany. It was the start of a campaign that would see Allied bombing kill an estimated 305,000 to 600,000 German civilians, including large numbers of the elderly people, and young women and their children. Over 6,000,000 homes were destroyed.

Heidi Koch emphasises what many ordinary people were saying at that time:

The area-bombing thing was just the kind of thing that you would have thought Hitler and the Nazis should have thought of. The funny thing is that Hitler did not invent such a terrible course of action as a British man named Harris did. Harris changed the whole situation from the bombing of the railways, gas, and electricity and water plants, and of course anything connected with the manufacture of ammunition and strictly military supplies, to that of actually deliberately bombing people. That is something I could never comprehend, and was something that would only push Hitler into retaliation whereby innocent civilians in England would also have to suffer. I would like to know this: Did Harris sleep properly after the war with the weight of all those corpses on his conscience? Did he ever have a conscience? I would like to have asked the man these things myself at the time, if I could.

The bombing of Germany still provokes very strong emotions in some, and much controversy remains to this day as to the rights and the wrongs of the area-bombing strategy and its influence upon victory in the Second World War.

Chapter Nine

Girls on the Land

The RADwf was the female youth section of the National Labour Service, a compulsory organization in which all young females had to enrol for a term of six months, usually after leaving the BDM at the age of eighteen.

With the outbreak of war, the duties being performed by young girls and women in Nazi Germany began to change rapidly. As with the women in England, German women, especially girls, were taught how to make new out of old. They were even assigned to tasks where they helped German soldiers with their washing and mending of uniforms, and other such related duties. The task of helping the German soldier was one considered to have been a great privilege, with special washing and mending stations being set up especially for this task.

During the first year of the war, in excess of 9,000,000 girls had been mobilized by the RADwf (and the BDM). Many were selected for agricultural work on the land. It was also with the advent of war that young women were brought into the previously male-only workplace of the armaments industry. Young women worked side by side with the men, most of whom were either unfit or considered too old for frontline military service.

During mid-1940, the SS began a programme of establishing settlements in the eastern occupied territories. Once the SS had removed the former inhabitants, BDM girls were given the task of cleaning and preparing houses for habitation by German settlers. Many of the BDM girls remained within these eastern territories for up to a year, specifically to help the new occupants by providing help in the home and the establishing of schoolhouses.

It was during this new phase in the occupied eastern territories that many of the girls would discover the brutality of the Nazi regime, of which they had become a part. Although the SS had ethnically cleansed these eastern territories with great efficiency, they were not always so careful to dispose of the evidence of their brutality. A woman named Ingeborg Schaller was one of the girls at the time sent to help set up the new eastern colonies. During a rare – and slightly reluctant – interview in May 2000, she shared some of her experiences:

I was a nineteen-year-old at the time. I did not really like the idea of having to leave home and work on a farm or on the land, particularly in former enemy territory in the east. I did, though, volunteer for this 'special work', as they were calling it at the time. This would involve working closely with our military, but performing many domestic duties in the settlements.

The placement was originally for only six to eight months, so I thought it would be fine, but my posting there was extended to twelve months. I left my home in Pirna, which is near Dresden, in late July of 1940, with a group of other girls. Some were taken from the BDM and others from the RADwf. Most of us knew each other, so we felt quite comfortable as we set out by train on our new adventure. It was a very long journey and night had fallen by the time we had arrived at our destination, which I do not wish to disclose.

Over the following weeks, we were cleaning houses and tenements. Each had to be thoroughly scrubbed with water and they were then disinfected under the direction of the SS. There were no traces of the former inhabitants at all; everything had been stripped from the houses.

I remember one incident that occurred one afternoon some distance away in a field. One of the dogs that belonged to one of the SS guards ran off and began digging at the soil with both of his front paws. Before the guard could get hold of his dog and pull him away, the dog unearthed what looked like the human remains of either a man, woman or child. I saw part of a torso and an arm sticking out of the ground. We never discovered just what it was, as the SS shouted at us to go away as they covered it back up, but it made those who saw it feel very uneasy, including myself. I know that after the war many areas, including that one, were investigated and a large number of bodies had been found. These were the bodies of those who had once lived there. The SS had murdered them all and buried them before our arrival. When I returned home, I was warned by my parents not to say anything about this.

For most of the girls leaving the BDM and entering the RADwf, work placements were found in Germany. For these eighteen-year-old young women, there again lay ahead a strict regime of work, rule and regulation, but the system was different.

The girls were given a degree of freedom, and although they were closely watched, they often mixed with members of the opposite sex, particularly during the early years of the war, in ways they could not hope to do back at home. It was in this context that many viewed their placements with the RADwf as yet another adventure, an escape from the war and from the relative boredom of their home lives. This applied especially to the city girls.

Those given placements on farms worked hard. During daylight hours, they occasionally worked from early morning when they set off to either work in the fields harvesting the seasonal crops, or tending cows, pigs and chickens, and learning how to milk the dairy herd. They lived and worked in large groups, often taking turns to cook and wash in addition to helping the farmer's wife with her many chores.

Many returned home with some particularly happy memories of their RADwf service. While many girls drifted back home to work in the munitions factories, many elected to stay on the farms and the land to continue with their work for the duration of the war.

With the commencement of Operation Barbarossa, Hitler's ill-fated attempt at invading the Soviet Union, which began on 22 June 1941, things could only become worse for the average German girl and woman. After some initial early successes, Operation Barbarossa soon began to stall. With the onset of a particularly cruel and freezing Russian winter, German casualties soon began to mount in staggering numbers. As a result, more and more females were increasingly required to replace those men who were sent to the Russian front.

City-dweller Kirsten Eckermann has some fine reminiscences of her time spent with the RADwf:

> I could not wait to go, to be honest, and I had been looking forward to it for quite some time. It was early summertime of 1941, and after a medical examination, that I passed, I was sent with other girls from the BDM to do six months compulsory service to work in agriculture. I knew that this meant working on a farm, which I did not mind, as it would be in the countryside. The farm we were going to was near the small town of Osna, situated between Frankfurt and Gorzow. We did not have to worry ourselves about air raids, as at that time air raids were still only coming in during the night hours. We would also be much safer out in the countryside away from the city, though we did feel concern for our families.

I had always wanted to go and live in the countryside, anywhere away from the industrial *Mitte*.

There were a few tears as me and my mother said our farewells to each other. Father looked me up and down and held out his hand, his bottom lip beginning to tremble. As I held his hand, he just grabbed hold of me and hugged me and began to cry.

I said to him, 'Father, please don't be upset, I will return soon and I will try and write you a letter and let you know how I fare.'

This was the first time he had ever shown any emotion like that. Maybe it had dawned on him that I was now no longer just a little girl, and I had grown up – I am not sure. I then picked up my small suitcase that belonged to my mother and set off to join the other girls ready to embark the train to Osna.

It was not a very long journey, and I think most of the girls were wrapped up in their own thoughts. Some just stared out of the window of the train, while others read books and talked amongst themselves. It was the responsibility of each of us to look after each other and make sure that no one felt sad.

Once the grim views of the city with its big grey buildings and workhouses and tall chimneystacks had disappeared, the mood began to change. The countryside scenery was so beautiful and we knew we were going to be out in it for a long time. When we arrived at our destination, we all disembarked from the train and made our way out of the little station at Osna where we were transported out to the farm some six miles away. It was a beautiful scene, with streams, pools and lots of fields and small woodlands. When we arrived, our RADwf group leader introduced us to the farmer and his wife and the workers who we would be working closely with over the following months.

We were billeted in what looked like an army barracks room. This was a long brick building with a chimney at the one end and a metal corrugated roof. The beds were arranged in two rows along the centre of the billet. The billet was often uncomfortably hot in the summer and freezing in the winter, though we had the little fireplace, which did help a little. In the winter we often fought for the beds nearest the fireplace, so to prevent any infighting, beds were rearranged in a way so everyone was positioned around the fireplace. Before bed, we would put logs onto the fire and these would keep the fire burning all night.

The rules were also given to us and we were reminded of our moral conduct and how we should behave ourselves at all times as ambassadors of the Reich. There were strict regulations about when we would be expected to retire to bed and what time we would rise each morning for breakfast and work. We often started work at around 9.30am to 10.00am in the morning, and finished early, though we often worked longer hours in the summer.

We would be working from Monday to Saturday morning. Saturday afternoon was our own time, as was Sunday, though on Sunday we were all expected to attend church for the morning service. I did not really enjoy going to church but attended just out of courtesy. As it was a farm, the male workers started quite early in the morning too, and were often out working at 6.00am, the work often going on until nearly midnight, though we never worked that late, as the few old men had that task.

We were given a kind of acclimatization period in which to settle in and become acquainted with the rules and regulations, and we were given a set of work clothes, including two regulation dresses, thick socks, boots and an apron.

One of the first things I ever learned, though, was to drive a tractor. I just saw one and thought I want to drive that thing. I did not stop to think what I was letting myself in for. Gerhard, one of the young men who worked on the farm, had the job of reluctantly teaching me how to drive the tractor. He explained that he was surprised by my request, as women did not often want to do such things, as they did not like to get their hands dirty.

I took his remark as an insult and barked, 'Are you going to show me how to drive the tractor, or are you just going to stand there and criticize me all day long?'

I think he knew he had upset me, and looking a little taken aback by my anger, he began to show me the basics. I think he only did this because he liked me, and I have to admit that I felt attracted to him too.

'First thing you have to do is sit your arse on the damn thing,' he said.

He then took this metal bar that was bent in the middle and placed it in the small hole at the front of the tractor engine. He turned the bar a few times and the engine chugged into life and he said, 'Now do you see?'

Next time, following Gerhard's instructions, I grabbed the bar in both hands and turned with all my strength as instructed. I turned the bar over a couple of times before it slipped out of my hands with a loud clank as the bar fell to the floor. Gerhard burst out laughing, so not wishing to look a fool, I quickly picked up the bar, put it back into the hole, and said 'ready' before turning it over again.

With a splutter, the engine started, and he said, 'Make sure you take the bar out of that hole and place it in the box behind the seat, and then climb up here.'

I placed the starter back in its box and climbed up beside Gerhard who was busy revving the engine up and smirking.

'You see that pedal there, that is the accelerator. This makes the tractor go slow or at its maximum speed, which is not very much at all.'

I interrupted him by saying, 'Alright, alright I know that now.'

He then went on to explain what the other pedals were for, before telling me to get into the driving seat. We quickly swapped places and I grabbed hold of the steering wheel. Gerhard remarked that, on a frosty day, the tractor would be harder to start, as the engine will be very cold. He also said the metal seat would give me a cold arse! So, I must find some old material and make myself a cover.

After instructing me on how to control the tractor, I then began to pull away, a little jerkily at first, but it was a great feeling, and I could not help but whoop with joy as I drove up the lane past the other girls with Gerhard at my side.

The thick black smoke from the tractor's exhaust blew right into my face, and it was not very pleasant, as on a long drive it actually made your face black, which made Gerhard laugh at me even more. I once nearly crashed the tractor trying to stop it quick enough so as I could jump down to go and hit Gerhard for teasing me, but he ran off as soon as I got down. I shouted 'bastard' at him, only after making sure there were wasn't anyone around. I nearly ran down a chicken shed once.

Over a period of time, I learned how to pull trailers, plough soil and things, and I did many other jobs. It could be unpleasant at times, as if any problems with the engine arose and there was no one around, I would have to fix it myself. Tractor engines were filthy, dirty things, and the grease and oil stained the hands and was difficult to remove.

I also learned how to drive a lorry and would often drive the girls into the small town of Osna to buy things, and to go to watch the latest film news on the war and things. We were aware that our army was on the offensive in Russia and, according to the newsreels we saw, the campaign would soon be over. I did not know much about how wars were fought, and you could probably say that I was ignorant to what was happening in Russia. We were told that we were winning and who was I to question, it was as simple as that. The authorities only told you what they thought you should know and nothing else.

While at Osna, we kept in touch with our families by means of letter writing, and sometimes, if we were lucky, we could speak to them by telephone. Some of the girls I was working with told me they had fathers and brothers fighting on the Russian front. It was sad that many of them would soon be dead.

Often while out working in the fields on the tractor, I would see our Messerschmitts. I would often pull up and wave my arms at them. One morning, one of them turned around and made a very low pass to my right, the pilot wobbling his wings in some kind of a salute. I could see the pilot's face with his black leather helmet and his flying goggles. The Messerschmitt roared past and it was a sight that enthralled me, as in all my years I had never seen one up that close before. I watched the Messerschmitt disappear behind the trees before carrying on with my work.

We also used to see Dornier-217 bombers quite regularly; I think many were on training flights from the local *Fliegerschule* [Luftwaffe Flying School].

Summer soon ended, and the winter that year seemed much worse than those of the past. Maybe it was because we were in the countryside, I'm not sure. I vividly remember having to break the ice that formed over the animal drinking troughs every morning. I had to go around each one and break the ice with a stone so as the animals could drink. We took it in turns to do this, as it was a job every one of us girls hated.

Christmas that year was the best I had so far, and we had spent weeks preparing everything for it. We even had turkey, duck, rabbit and goose for the first time in our lives; these were things our parents could never have provided or afforded to have given us. Back home we were very lucky if we had a few sweets and maybe some fruit, but here we had everything in abundance.

We girls often made gifts for each other, such as corn dolls and small embroidered cloth items. We did get scolded the one time though, when we were caught making perfume from wild flowers. We were told bluntly that perfume was of a contraband nature and should any girl be caught either making it or wearing it in future, there would be trouble. The homemade perfume was then poured away. It was just a little reminder that we were not completely free of our senses or obligations to the Reich.

However hard the authorities tried to keep the young German girls under strict control and supervision, there was always a rebel element within each group who would exploit the slightest opportunity to 'get up to things'. Though the girls were always heavily chaperoned, either by their group leaders or the owner of the farm where they were employed, there were always one or two who managed to slip through the net, away from the watchful eyes of their prefects and employers to partake in illicit activities such as drinking, smoking and sex. Contrary to popular belief, there were many secret and illicit liaisons taking place amongst the girls of the RADwf, much as there was with the land girls in England at the time. Gabrielle Haefker recalls:

It does make me laugh because people still have the view that we were all like saintly virgins or something and conformed totally. There were quite a few girls who were caught sneaking out of their beds at night to meet up with young men from the farms and nearby villages. There were also many who did not get caught out and managed to get away with it. It was human nature taking over and the authorities could never have hoped to stop it happening.

I know one young girl who sneaked out of her billet most evenings to meet up with a young admirer from a local village. They often went into the woods, as did most courting couples. She confided in me as a friend, and told me everything that she had done with this young man and that she had let him put his hands inside her blouse and feel her breasts while she smoked one of his cigarettes. I was quite shocked by it and listened to her with my eyes wide and a hand over my mouth. She later admitted that she had intercourse with him several times.

When I asked what about if she falls pregnant, she laughed and said, 'Oh, I don't think that can happen as he pulls it out of me before it sprinkles.'

She then said that she would go and wash herself out in the stream to make sure there was no semen inside her. I asked her what it was like to have sex with a man and she replied '*Gut.*' [Good].

Other girls met up with each other and drank alcohol and smoked cigarettes. Both of those things were considered unladylike by some. I drank alcohol on many occasions and smoked the odd cigarette.

There was this girl named Bertha who was in our group who could roll cigarettes with her fingers. We used to watch amazed as none of us could ever get it right. I asked her how she learned to do it and she replied that her older brother had showed her. Bertha returned home to Hamburg after her RADwf service and we kept in touch for a while until she was killed in an RAF bombing raid. I still cherish her memory now, as she was such a character. It was Bertha who once gave me some snuff to try. She never said where she got it from, but she had quite likely bribed one of the men to give it to her, but I hated it as it made me sneeze and made my eyes water, while Bertha howled with laughter at me. We often used to say that Bertha laughed like a horse, it was one of those funny sounding and infectious laughs.

Olga Kirschener, an eighteen-year-old who went to work the land, reveals a liaison with a young man from the local village that she managed to keep secret:

I will not mention his name here, but it all started with admiring glances, then we got talking and it started from there really. We arranged to meet after dark one evening. I sneaked out unnoticed from the house I was staying in with the other girls, and met him at the gate to the meadow. It was a beautiful moonlit evening and we ran off into the meadow and went into some trees by the lake. We were both a little scared but excited and we took off our clothes and embraced for a few minutes. We lay down and made love there in the trees. We were both so excited that it did not last long, so we shared a cigarette and made love a second time. He began to make a lot of noise and I put my hand over his mouth. Afterwards we walked back through the meadow hand in hand in the moonlight. I left him at the gate and sneaked back into the house. It was always a risk as if we had been caught my parents would have been informed and they would have killed me.

Ursula Sabel also has some memories to share of her service with the RADwf, which began on 1 April 1941.

During the last months of my time at school, word was going around that we girls would soon be called upon to do our compulsory work service with the organization of the RADwf. Some of the girls I knew as friends had already received a letter requiring them to attend a medical examination prior to their initial training period, before being given a work placement. I too received my work training notice and had to have a medical examination where I was passed as fit.

In only a few weeks, I prepared myself, getting everything ready to leave for the training course. The training was basically to prepare us for the kinds of things we would be doing within our work-placement situations. The course was arranged at the end of our school time, and not while we were still attending school on a fulltime basis. I travelled to Westerwald and began my pre-work training on 1 April 1941 at a village near the town.

Our living quarters were situated at the edge of the village, and were a two-storey stone building, with two additional barracks nearby. It was surrounded by trees and flowerbeds, and the flagpole was given the centre place as usual at the camp. Upon arrival, I was shown along with the other girls to the sleeping hall situated in the barracks. My bed was on the lower floor next to a window, and there were twelve to fourteen of us, including a guide or prefect, and she was given complete authority over us all.

The conditions were very good at the camp and we were issued with our work wear. I was very relieved to find that everything I had been issued with fitted me correctly for once! I had to make sure that repairs were made to my work clothing whenever necessary. Fortunately, this was not very often, unlike some of the other girls who had to make constant repairs to their clothing. The issued clothing consisted of a pair of blue cotton dresses with short sleeves, two white aprons, two red head scarves, two pairs of boots, two pairs of thick socks, one brown dress-skirt, two white blouses, one jacket-dress and a hat, and in addition to this we had our own underwear.

The total number of staff consisted of around forty-five girls, a camp guide and two leaders. Everything in the camp was self-contained, including washing and cooking facilities.

During the first six weeks, we were given extensive instructions on every possible topic. The topics included realm work service, behaviour on the camp and within the field service, and information on the farming families who we might be working for soon, and of course the geography of the Westerwald region. Lastly, we were given detailed instructions on what we were expected to do most days.

The six-week course and the ban on all camp leave soon passed by, and then the field service began. I was assigned a place with a family that included three children and a grandmother. The agricultural work was good in the sense that I was able to do so much outside in the fresh air. I helped throughout the whole of the hay-harvesting season, which back then was very hard and laborious work. I often had difficulty in keeping up the correct rhythm when turning over the grass; it was a completely unusual physical effort for me back then.

Our day was a relatively short one as we only started work from around 10.00am of the morning. We were required to be back at our camp in good time to complete our other duties such as cleaning and housework, etc.

My second work placement was in Gershasen, and four other girls joined me and we had bought ourselves a bicycle each, and we rode to work together each morning. I had to work in the fields, and the farming families were heavily dependent upon us girls, as more and more of the young men were going off to fight in the war. So it felt good to be helping our country and its people in a meaningful way.

My next order was 'six weeks indoor service'. This was not so good as it meant performing all manner of menial tasks often within the confines of the camp. The best part of this service was that referred to as the 'flower service'. Flower service was when you had to go out into the fields and the forest to pick fresh flowers for the vases in the camp. I did not like the housework or working in the kitchens at all [this was known as *Waschkueche*]. It was while confined to camp doing this house and kitchen work that one of my friends suffered an accident on her bicycle. She had hurt herself so badly that she could no longer do work in the fields.

My next placement was with a family in Westerburg in a bakery shop. I helped in the house and the bakery shop, but regulations of that time prevented me from being able to serve customers. I also helped out on the local farms by working in the fields. The people of Westerburg were very nice to me and the work was pretty easy to master. I remember once at the camp while we were waiting for our dinner. Our camp guide would often leave us unsupervised in the dinner room for quite a long period. During one such occasion, I smuggled a book in with me titled *Feldpostaugaben*, a book that was produced specifically for our soldiers. It appealed to me and the other girls in particular, because it contained poetry and readings of a philosophical nature. When the guide appeared, we all had to stand up so I slammed the book shut and held it in my hands behind my back, before dropping it onto the seat. When we were given permission to sit, I would sit down on the book and the guide would not know it was there.

There were many happy times and I remember visiting the old house and bakery after the war. I was shocked to find that so much had changed, it was all so different to how I had remembered it all, even many of the faces I had known had gone. When I called at the bakery, the original owner answered the door and I was given the terrible news that during the war bombs fell and hit the bakery and other houses. The baker had lost his wife, son and daughter in just one bomb attack and his business was also wrecked. Though he later rebuilt the shop and also found love again and remarried.

In all, there were many happy times back then and I still recall how we girls talked amongst ourselves on a quite personal level when no guides were around. We talked about many things including literature and about our own personal identification. The one guide in particular was very kind to me as she let me play and practise with my violin on many occasions throughout my time with the RADwf and that was something which meant a lot to me back then.

For a great many, the RADwf experience proved to be a worthwhile one, from both a personal perspective and in the way that it provided a much-needed secondary workforce to replace men who had left their jobs in the

Hanna Buttinghaus, who won the ball throwing event at the Tokyo Youth Olympiade.
(©Pressebild-Verlag Schirner/Deutsches Historisches Museum, Berlin)

Gabrielle Haefker takes the oath as she joins BDM. *(Image courtesy of G. Haefker)*

Girls of the BDM at a local rally.
(BDM Archive)

Female Flak auxiliary. Many young women were recruited into the German Flak arm during the Second World War. *(Image courtesy of E. Blandford)*

Kirsten Eckermann on the left is pictured here at a Nazi Party rally collecting donations.
(Image courtesy of K. Eckermann)

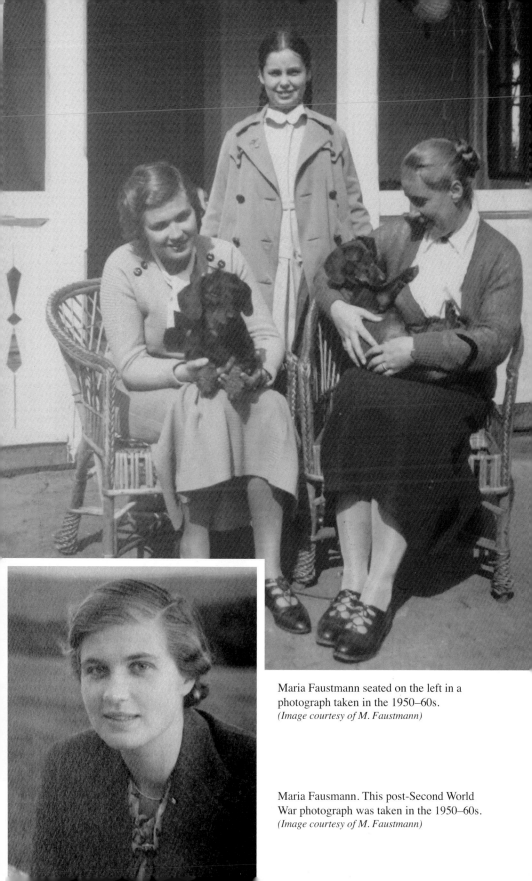

Maria Faustmann seated on the left in a
photograph taken in the 1950–60s.
(Image courtesy of M. Faustmann)

Maria Fausmann. This post-Second World
War photograph was taken in the 1950–60s.
(Image courtesy of M. Faustmann)

Ursula Sabel.
(Image courtesy U. Sabel)

Carly Hendryks.
(Image courtesy of C. Hendryks)

BDM girl in sports attire.
(BDM Archive)

Brigitte Schutternkopf.
(Image courtesy of B. Schuttenkopf)

A photograph showing BDM girls on summer camp.

Apprehensive looking girls of the Jungmael Bund – the Hitler Youth for girls aged ten to fourteen.

BDM girls at camp roll call.

BDM girls watch a sporting tournament in progress.

German girls operating communication equipment during the Second World War.

German girls manning a search light during an air raid in the Second World War.
(Image courtesy of E. Blandford)

Girls of the BDM on the Willhelmsplatz.

Girls of the Bund Deutscher Madel – the Hitler Youth for girls aged fourteen to eighteen – collecting funds.

Girls of the Jungmadel Bund. *(Image courtesy of the Bundesarchive)*

Hitler with BDM girls. *(BDM archive)*

Nuremburg rally in 1936. *(BDM archive)*

Jung Madel poster.
(BDM archive)

RADw girls working on the land. *(Image courtesy of the Bundesarchiv)*

Theresa Moelle at front. *(Image courtesy of T. Moelle)*

factories and fields to fight in the war. Skilled men, with highly valuable knowledge of their particular trades, were not permitted to leave their jobs to join the army or air force. Instead they had the task of training up young girls and women who were now entering the male factory world to work on tank, artillery and aircraft production lines. Young girls were also employed in the munitions industry where their small hands became valuable assets for such tasks as the polishing of the insides of artillery projectiles.

Heidi Koch was one of the girls who, after turning eighteen, apprehensively entered a local ammunition production facility.

I was not very happy about having to go and work in one of the factories. They were dirty and noisy and full of old men who would stare at you for hours. I had always wanted to move out of the city and work on the farms in the countryside, but certain social changes meant that more and more girls and women had to replace the ordinary workingmen and labourers in our factories. Only the skilled men (and those too old to fight in the war) remained, so as they could then pass on their knowledge to the women workers. I was given an overall to wear, and this was too big for me and I had to wear a scarf over my head to keep the dirt and grime out of my hair.

I was taken into the factory and given a brief on safety procedure and where I must go if the air-raid siren sounded. There was much danger in these places and women were warned to beware of all of the moving machinery inside the factory. I heard that one girl had got her headscarf caught up in a wheel; this pulled her into a large drive belt and she was decapitated.

My first job was a relatively simple and very boring one. All I had to do was polish the insides of shells with a piece of cloth. The shells came down very steadily on a moving belt and you picked them up and cleaned the insides with the cloth. With my small hands and nimble fingers, I was ideal for this job, but it was terribly boring.

Many of the men constantly smoked rolled cigarettes as they worked on their machines and the combination of the smell of oil, smoke and hot metal gave me a headache. I only stopped very briefly for a light lunch and we either had coffee or water to drink.

After working in the factory, I would return home where I would have to help Mother prepare our meal. I often felt too tired to do anything, but knew I had to help as Father never helped her very much. I also had to wait until he had washed himself before I could wash. If he came home and I was washing in the tub he would consider that I had been disrespectful to him, just because he had to wait a few minutes. I often lay awake at night wondering just how long I could go on living like this, the routine of getting up, going to the factory, doing the boring work and then returning home. Other girls that went to work with me felt exactly the same way.

Later on we even had slave labourers come and work in the factory, but we were not allowed to talk to them or go anywhere near them. We felt so sorry for them, as they received little to no food or water and were forced to work much longer hours than we did. Often when the daylight raids began, when the siren sounded while all of the German workers were being evacuated to the air-raid shelter, the slave labourers were forced to continue working under the threat that if they stopped working they would be shot.

I once broke the rules and risked severe punishment when I saved up some lunch which I should have eaten myself, and by crawling along the floor on all fours I managed to get near to a young Polish woman working at a machine. She must have been a little scared and probably wondered what I was doing, and she tried to pretend that she had not seen me so as not to attract attention. As I crawled nearer, I was then able to throw the small wrapped bundle of food over to her feet. I then looked up at her and gestured for her to have it. I smiled at her and she smiled back and I then crawled away back over to my area. She pretended to drop something and I saw her bend down to pick up the bundle of food. A few weeks later she was transferred away and I never saw her again.

Around three weeks later, I fell ill, and as a result was moved out of the factory and given a placement at a small chicken farm. I was overjoyed at the news, as it would mean I could escape the factory. The chicken farm was not necessarily any more exciting, but it was out in the air. I woke up each morning at around 7.30am as I wanted to go with the owner's wife, Marlene, who I called Frau Marla, and she would take me out into the field runs to collect the eggs from the birds. We would return to the house where we then had breakfast, including brown bread and some of the eggs that we had just collected. I would go and help her with things like shopping and with her washing and housework.

On weekends, I often went swimming in a large lake that lay at the bottom of one of the fields, though only in the warm weather.

One evening Frau Marla said to me, 'Tell me something, are you happy with everything, you know, with home and everything else?'

I replied, 'Yes, I am happy.'

She then said, 'I am not so sure, there is so much sadness in your eyes child, and you never talk of your family or ask if you can write to them.'

She then said that if I ever needed to confide in her with anything then I could always tell her. I told her about how I hated life in the city and the fear that everyone felt with the bombing. I also told her a little about my home life and about how I disliked father's discipline and his habits. I told her that I did not want to go back home and that I wanted to stay with her at the farm. At that, she gazed at the tall grandfather clock which stood in the corner of the kitchen area and said, 'Look, it is time that you were in bed, now get some sleep and I will see you in the morning.'

After about a week after our conversation, she informed me that she had been speaking to the local authority responsible for the labour service. I thought for a minute I was in trouble and was maybe going to be sent home for what I had told her.

She said to me, 'I am going to need help for much longer than I expected, and rather than have another girl sent here I felt it would be easier if you stayed on, as you are aware of the routine and what to do.'

I am not sure how she managed to arrange this, as the rules were rules, but I think she knew people in high places, I am not sure. I remember throwing my arms around her and hugging her. Later I also wrote a letter to my mother explaining that I was not coming back home just yet as I was still required on the farm.

Other girls were sent to us from the labour service and I was given the task of showing them what to do, and I later became a leader and was in charge of around thirty-five girls. With the emphasis of land work and agriculture becoming ever more important, Frau Marla had to expand her farming and we soon had pigs, and planted crops which all helped to provide food for the German people. The expansion also helped me to remain out of the city and I never returned home. I remained in touch with my mother and sisters by letter and I had arranged meetings with them, as I often paid for their train fares to come and visit me. I never returned to our house until my father passed away. In a way I regret not seeing him, but you have to understand that we had grown apart in our attitudes.

Frau Marla did not like Hitler and neither did I after what I had experienced in the ammunition factory. My father was convinced that Hitler was the right choice of leader for Germany. How could I have lived under the same roof and lived the way that he had wanted me to? It was not possible, and if I learned anything from the RADwf, then it was that you as a woman could use the system to your advantage and to escape. As regarding our service in helping to aid the Nazi war effort, that is rubbish. Almost everything that we produced on Frau Marla's farm was for the civilian populace. Often the food was sold much cheaper than it should have been in order that families who we knew were poor and had little income could eat.

Later in the war most of the livestock on our farm, and indeed many others in Germany, also became the focus of the Allied attacks. Fighter aircraft would often dive down and machine gun cattle and pigs deliberately to kill them. Whether this was just for sport I cannot say, but we were resourceful, and we were able to collect up the dead animals and then prepare them in mass storage. Usually the meat was butchered, salted and then dried or smoked, it would keep longer this way. Other farms just stopped the rearing and keeping of livestock to concentrate on crops and vegetables. Though I know that Allied planes took great pleasure in shooting up grain silos and storage units, even carts were fired on and sometimes destroyed. It was only a matter of time before someone was killed and this person was a girl aged only seventeen. American fighter planes fired at the horse-drawn cart she was on, killing her and the horses. Then the planes just flew off.

It is certainly true that marauding Allied fighters became frustrated at the lack of action. As a result, they began shooting up anything that took their fancy. Farm livestock was viewed as an enemy resource that could be utilized, so cows, pigs, horses and goats were often strafed with machine-gun fire, without particular regard for any civilians within the immediate vicinity. Grain storage facilities also provided a fun target to shoot at. Pilots often liked to watch the puffs of smoke as their bullets found their mark, though this was a practice also favoured by certain Luftwaffe bomber and fighter crews.

This was just another thing that the German girls, along with countless thousands of German civilians would have to learn to contend with on an ever-increasing scale during the course of the war.

Gabrielle Haefker:

As young women, soon we were doing everything. We worked on the land, in the factories, we drove buses and trams and we did nursing duties. Yet, still in a way we gained little respect in the eyes of the men. Some of the men I came into contact with, particularly during my labour service, made me feel sick with their stupid remarks and comments.

One morning, I was on the way to do my work on the land when two men passed me on their bicycles. I smiled and greeted them with a customary 'Heil Hitler' followed by a 'good morning', and then one of them turned around and said, 'That is what I like to see, German girls on the land,' while the other quickly butted in and said, 'German girls on the land, but better on their backs.' They both laughed and cycled on.

Was this all that men could think of? Were we just objects for screwing? That is how I felt and I don't think we were ever respected in quite the way that we should have been. Not until after the war, even though what we did with the RADwf proved us as more than equals to the men.

Chapter Ten

Terror from the Sky

In many ways, 1943 was the beginning of the end of the Third Reich. Hitler's failure to invade England, followed by the crushing defeat of his armies in Russia, were events that would seal Germany's fate. Again, Hitler's interference had cost the German forces dearly. By not allowing his armies to conduct tactical withdrawals and retreat at the critical points during the battles in Russia, Hitler had resigned his military machine to certain annihilation. To make matters worse, by May 1943, the German military campaign in North Africa had also began to falter and lose ground to the Allies.

America's entry into the Second World War, following the Japanese air attack on Pearl Harbor on 7 December 1941, would prove to be the real nail in the coffin for Germany. American forces could not mount attacks on Germany from their own shores, but bomber and fighter-bomber aircraft based in England could. Up until January of 1943, the RAF had fought the air war against Germany alone, sending its bombers to attack German cities at night.

The whole strategy of the Allied air offensive against Germany, however, was to change from January 1943. The changes were relatively simple, but ones that would prove to be devastating to the German infrastructure, which would find itself rapidly overwhelmed by the sheer volume of attacks launched during the new phase of the Allied bomber offensive. By 10 June 1943, it was agreed that, while RAF Bomber Command would continue to attack Germany by night with saturation-bombing raids, the United States Army Air Force (USAAF) would attack by day, in what were termed precision-bombing raids. A system of round-the-clock bombing was planned, which was steadily intensified in the hope that German civilian morale would collapse.

It was on 27 January 1943, that the USAAF made its first daylight raid against Germany. With a force of B-17 Flying Fortress and B-24 Liberator heavy bombers, the USAAF attacked Emden and Wilhelmshaven.

On 29 January, the Nazi Party's tenth anniversary celebrations were disrupted when RAF Mosquito fighter-bombers came in at low level on what was the RAF's first daylight raid on Berlin. Without any opposition from the Luftwaffe they strafed buildings with 20mm cannon and .303 machine-gun fire, before roaring off over the rooftops. Such an attack proved not only to have been a huge embarrassment to Goering, but also a huge psychological blow to the German civilians taking part in what was an important celebration in the Nazi calendar.

The USAAF would suffer appallingly high losses amongst bomber crews during the daylight raids, particularly against Berlin. The city had more anti-aircraft guns per square kilometre than either Hanoi had during the Vietnam War or Baghdad during the 1991 Gulf War. More bomber crews were lost while attacking targets over Berlin than any other city of the Third Reich. In comparison, German civilian loss of life was even greater, but quite apart from destroying the German civilian morale, the bombing only had the effect of hardening civilian resolve. Life still went on, but it was incredibly hard, especially for schoolchildren, whose lessons would now be constantly disrupted by the howl of the air-raid siren.

Anna Dann recalls:

> I remember the first daylight air raid very vividly. We found it hard to believe when the siren sounded, as previously the bombers had only attacked at night. We hurried out of the classroom as quickly as possible and out of the school building. As we ran out of the building and headed for the air-raid shelter, which was a large semi-recessed concrete structure, we could hear the distant drone of aircraft. As I ran with the others, I thought of Mother and Father and my brothers, and wondered if they were going to be safe. The fear started to turn to blind panic and I felt my heart begin to race in my chest, my mouth started to go dry, and that familiar headache start to instantly develop. This would become something I felt every single time I heard that horrible siren. When we got to the shelter and it was made clear that everyone who should be present was present, the heavy door was slammed shut and there we crouched down in an almost subterranean darkness lit only by a dull light from the ceiling. Even though we were relatively safe inside the shelter, we clearly heard the bombers approach and we knew from the sound that there must be many planes. The guns began to fire and their fire was so intense and rapid that it drowned out the noise of the planes. It was absolutely terrifying, and at one point, for a few seconds, the lights went out and it was pitch black; some of the

girls began to scream and panic. The teachers who were in with us shouted, 'Girls, don't panic, remain where you are and please try to remain calm, everything will be alright soon.'

The light flickered and came back on, and in the dull light I could see the frightened faces of some of the other girls, tears running down their faces as their eyes stared wildly up at the ceiling, as if it might come crashing down upon them at any moment. We all began to huddle together and we were shaking from the fear, and dust began to fill the air inside. I was aware that one of the girls next to me was so scared that she had grabbed hold of my hand; her grip was so tight that it almost hurt. One girl urinated herself with fright it was so bad, but at that moment nobody seemed to care. We sat crouched together like sardines in a can in that shelter before the all-clear siren meant that the danger had passed. The smell inside the shelter had become unbearable; it was the smell of sweat, urine, masonry dust and fear, an indescribable mixture of smells.

When the shelter door was opened and the rays of natural light flooded in, it hurt everyone's eyes and we came out stiffly like moles from soil. There were one or two girls who were so shaken and petrified by the experience that they could not come out and they had to be helped out from the shelter. One of them was the one who had urinated herself. She did not come back to school after that and her parents moved away to relatives in the Kiel Bay area near Schleswig. When we came out of the shelter, huge plumes of smoke rose into the sky around us. We soon learned that bombs had fallen onto nearby factories.

It brought home the dangers to us in a way that no propaganda ever could have done. We didn't believe the propaganda anymore, which told us we were safe in Berlin. I heard stories that many American bombers had been blown to pieces in the skies above the city.

A few weeks after this first big raid, my two brothers Franz and Josef volunteered to join the local flak unit and were accepted. This caused Mother and Father no end of worry, as this would mean that they would be right in the thick of the action and the danger. When not in action, some nights they used to shoot rats, using their home-made catapults and a hand torch to amuse themselves and pass the time away. They would have competitions and bets to see which one of the crew could get the most rats by the end of the night and be hailed as the Rat King!

Before bedtime, every single night I prayed for their safety and safe return to us each morning. In fact, I often used to listen out for them to come in through the door during the early hours of the morning, only then could I really sleep. Once I heard that door quietly open and close and the two young men bumping around and saying 'shhhh' to each other, trying to come inside without being too noisy, I knew they were alright and I thanked God before dozing off only to be roused a short while later for school.

On 5 March 1943, the first really effective bombing attack was launched against Essen, a city lying to the north of the Ruhr, with a population of 682,000. It was this first successful raid on Essen that hailed the beginning of the so-called Battle of the Ruhr. The intention of the Ruhr air campaign was to crush the heart of German industry. It was an attempt to sever the very jugular vein of the Third Reich war machine, but it would again prove to be a very costly campaign in terms of the lives of both Allied aircrews and German civilians.

During the evening of 16 May 1943, the RAF aimed to deliver the heaviest blow to date to German industry in the Ruhr Valley, in a raid that became known as the 'Dambusters Raid'. The attack was carried out with nineteen specially modified Avro Lancaster four-engined heavy bombers of the specially formed No. 617 Squadron, RAF. The targets were the Möhne, Eder and Sorpe dams situated in the Ruhr Valley. The attack achieved the objective of breaching both the Möhne and Eder dams, sending a massive destructive tidal wave down into the Ruhr Valley below. The damage caused severe flooding in the region with a massive civilian loss of life. Most had been asleep in their beds as the twenty-five-feet high wave of water came crashing down through the valley at a speed of twenty feet per second. Brigitte Schüttenkopf, who was only a young child at the time of the raid, remembers the terror that came that fateful night:

We were amongst the very lucky people whose houses were not swept away, as we lived at the far end of the Ruhr Valley region. I remember the distant noise, like a kind of muffled roar. It was loud enough to wake most people who then began to panic and scream, and we then heard the water arriving like an express train, followed by crashing and banging noises coming from downstairs, as the floodwaters rushed into our house, bringing debris with it.

We had no power in any of the houses, and when we got up to investigate, the whole of the downstairs was full of water up to the ceiling, which must have been over ten feet deep and we could not get out the house. We were trapped upstairs and when we looked out of the window, it was like we were living in the middle of a river. We could see the water rushing by in the moonlight with pieces of debris floating along on the surface. It was very frightening, as we did not know what had happened, but Father had said there must have been an accident at the Möhne Dam, as the floodwater could not have come from anywhere else. We prayed that our house would hold steady and not collapse under the water pressure.

At first light, we knew as boats came to rescue people and the news went around that enemy planes had bombed the dams and that thousands of people living at the lower Ruhr basin had been swept away in a huge wave of water. It took weeks for everything to get back to normal again, but the floods did not affect the industrial plants too badly, and many were operational after only a few days.

Afterwards, it was very difficult to rest in our beds at night. I later heard stories of young children in the small village of Himmelpforten swept from the arms of their parents as they desperately tried to escape from their flooded homes. The village priest had heard the explosion as the dam was hit and began to ring the church bells to warn the sleeping villagers. He had feared that such a thing might happen for some years and had arranged such a warning with the villagers. The priest's warning was hopeless though, and the village, along with that church, was swept away, just like matchwood. The bloated and rotting corpses of cattle, horses, pigs and human beings were found in fields, rivers and woodlands for many weeks after that dreadful event. It made me hate the English and the planes that did this.

The attack on the Eder Dam was also a success, and from the attacking aircrews perspective, it was an even more spectacular sight than the breaching of the Möhne. Two-hundred-million tons of water, in one great tidal wave, rolled down the steep valley at a speed of thirty feet per second. The RAF paid a high price for the attacks on the dams, with fifty-six airmen of the nineteen aircraft killed. When the result of the mission was found to have not proved that disruptive to the industries in the Ruhr, one has to ask the question, was it worth the cost of all those lives? Of the 1,294 civilians who perished in the floods, 749 were slave and prison labourers. There had been a Russian prisoner of war camp in the valley below the Eder Dam, and this too was swept away, leaving no survivors.

The terror from the skies could come at any time of the day or night. Anna Dann was lucky to survive an attack on a train she was travelling in with her BDM group. She recalls:

I had not been a member of the BDM for long having just turned fourteen years old. I had been looking forward to my first summer camp and there had been talk that there would be no summer camp that year because of the risks and everything. In the end, it was decided we should continue and go to summer camp as usual. In the days prior to our trip, we were told what must happen in the event of an air-raid alert. We were told that in the event of an air raid while we were on the train, the train would be stopped and we must immediately get down onto the floor and curl up under the seats, and remain there until we were cleared to come out. Under no circumstances was anyone to come out until instructed.

The day we left for the trip to the camp we all got onto the train and were a little anxious to get away from the city. I was also anxious about leaving my home, as it was the first time that I would be away and sleeping in a strange bed and in a strange place. The ride through the city and its immediate outskirts was fine and we soon began to settle and lift our spirits. It must have been half an hour to maybe an hour later when the train suddenly shuddered and we thought it was going to come off the rails as it shuddered and the breaks screamed.

Immediately our leader sprang from her seat shouting, 'Get down, get down!'

We knew what we had to do and got down beneath the seats and I placed my arms over my head and waited. We heard the roar of engines and they sounded very close – the engines faded and then grew louder.

We heard someone shout outside, '*Achtung*! [Attention!] They are turning back around.'

There was a loud cracking noise and a small series of explosions and whistling sounds, then the roar of engines again, only much louder and we heard the planes going right over our heads. We remained motionless beneath the seats of the train, when a man came through into our section of the carriage and told the group leaders, 'You must all disembark from the train immediately.' They gave the order for us to get off quietly as possible with no pushing. When we got off the train we could see that the locomotive pulling our carriages had been hit as it had holes in its boiler and the steam was pouring out at very high pressure. We were told that we had to get as far away as possible from the boiler in case it exploded. We had to line up and leave by walking back along the track we had travelled along staying close to the trees at all times. I don't know what upset me the most, the fact that I had just been on a train that had been attacked, or the fact that our summer camp was now over. The walking was no problem as we were quite used to walking, but all the time we were nervously looking back behind us up at the sky.

Minutes later, we heard more planes coming, and someone shouted up through the line that we should not panic as they were ours. They roared overhead and were probably looking for the planes that attacked our train. One of the Messerschmitts turned back around and circled around us for some minutes before flying away, maybe it was protecting us from further attack. We all waved at the Messerschmitt as it came around. We had to go to the nearest station where another train was waiting to take us back into Berlin. We discovered later that the planes that had attacked our train had been two British Mosquito fighters.

When we arrived back in Berlin we were told that an alternative camp would be arranged before the end of the summer, or maybe a few weeks' time. When we arrived home our parents were waiting for us, and we were amazed at how quickly they had been informed. As I got off the train my mother grabbed me and hugged me, she was crying and saying, 'I have been so worried, are you alright?'

After that, she was very concerned about me going anywhere alone, and wherever possible she sent Franz or Josef with me, even to buy sweets from the shop.

On 24 July 1943, the RAF launched Operation Gomorrah, an attack on the city of Hamburg, utilizing 746 RAF bombers. The attack was a devastating success, the bombers dropping 2,300 tons of high-explosive bombs onto the city within a period of forty-eight minutes. The fires of Hamburg were clearly visible from a distance of 200 miles away.

On the 25th, the city was attacked again by the USAAF in daylight. There were already 100,000 people homeless as a result of the attack on the 24th. The situation was becoming extremely untenable in the city, forcing the authorities into planning the mass evacuation of the city. Essen also received the attention of the bombers on the 25th, with over 2,000 tons of high-explosive bombs being dropped on the city. On 29 July, the authorities officially ordered the mass evacuation of the city of Hamburg. Casualty figures were quoted at the time as being in excess of 50,000 dead.

On 23 August, it was the turn of Berlin to receive the full attention of the Allied bombers, in what would be a series of sustained, heavy raids on the city by both the RAF and USAAF. During the night of the 23rd, 727 RAF bombers took off from their bases in England to drop some 1,700 tons of high-explosive bombs on the city.

Dana Schmidt remembers the nightmare that came in the blackness of 23 August 1943:

I was thirteen years old, still at school and living with my mother. Father was in the German army as an artillery officer, and I also had a brother who was also serving with our army and he was a corporal serving with an infantry unit. This meant me and Mother were left on our own, though we tried to get on with our lives as normally as we could under the circumstances. There had been attacks on Berlin before and we knew what we had to do to keep safe and where the nearest air-raid stations were. There was a large one that was only some four hundred yards from our house, so at a run we could get there very quickly. The shelter was one used mainly by machine workers of a nearby factory. For safety's sake, and to avoid any confusion in the dark, Mother and me decided to sleep in the same bed.

Things were very much as normal during the early evening of 23 of August 1943 and me and Mother had eaten our meal, which was not very much, just a few small sandwiches with a little milk. It was a warm evening and before getting into bed Mother opened the window of our room a little to prevent the room becoming stuffy. We got into bed and were asleep in a matter of minutes, and the next thing I was aware of the air raid siren blaring very loudly as it was only a short distance from our row of houses.

Mother immediately jumped from the bed and said, 'Dana, quickly put this on, we must get out of here now.'

She handed me my jacket, which I then put on, back to front at first, so I took it off and wrapped it around my shoulders. I went to put my boots on but Mother said, 'No leave them here just get your socks.'

I quickly pulled out a pair of thick socks from the cupboard and as there was no time to put them on, I stuffed them into my jacket pockets. Mother put her coat on and then grabbed my hand and we both ran down the stairs. We went straight out of the front door and mother slammed it shut behind us without locking it. We ran down the road and I was aware of others coming out of their houses. With nothing on my feet, the road felt quite cold, but Mother and me ran like champion sprinters to the shelter and were soon safely inside. Many others had decided to leave the shelters in their gardens to seek the safety of this larger and more heavily protected one made from concrete.

Once inside, Mother and me huddled up in a corner and wrapped our coats around ourselves. I put the thick wool socks on my feet and tried to settle down to sleep. It was still relatively quiet even after half an hour had passed, though there was the distant rumble of the flak on the outskirts of the city.

One by one the other gun teams protecting the city began to fire, the noise grew increasingly louder. We could hear the drone of the planes above and whistling noises. An explosion shook our shelter and put out the lights inside it. Nobody dared move and you could hear the cries of frightened children and their mothers trying desperately to comfort them. One of the old women had managed to light a candle, even though the explosions continued nearby, making the ground shake and more dust fall from the ceiling. The candle did not throw out much light, but it was better than sitting in complete darkness. Some of the men were mumbling obscenities about what they would like to do with 'those bastards dropping bombs'. One of the younger women reminded them that there were young children and babies in the shelter too and to 'keep their voices down'. It was strange, as for a minute it felt like a full-scale argument was going to develop.

Someone had boiled up some water and made some coffee, and this was passed around in small metal military cups. I had a few sips but shuddered as there was no sugar in it and I quickly passed the cup to Mother who finished it off, and I tried hard to drift off to sleep by covering my ears with my coat.

The next I knew Mother was shaking me to wake me up, 'Dana, wake up, it's safe now, we must go outside and see if everything is alright.'

I rose to my feet and felt a little stiff and Mother helped me into my coat and put her arm around me as we made our way out of the shelter, it was getting light by this time. The all-clear had sounded some time ago but there was a scare and some confusion that some bombs had landed nearby without exploding, and before anyone was let outside, this had to be verified. Even from the shelter, the sheer damage was evident, the sky was blanketed with thick black smoke and as we walked along the road, we could see piles of rubble that had once been houses and fires burning out of control. The sky was blood red over the city and glowing like hot coals from the fires.

'Maybe, they did not get our house,' I said to Mother, but she was silent as we approached our street.

I prayed under my breath that our home was still standing. Smoke hung above the street where we lived and RADw men and firemen were busy digging into the rubble piles of many of the houses in our street to free trapped people and fires were still being fought. We walked a little further and could see that the whole row of houses including ours had gone; just piles of broken bricks and timber remained and yellow flames poured out of a broken gas main. Women and children who we knew as neighbours wandered around in a daze crying. Mother broke down into tears as bodies were brought out of some of the rubble. To me they did not look like human bodies, they looked like dust-covered rag dolls, and some had patches of blood on them while others had legs or even heads missing. Some of the corpses did not have a mark on them, but it was a horrific sight and as Mother wept uncontrollably, I tried to comfort her.

Some friends of ours from the next street took us down to the church hall where everyone who had lost their homes had been taken. There we were given blankets and coffee and told that later we would be escorted to our home where we could try and salvage some of our property. The authorities basically asked if any relatives lived nearby whom we could stay with and they helped to arrange everything for us.

The Moelle family, living on the edge of the city in the relative safety of pastureland, were astonished by the sight that greeted them when they came out of their shelter beneath the house.

Theresa relates:

I ran straight up to my room and pulled back the thick black curtains, and I said, 'Oh, my God.' The other Moelle children followed and said, 'What is it, Theresa?'

We stared from the window towards the direction of the city and there was this huge yellowy-red glowing halo that filled the sky above and around the city. We knew that this meant that Berlin was on fire, and that it must be very bad indeed. I pushed up the window to open it and leaned out, and I could smell the smoke.

Walter Moelle came into the room and from the doorway he could clearly see the city burning. The look on his face was one which I will never forget, and he quickly left the room and went downstairs to talk with his wife. I followed him and crept quietly half way down the stairs to try and listen to what they were talking about. I did not hear everything but I heard them talk about getting us children out of here where it would be safer.

At first light, thick smoke hung over the city and this failed to disperse throughout the whole day. We heard more British planes had been shot down and another one had crash-landed six miles away. I was told that three of the crew had escaped and had later surrendered to soldiers from a nearby flak unit. At that time I didn't care. I was angry about the bombing and felt that maybe we should kill all of them if we capture them?

During the following days, we often saw bands of people trailing out into the countryside, carrying bags and small carts filled with their few possessions. I found that most were women who had lost their husbands either in Russia or in the recent bombing attacks, and I got talking to one of them. She had two small children with her, a boy and a girl. I asked her where she was going and she replied, 'We are going away from Berlin, as we have nothing anymore, and maybe I will be able to find work somewhere on a farm so as my children can eat, I just don't know.' She gazed back towards the direction of Berlin and said, 'The terror from the skies will be back, with an even greater harvest of corpses.'

Before she went on her way, I quickly ran inside the house and took some eggs, a large piece of bread and some milk out from the kitchen and gave this to her. She looked at me and said, 'Bless you child, but what of you? What are you going to do?'

I said to her, 'What do you mean?'

And she replied. 'Have you not heard that our armies are being defeated everywhere and they are having to fall back and surrender?'

'Is that really true, are you sure?' I asked.

She nodded her head, looked back again in the direction of Berlin before wishing me farewell and walking on her way.

Only a couple of days later, three enemy aircraft came across our fields, very low and very fast. They roared overhead and seconds later, there was the sound of gunfire. They had passed over the fields and had fired at the livestock again, killing some cows. Some children playing nearby beneath some trees were nearly also hit. This became a regular game and they seemed to enjoy flying low over our fields and killing our animals.

One afternoon a group of young Hitler Youth soldiers pulled up at the farm with a truck with a gun on the back. I soon learned that they were flak gunners and had this gun with four barrels that was designed to shoot down fast-flying enemy planes. The gun crew set the gun up beside a tall hedge and covered it with some straw to help camouflage it. Sure enough the planes came again around two days later only this time the flak guns were waiting for them and once the enemy planes came into view the camouflage was pulled off and the crew began firing. One of the enemy planes was hit and rapidly lost height – trailing flames behind it. It dived into a field and exploded in flames and the crew perished inside. The others did not return to see their comrades' fate and we all cheered. When the people from the Luftwaffe had finished inspecting the wreck, it was left there in the field and the kids used to go and play with what was left of it. The flak gunners, being only young men from the Hitler Youth, often gave us the empty cartridge cases from their gun that we would then keep for souvenirs. Though they should not have given them away as metal was desperately needed for recycling in the factories, I put my cartridges cases under the mattress with the piece of Wellington bomber I had.

Berlin was attacked again with an ever-increasing ferocity and tonnage of bombs. On 31 August, 1,000 tons were dropped on the city, and between 18 November and 16 December 1943, a total of 18,000 tons of high-explosive bombs had been dropped on Berlin. While the Luftwaffe were successful in intercepting the bomber formations by both day and night, and inflicting heavy casualties on the attackers, the sheer weight of responsibility placed upon its weary shoulders since the outbreak of war back in 1939 was now beginning to take its toll. The terror that had come from the sky was one that was seemingly unstoppable. For many these were omens of the destruction to come.

Anna Dann concludes:

> The saddest thing of all was the sight of mothers being taken to the makeshift town hall mortuary to see if the bodies of their children were amongst the dead. Several bombs had struck a school and there were few survivors. It was a horrifying sight to see all of the bodies lay out and these wretched women having to look at each one of the dead children to see which one was her child. Most were just too hysterical with grief and it was often left to the grandparents to make the identification. The bombing was no longer against the military or industrial targets, the bombers were trying to kill the civilian population now, and that's how we looked at it.
>
> Each time they came in ever greater numbers, as thick as swarms of flies.

Schweinfurt also became a popular target for the Allied bomber offensive. The main concentration of flak guns set up to defend Schweinfurt were situated across the river to the south. There were over thirty 88mm medium-calibre anti-aircraft guns in this particular flak zone, making it a fairly formidable defensive feature.

There was a large air-raid shelter near the Schillerplatz that was mainly for the workers at the VKF ball-bearing plant and their families. Martina Schepel, who lived in one of the many factory residential houses on the Schrammstrasse, which was just across the street from the VKF plants, recalls the terror of the Allied bombing attacks.

> I was only a little girl at that time in 1943, but could never forget the terror that we lived with every day. My father worked at the VKF *Werke* [works] as a machinist, making ball bearings for aero-engines and other equipment. The worst of the bombing attacks on our city were those of October 1943. They were particularly bad and many of the residential buildings where the workers lived with their

families were bombed. It became so bad that people began to queue outside the Goethe air-raid bunker, though there was another on the Ernst Sachs Strasse, though this was mainly for the factory workers and their families.

I lost many of my little friends during those air raids, they were so cruel, and I am still so angry about it all. When the siren would sound, we ran for our lives. We often remained petrified for hours on end as the bombs rained down around us. You could feel the shockwaves from the bombs as they exploded outside the shelter, and when one landed close by, the air was often sucked out from the shelter by the force.

When it was over, there were the usual scenes of carnage day after day; the bodies of cats and dogs which had been blown apart, families weeping outside of their bombed homes, while others went to hospital with their injured wives, children and husbands. Often the gas, water pipes and sewer drains would be blown open, and as the gas pipes spouted bright orange flames, water and sewerage would pour down the streets. The smoke would hang over Schweinfurt for days and it seemed that on some days it never really fully got light. There was not one part of that city that escaped the bombs, everywhere was hit and it was quite indiscriminate, with no regard for civilian safety.

Out in the streets there was shrapnel everywhere, even lodged in the guttering pipes of the houses. Our father had to climb up with a borrowed ladder and remove the metal from the pipes. Often there were holes in the roof caused by shrapnel and these holes were blocked with anything that Father could find. Father was later killed during one of the air raids in 1943, and the whole of the residential area had been badly bombed, so Mother made arrangements for me, and my older sister and brother to move away and stay with relatives. She still needed income with which to support herself and help provide for our upkeep, and so Mother went to work in the VKF *Werke*. We saw little of her and I was convinced that we would lose her too, and I begged her to come to us in the very few letters I was able to send her. She kept working, doing the same work as a man would have done, right up until the end.

We survived the war, but will never forget how the bombing robbed us of our father and my mother of her husband.

Chapter Eleven

The Volkssturm and the Werewolf

Although not officially instituted until February 1945, preparations to create what became known as the 'Werewolf Project' began somewhat earlier. Contrary to popular belief, females were to form as much a part of the project as the males. The idea behind the Werewolf Project was to train the youth and young children of Germany in the use of firearms and the principles of sabotage and sniping, so that they too could join the fight against the Allies should they enter German territory.

The exact date that the militarization of female youth began in wartime Germany is not clear, but there is much evidence to suggest that it began before the Werewolf Project came into existence in any official capacity. As the war dictated change, young women from the age of eighteen were accepted into the German military as auxiliaries. As a result, many ended the war attached to the Luftwaffe as ground controllers, drivers and flak-gun crews.

Prior to the implementation of the Werewolf Project on 25 September 1944, Hitler created the *Volkssturm*, or 'Peoples Storm'. Hitler announced the creation of the *Volkssturm* concept via a radio broadcast to the German people on 18 October 1944. The man given overall control of the *Volkssturm* organization was, unsurprisingly, Martin Bormann. Bormann was also head of recruitment and political leadership of the *Volkssturm* units.

The idea of the *Volkssturm* was to create a national militia made up of all able-bodied civilian men, from sixteen to sixty. There is, however, ample evidence to suggest that much older males were drafted, threatened or frightened into joining the *Volkssturm*. The objective of the *Volkssturm* was to fight to the death, if necessary, and defend Germany at all costs and with whatever means available. While the *Volkssturm* was intended as primarily a male national militia, females did join the *Volkssturm* fighters, defending towns and cities of the Third Reich.

The Werewolf Project was only a slightly different concept, utilizing members of the four main Nazi child and youth organizations: the *Jung Volk*, *Jung Madel*, Hitler Youth and BDM. German children legible for service under the Werewolf Project started as young as eight years old.

German female guerrilla units and battalions were also being specially formed at about the same time as the *Volkssturm* mobilization began. *Jung Madel* and BDM girls, aged between ten and eighteen years old were called up for service in remarkable all-female guerrilla units.

As already mentioned, one of the most notable female Nazi leaders given the task of overseeing the militarization of young girls and women under both the *Volkssturm* and Werewolf Project, was Gertrud Scholtz-Klink. Some of these female combat units organized by Scholtz-Klink would later see action in the fighting near Warsaw and during the fall of Berlin.

Hitler Youth leader Artur Axmann fully supported the use of children in the war effort. It was apparent to many that the likes of Axmann and Bormann would be nowhere near the fighting, choosing to remain with Hitler in a bunker deep beneath the Reich Chancellery, plus, neither could consider themselves as soldiers.

In the German cities at that time, there was no exact shortage of weaponry. Most families possessed a shotgun or firearm of one type or another, some of it originating from the First World War. Those who could not, for whatever reason, obtain firearms or grenades, were taught how to make improvised materiel such as Molotov cocktails, which were simply glass bottles filled with petrol or other flammable liquids and fitted with a piece of rag in the top. All the user had to do then was light the rag and then throw the bottle at the target area. On impact, the bottle would smash and the whole thing would ignite. Such improvised weapons were lethal against unprotected soldiers, but were useless against armoured vehicles such as tanks, unless they could be dropped through the open crew hatch.

It appears most likely that it was during this phase of civilian military mobilization that many of Germany's young girls were first introduced to weaponry they had only previously seen being either used or carried by their soldiers. The *Jung Madel* and BDM organizations openly encouraged their members under the Werewolf Project to handle firearms and learn how to make booby-trap devices and explosives.

Hitler was conscious of the military catastrophe facing Germany, yet the Werewolf Project was, in reality, just another one of Hitler's contingency plans for the last line of defence of his crumbling Reich. Many German *Wehrmacht* officers expressed grave concern, especially at the prospect of young girls and women becoming involved in the fighting in and around German villages, towns and cities.

Former SS soldier Theobald Hortinger spoke exclusively with me during a brief meeting in the winter of 2000, when we discussed the militarization of the female youth in Germany. Theobald explained that once during a conference in Berlin, he had overheard senior officers talking with Hitler about the subject of females being involved in armed conflict. One of the *Wehrmacht* generals present at the meeting – possibly General Heinz Guderian – argued with Hitler that he was not convinced that girls, owing to their limited training and lack of military knowledge and experience of battlefield situations, would be able to operate either cohesively or tactically alongside regular *Wehrmacht* soldiers.

Hitler was said to have cut him short, barking, 'Rubbish, are you trying to tell me that our womenfolk should be exempt from the honour of dying for their Führer?'

Theobald had explained that such statements were very typical of those made by Hitler at that time. In another one of his incoherent rages, Hitler said of the German youth, 'If it has to be, then the enemies of Germany will drown in the blood of Germany's youth.'

Theobald also mentioned that a directive had definitely been issued on paper authorizing the militarization of all young girls, though no significant documentation has been found to confirm the subject. As a result, the existence of such a directive is still largely confined to myth. There is little actual archive material available today, due mainly to the fact that the militarization of Germany's female youth began so late, that Russian, British and American military intelligence departments had little time in which to gather sufficient data. It has to be said, however, that the Soviets did make a concerted effort to compile detailed reports on child combatants.

Heidi Koch, however, during an interview with the author, confirmed that a directive of sorts had in fact been issued:

> We were told by the BDM and in directives issued to youth leader Artur Axmann, that if we failed to defend Germany, our people, our cities, we would be a worthless race once more, and that the Jews and Communists would return in their masses and we would face worse misery than those after the year 1918. We were informed that we as a people must not lose this fight; as if we lose then none of us will have deserved to live.
>
> That was the message given to us which had apparently been dictated by Adolf Hitler himself and then issued to all of the Hitler Youth groups and their leaders all over Germany. We were also told that we must not abandon Berlin, regardless of the dangers we faced,

but must dig in if necessary. We were told that if we attempted to leave it could be viewed as cowardice or even desertion. Desertion was a crime punishable by execution.

The military training and instruction given to girls of the *Jung Madel* and the BDM varied according to the strengths of the individual female involved. The small and slightly built girls were given instructions on how to use stick grenades and how to make Molotov cocktails, known more commonly today as petrol bombs.

To enable the girls to put their instruction into practice, they were taken to old firing ranges usually reserved for the Hitler Youth boys. Dummies were then assembled at which the girls could practice throwing inert grenades – usually constructed of solid wood but made to look exactly like the real thing – at the dummies. Once the instructors felt that the pupil was competent enough at the task, they were given a limited supply of real grenades to throw.

Molotov cocktails were potentially dangerous to use, as the thrower had to ensure that the device was thrown in a manner that did not put either herself or a comrade at risk. Molotov cocktails were usually dropped onto enemy soldiers or soft-skinned vehicles from buildings. The girls were therefore taught to climb up ladders, climbing frames or other objects, light the rag, and then drop the device down onto a designated point on the ground. This is perfectly illustrated by an incident that occurred in Berlin, when two 15-year-old BDMs dropped a Molotov cocktail onto Russian soldiers advancing through an alleyway.

The girls were also shown how to make booby-trap devices from captured grenades, using empty meat tins and cord or wire. The grenade pin would be removed, and the safety lever held tight as the grenade is pushed down into the restricting confines of the tin, thereby retaining the spring-loaded striker in place. A length of cord or piano wire was then threaded through a hole in the top of the grenade and tied in a small knot. A trip-wire was then connected and camouflaged with whatever foliage or debris was available. An unwary soldier would snag the wire with his leg, pulling the grenade out of the tin, the safety lever would fly off and the grenade would explode. It was a very simple yet effective device.

Such devices were also rigged up at potential crossing points on rivers and deep streams where their effect was even more lethal to the victim from the shock wave generated by the underwater blast.

Girls were also shown how to make what later became known as 'toe poppers'. This was nothing more elaborate than a standard rifle cartridge inserted into a piece of hollowed-out wooden cane or any other suitable material, roughly the same length as the rifle cartridge. Either a pin or nail was placed with the point positioned against the primer at the base of the cartridge. The cartridge was then placed in the ground with only a small area of the bullet head protruding from the surface of the ground. When stepped on by a soldier, the force of his weight would cause the pin or nail to strike the primer, causing the cartridge to fire. The result was quite effective for such a small booby trap, as the victim often lost half of their foot or their toes, hence the nickname toe popper. It was mainly used to incapacitate rather than kill, thus adding to the commitment of the enemy's resources.

Stronger girls of both the *Jung Madel* and BDM who were competent in handling a rifle, were taken to firing ranges where they learned basic musketry skills. Using blank ammunition at first, they were trained how to load, fire and maintain the weapon, as well as how to clear any stoppages. The weapons used were usually standard German infantry rifle, the 7.92mm-calibre Mauser *Gewehr 41*. Girls who became particularly good shots were offered the chance to become *Heckenschütze*, or snipers.

Helga Bassler, familiar with the use of firearms, was recruited to become an *Engel Heckenschütze*, or angel sniper. The term *Engel Heckenschütze* was used by some of the *Wehrmacht* soldiers to describe some of these pretty maidens with rifles. The soldiers would say that they looked like angel snipers, hence the sobriquet.

Helga recalls:

> I was a good shot with a rifle, mainly for the reason that I often accompanied my father on many of his hunting trips with his friends in the Bavarian Black Forest before the outbreak of war. My father and his friends used old army rifles to shoot wild boar in the forest.
>
> The first time I ever had a go with my father's rifle I could not hold it properly, and he had to steady the end of the barrel for me. Although my aim was not brilliant, I fired and I hit the boar within the rifles sight. My father was as amazed as I was when the animal fell dead to the ground with a single shot to the chest. In fact he actually excitedly cried out, '*Schiesse!*' [shit!] with astonishment.
>
> As I grew older and stronger, I learned to use the gun more independently, and before the war ended the yearly hunting trips into the Black Forest, I had claimed a few more animals. I knew very well that humans were as easy to kill as wild boar, and that if

I had to, I would defend my family and my country against those who wished us any harm.

A rifle is not a difficult thing for anyone to learn to use. It is like learning to use a knife and fork or maybe play a piano; with time and patience, you improve. My little proportion of natural ability caught the attention of the local *Volkssturm Gruppenführin*. I was guilty of showing off to them a little the skills I had learned in the past and was asked if I wanted to become a *Heckenschütze*. They told me that all I would have to do in the event of any military threat from our enemies was find cover and shoot at any enemy soldier who presented himself. The *Gruppenführin* explained, 'We know that you have killed *wilde sau* [wild boar], your father has bragged of his daughter's prowess with a rifle by saying that his daughter can shoot straighter and better than our soldiers.'

A couple of days later, I joined some eight other Hitler Youth boys and girls at one of the rifle firing ranges, a large bank of sand with a concrete wall behind it. We were told to form a line and two men with *Volkssturm* armbands came down the line, handing each of us a rifle that we then had to place down on the ground in front of us. Another man came down the line and placed some cartridges beside the rifles. The instruction was quite basic and we were firstly told how to make sure our aim remained true by adjusting the sights. To avoid any confusion as to whose shots belonged to whom we had to do our firing exercise one at a time, which meant we had to wait around for our turn and it became quite boring.

Our targets were made of board, and out of the eight of us, three girls and five boys, only four of us attained a required score. These were three Hitler Youth boys and myself. It was noted that my shooting was better than the boys. The boys did not like it very much and they glared across at me rather contemptuously.

After that, we who could shoot well were given regular training, and as kids, we found it exciting. We were taught not to stay in any one place for too long, but to move around wherever possible so as to confuse the enemy. At the time I never thought of our enemies as possibly being men with wives and children and maybe daughters of their own like me, they were like ghosts, without faces. I never thought that they would really come, and that I might have to shoot them. We were warned that we must not feel sorry or hesitant if the time came to shoot to kill real soldiers, as they would do exactly the same to us or possibly worse.

Propaganda warned us of what might happen if the enemy does come to our cities, we were particularly afraid of the Russians; our fears were justified as reports suggested that the Russians were now advancing closer. The Russian hordes had good reason to want to hate and destroy Germans, for everything they had suffered because of the war on the Eastern Front. There were few illusions by this time.

Instruction on how to use the ubiquitous *Panzerfaust* anti-tank rocket launcher was also given to the girls. This was one of the most prolific of all weapons given to those civilians of both the *Volkssturm* and Werewolf Project defending German cities. It was light and easy to use, but its use required a great deal of bravery and self-discipline, as in some cases one had to get to within thirty metres of the target, usually a tank, before it could be used with any certainty of success. This meant that the user would be well within the range of the tank's defensive armament. The girls given the task of tank-killers would have to operate amongst the rubble, utilizing it as cover while waiting for tanks to either drive by or be decoyed towards them. The idea was that they would then kneel down right in the path of the tank, and fire at almost point-blank range at the frontal armour before running back into cover. From the female perspective, this was a task that required exceptional courage. Some of the girls were, however, to prove themselves more daring than battle-hardened soldiers, as Dora Brunninghausen explains:

The *Panzerfaust* was the easiest weapon of all, and I decided that this was the weapon of my choice. I soon began to regret that decision, as I was taken with some other girls to a field and given a wooden replica *Panzerfaust*. We were given instruction individually and I was to go first. A Panzer tank faced me at the end of the field, and I saw several men getting into it and start it up, and I was shown what to do. I was horrified to discover that the tank would drive directly towards me, I had to lie down in a shallow trench in the field, and at the designated point, I would pretend to fire off the *Panzerfaust* and shout out 'BANG!' to let the instructors know that I had discharged my weapon. Well, I did that and as I shouted 'BANG!' the instructor shouted back even louder, 'Now lie perfectly still and don't move.'

I retorted back that 'the tank was going to drive over me.'

He then yelled, 'If you lie still you will not be harmed, now do as I tell you.'

I lay on the ground and admit that I began to whimper and just froze as that thing actually drove right over me. I vividly remember the tracks and wheels and the horrible grinding and screeching noises as it passed over me. As soon as it passed over me, I got up and quickly sprinted to the side of the field.

The instructor then said to me, 'You see if you lie down in a shallow dip in the ground and parallel to the centre point of the vehicle, and away from the wheels, you cannot be harmed.'

I asked visibly shaking, 'What was the point of doing that if the tank had been hit by the *Panzerfaust*?'

The instructor said, 'Well, Fraulein Brunninghausen, that had nothing to do with the exercise, it was a test of your faith in me and yourself to do as was desired.'

Some of the girls were laughing at me saying that I was as white as a ghost and my legs were quivering. They soon fell silent when the instructor called out 'NEXT!'

There were three main types of *Panzerfaust* anti-tank weapon. These were classified 30, 60 and 100 respectively. The numbers indicated the effective range of the particular weapon in metres. For example, the *Panzerfaust* 100 had an effective range of 100m. The hollow-charge warhead could penetrate 200mm-thick armour, which meant that this one, relatively small and lightweight weapon, was a match for any tank in the Allied inventory, and would wreak havoc amongst Allied and Russian tank crews alike in the coming battles, often fought at close quarters.

In order to get the girls used to seeing dead bodies, they were often taken in groups to the makeshift morgues around the city. There they were shown the bodies of the victims killed during the bombing.

Heidi Koch attended one of these gruesome tours:

Our whole group of forty girls was taken to one of the church halls, which the authorities had taken over as a temporary morgue. The bodies were down in the basement and were covered with blankets. Each body had been labelled so as you could see the person's name and age details. The blankets were then pulled off by one of the orderlies so as we could see them. It was a horrible thing to see, the faces of babies with their eyes wide open, children, old men and women. Some of the bodies had no heads, arms or legs, and some just looked like heaps of meat. Some of the girls began to be violently sick, and they coughed and vomited onto the floor, but we were told to look and to remember what we had seen as it was the very reason why we might have to someday fight the barbarous hordes, as our leader put it. I shut my eyes and swallowed hard desperately fighting to stop the contents of my own stomach from hurtling up my throat. We were then led back up the stairway out of the morgue. On the way up the stairs, two women passed us with buckets and mops, cursing to themselves about having to clean up yet more vomit. Clearly, we had not been the only young visitors to that morgue. Although many of us had seen some dead bodies being pulled from bombed houses, nothing could have been as graphic as what we had seen in that morgue. I would often wake in the middle of the night, with sweat pouring off me and crying hysterically. Sometimes Mother and Father would have to run into my room as I began to thrash about in my sleep, so violently that I knocked things over and might wake up the others.

There were far worse horrors to come than those witnessed in that morgue.

Hitler had given his personal approval for the sacrifice of female youth. He was of the opinion that both young males and females would act as a kind of tactical stopgap against the Allied and Russian forces, which would not necessarily expect children to attack them. A former *Wehrmacht leutnant*, Albert Freist, recalls the horror of his senior commander when hearing news of the planned Werewolf Project:

Our commanding officer had held numerous meetings with those officers closest to Hitler, in other words his subordinates. Our commanding officer, when hearing of the Werewolf Project, shook his head in disbelief. He had much reservation about bringing young Hitler Youth boys and girls into any defensive plan, on the grounds that young females in particular, once brought into any situation of conflict, would immediately feel fear and lose all nerve and sense required to mount any effective attack. He wrote a short letter stating that perhaps the older females and BDM girls would best be used to assist the wounded in a medical capacity instead. He did not agree at all with the proposal of any female militarization.

His note was forwarded but I do not believe that it received any reply in return. I know there was a phone call from Bormann regarding this issue, but I have no idea what Bormann had said. The Führer's plan was, though, reaffirmed later on and his demands were unchanged. The commanding officer was very worried indeed as he confided in me a little while later that he had two teenage daughters in Berlin.

As officers agreed and disagreed with the moral principles regarding the militarization of Germany's females, the Hitler Youth continued to encourage and instruct its members in the use of deadly force.

Sophia Kortge:

The first weapon I ever held was an army rifle. This I found to be much too heavy and clumsy for me to use, I was hopeless with it, although that did not excuse me. The rifle was taken off me and I was then handed a pistol, and I found that much easier to hold. I was told to aim it and pull the trigger, as the weapon had no bullets in. I could not hold the weapon in one hand so had to use both hands. I aimed the pistol at a poster on the wall and pulled the trigger, the pistol made a loud click. I was shown how to use this weapon by a newly appointed BDM group leader who we soon nicknamed 'The Beast'. She was a big and sort of imposing young woman, who rarely ever smiled and was totally committed to Nazism in its every possible form. She took the pistol apart and showed me how the weapon was put back together.

She then said to me, 'Now you must try this,' and she passed me the pistol.

I had forgotten almost straight away what to do and she began to lose her temper with me by raising her voice and saying, 'You are not concentrating. Now I will show you again and you will do what I have shown you.'

Her face seemed to twist when she became angry and that is why she got the nickname 'The Beast'. I watched again how she took the pistol apart, visualizing it in my mind, and then reassembling it again. Afterwards she then handed me the pistol again and nodded to me, as if to say, 'Well, go on then'.

This time, I managed to get everything more or less correct, though it took me some time. The Beast then explained that I must practice this until I can do it much quicker. At that time, we were not allowed to take weapons home with us, as these were only to be distributed upon the orders from the *Volkssturm* and Werewolf authorities of our block area. The *Volkssturm* and Werewolves could only be issued with weapons when the *Gruppenführers* of the block in question were instructed to mobilize by Hitler.

All weapons were held at pre-arranged collection points around the city. The idea was that, in the event of an emergency, the citizens would go to the designated collection points, where they would be then issued with a weapon, before being transported to where they would be needed to engage the enemy. We were, however, encouraged to take home manuals that explained how the weapons worked and how to look after them, including taking them apart to clean and putting them back together.

We also learned how to use grenades and the most famous weapon, the *Panzerfaust*. At that time, there were probably more girls acquainted with the use of this weapon than men were. My father had an old rifle that he kept in the downstairs cupboard of our house. As school was now often being taught down in the air-raid shelters because of the disruption, I often came home early, and it was during that time that I first saw my father sit down and strip the gun, clean it, and then load it with live bullets.

He looked across at me, smiled and said, 'Well, Sophia if they come we will be ready to defend ourselves.'

Over the next few weeks The Beast taught me how to shoot the pistol. She was a very good shot and learned her art from air-rifle shooting in the past. The pistol did not have a very long range and you could only shoot over a short distance, where accuracy was not that important. The Beast wanted the shots to hit the head or chest area of the targets that were in the shape of soldiers. It took a little while, but after a time I could do this and The Beast would be pleased. She also told me, 'When you fire into the enemy, you must fire two or three shots in quick succession, so as to be sure of killing him. A wounded soldier might shoot you in the back as you walk away from him.'

She also delighted in telling me that if you hit the enemy in his chest, the bullets may puncture his lungs and he will then drown on his own blood. There had been rumour that The Beast had been chosen to instruct girls in these tasks by the NSV [*Nationalsozialistische Volkswohlfahrt*, or People's Welfare Organization], which was the female section of the SS. The female SS were called, or rather nicknamed, the 'Brown Sisters', and everything about The Beast pointed to SS involvement, and there was also a rumour that she had come from one of the death camps. The Beast was very good in the respect that she could frighten you into doing anything she wanted you to do. Of course, I later discovered that this woman had been personally selected to train girls in the use of firearms by Gertrud Scholtz-Klink herself.

The girls also had to be taught the rudiments of guerrilla warfare, and had to dig trenches and dug outs as part of their national-militia duties.

Sophia Kortge explains:

We were told to pick up a shovel each and then we were taken to various points such as gardens or sports fields and were shown how to dig what they called a slit trench. It was quite hard and monotonous work and we broke up the boredom by messing around. I remember pulling an earthworm out of the soil of my trench and, after dangling it in the air for a few seconds, I tossed it to one of the other girls who then shrieked and jumped out of the way, flailing her arms in the air in disgust, as she did not like worms. We laughed amongst ourselves as the worm was thrown back in our direction, and a full-scale worm fight broke out, and there were handfuls of dirt flying in all directions as more girls joined in.

Another girl quickly picked up the worm and held it to the front of her work trousers and shouted out, 'Look, a penis!'

By now we had dropped our shovels down and were in fits of laughter, the tears streaming down our faces. Then the *Volkssturm* man in charge of us all came back and, upon hearing the laughter, ran across to us and began to shout at and curse us for messing about.

He said, 'What the hell do you think you are playing at? You are a disgrace, this is not some kind of a big joke, *fraulein*, now stop messing around and get on with your work before I report you to your superiors.'

He glared at us with his angry red face and walked away tut, tutting to himself. We started shovelling again but could not help looking at each other and giggling. I suppose we were ignorant to how serious all this was, and couldn't really imagine that our city would really be invaded. There were many lighthearted occasions like that though, and it was not all doom. Later on, we were not smiling as we had big blisters on our hands which became very sore, as they were too soft for that kind of work!

The girls also had to learn guerrilla-warfare techniques such as firing their weapons on the move from buildings or from any other available cover, along with concealment and escape and evasion tactics. To many Hitler Youth boys, this was something that had become second nature almost from their first day in the Hitler Youth.

For girls, it was completely alien as they had only really learned how to be mothers, proficient first-aiders and housekeepers. If they were to fight, it was important that they learn as much as possible and very quickly if they were to prove successful and survive the coming battle. The very lifeblood of both the *Volkssturm* and the Werewolf Project would lie in the individual's will to fight and survive.

Under the *Volkssturm* and Werewolf Project, Anna Dann, the little fifteen-year-old Berliner, was also given basic introduction on the use of weapons during the mass militarization of German society.

It was quite frightening, as in our BDM meetings we suddenly went from learning about first aid, childcare and homecare, and making things like gloves and hats for our soldiers in Russia, to learning about guns and how to kill people. There had suddenly developed an air of depression that seemed to sweep across the whole of the city. We were told that we must learn to use weapons so as we could help defend the city if the enemy invaded. There was no way I could lift up an army rifle; I was only a small girl. In fact, many of my friends in the BDM group giggled as I struggled with one of the rifles, trying to lift it up. It was swiftly taken away from me when I almost dropped it on my toes. I was then shown stick grenades and *Panzerfaust* rockets, both of which were quite easy to use.

We were also told that during the coming weeks we would learn basic marksmanship and would have to learn to fire air rifles at paper targets. If necessary, air rifles would be used to fire pellets at enemy soldiers, which, when you think about it, is pretty ridiculous.

My parents were quite horrified and were not happy at all with the idea of me having to handle weapons. My two brothers Franz and Josef were even more concerned, and they later told Mother and Father that the other men serving with the flak units had planned to flee Berlin if things became too bad, as they did not wish to see their families die in a futile battle. Franz and Josef knew how bad things were and hinted at this often to Mother and Father.

It was quite clear at that time that the war was going very badly and could be lost, and all hopes would have to remain with some crazy defensive strategy, which included us children. It was insane to see little girls carrying *Panzerfaust* tubes when they had previously carried dolls in their arms.

Over and over again we were told, 'If you do not do your own personal duty to your Führer and the Reich, then Germany will fail and you will all be made communists under Stalinist-Russian rule, and you will only have yourselves to carry the guilt.'

Each day though, more and more people were joining the refugee columns pouring through the city from east of Berlin. We often talked with these people and they said that the Russians were coming and that nothing could stop them. Some of the Berliners would shout '*Feigling!*' [coward] or '*Verräter!*' [traitor] at these wretched people.

Kirsten Eckermann, having completed her RADwf land-labour service had spent some time in Essen with her aunt. She returned to Berlin in late 1944 to find the populace consumed by the madness of the suicidal *Volkssturm* and Werewolf mobilization.

I had kept in touch with my family in Berlin via letter, and used to listen to the radio to find out about the events taking place in Berlin and all over Germany. You could never tell which were truthful or which was propaganda, though, with the nightly radio broadcasts. I found it very scary when Hitler announced news of creating a people's army. I did not want my mother or father to have to fight, and to be honest, I did not really want to have to fight either.

When I returned to Berlin in November of 1944, after spending some time with my aunt and four cousins in Essen, I was able to get work quite easily as I now had experience with driving various cars and lorries, and was able to turn my hand to more or less anything.

More and more men were being required to join the war, and we women had to fill in for them when they went away. After two months of working with the postal services and telecommunications, I ended up with three other young women as a train driver.

The BDM began to play a greater role, as more girls were required to replace the men leaving Berlin and other cities to fight. Though that did not mean that I escaped the *Volkssturm* mobilization, and I too had to learn to use a weapon. Most common was the *Panzerfaust* and stick grenades that we had to learn to use properly. Huge supplies of these weapons were poured into the city, ready in case they were needed. It was common to see small children practice throwing stick bombs in the parks, and *Volkssturm* members encouraging these proud little warriors. I also saw little boys of between eight and ten with stick bombs in their trouser belts, proudly showing off their weapons and giving passersby Hitler salutes. The *Volkssturm* armband worn on their coats or jackets identified those men as belonging to the *Volkssturm*.

As I travelled the familiar route through the city on the train runs, it was obvious things had changed considerably. It was a pathetic sight, in many cases old men, some of whom could barely walk, wearing the *Volkssturm* armband. The ordinary people were no longer happy; they were absolutely tired of the years of war and having to hide away in air-raid shelters throughout the day and night, and were physically and emotionally exhausted by it all. We were all suffering from the rationing of food, the constant threat from the air raids, and most were tired of the promises of better things that had not materialized under the National Socialists.

There were also whispered rumours that millions of Jews, Poles gypsies and many German non-conforming nationals had been slaughtered by our own soldiers in specialist death camps, which seemed to permeate every day conversation. Now they were being told to prepare to fight or die, and that only traitors would not stand up and fight.

The people of Berlin had always been a bright and fiercely proud people, but now that pride had gone and was being replaced by fear. We didn't want to fight, no one did, even our parents and grandparents were being called up to fight in the *Volkssturm* and both Mother and Father were taught how to use a rifle. During the evenings we discussed what would happen if the worst came, and we had a plan that we would throw away the guns and try and head in a westerly direction out of the city to safety. It seemed better to take our chances and head for the English and Americans to the west, it was considered suicide to head east. Though some had already left the city, new laws were soon put in place by the authorities and these laws were reaffirmed by the Gestapo, in an effort to dissuade or prevent people from leaving Berlin. Soon anyone attempting to leave Berlin would be arrested if caught and would be a traitor to the Reich and the Führer. This carried a death penalty and even children were told they could be shot for trying to flee. Often they were told that if they refused to stay and fight, their parents would be executed. We were also told that if we were called upon to defend Berlin, then it would only be until our armies arrived to take over.

Goebbels was still churning out propaganda, calling for every man, woman and child to stand firm and that Germany would be like a phoenix rising from the ashes, saved by our Führer Adolf Hitler, all this to a backdrop of corpses hanging by ropes from trees and lampposts.

The degree of shooting skills attained by the girls of the BDM at the Hitler Youth firing ranges varied considerably, as Sophia Kortge explains:

Some of the girls were absolutely hopeless shots and could not hit a thing, in fact they were dangerous. The rifle instructor was a young man from the Hitler Youth who had been given the task of training us to shoot properly. He once went berserk and refused to train one group of girls after one of them fired a rifle by accident and the bullet just missed him. He later complained and had said something about 'life being much safer fighting the Russians than training that lot to shoot'. Yet some of the girls were pretty good and just needed nurturing.

From talking with the one-time child combatants, it has become obvious that the defensive strategies of both the *Volkssturm* and the Werewolf Project were arranged so that the children and civilian fighting units would in a way bog down and severely hinder the enemy advance. Hitler had, by this time, removed any feeling of guilt over the use of Germany's children to achieve his military aims. He once said, 'I have no scruples and I will use whatever weapon I require.'

On 3 January 1945, a document was issued outlining a new proposal, stating that girls of the BDM and boys of the Hitler Youth would be called upon to replace post office officials in German cities. The idea was that 60,000 male postal officials could then be released for army service, or, in some cases, for employment in war industries, though this duty would not affect their military mobilization should it be required. The previously secret document obtained by David Jackman states the following order:

> The *Reichsjugendführung* [Reich Youth Leadership] has declared service in the postal service to be a *Jugenddienstpflicht* [Youth Conscript]. Boys and girls between twelve and fourteen years old wearing Hitler Youth or BDM uniform will be employed, for five hours a day, on light duties such as letter-sorting, messenger services, assisting in the telephone exchanges, etc.

On 1 March 1945, copies of a document was issued to all Hitler Youth leaders or their authorized deputies.

The document outlined the importance and the immense damage that can be caused to the enemy by basic sabotage techniques. The techniques outlined were instructed to young girls and boys under the *Volkssturm* and Werewolf Project, along with weapons training programmes. In this declassified document, also sourced by David Jackman, the thirteen basic rudiments of sabotage are explained:

1. Sugar in gasoline. This causes pistons to get stuck and the motor becomes unserviceable.
2. Sand in gasoline. Fuel lines and valves become clogged and the motor is rendered temporarily unserviceable.
3. Tar in intake valves on motors and wheels (in case of railway cars). Bearing burn out and vehicles get out of control and become unserviceable.
4. Placing of metal spikes at road curves during the night. Tyres of vehicles blow out and vehicles get out of control and become unserviceable.
5. Stretching piano wire across the road in the dark (in this case consider the colouring of the wire). Vehicles and especially motorcycle couriers can be put out of action.
6. Laying boards with nails at road curves. The result same as in 4.

7. Placing rocks into switches. Switches cannot be set and trains will derail or collide and the enemy suffers heavy losses.
8. Laying drag-shoes on open track stretches. Trains derail.
9. Destroy wire mechanism for controlling semaphore signals. Trains go past signals and derail or collide.
10. Connecting power and telephone lines by throwing wires over both lines. At all exchanges connected with that line the apparatus will burn out.
11. Piercing membrane in telephone receiver by means of a pointed pencil. One party can hear, but the other one cannot.
12. Tearing down enemy telephone cables. Interruption of enemy communications and command systems.
13. Steal from the enemy whatever you can. Weapons, ammunition, equipment, parts of uniform, food gasoline; in fact everything that belongs to the enemy and that he can utilize destroy in any out of the way place, so that he cannot find anything on you if you are searched.

It is difficult to see how any enemy, particularly those of the British, Canadian and American forces, could have psychologically prepared themselves to confront units of either the adult civilian *Volkssturm* or child Werewolves.

Allied intelligence warned that troops could find themselves under attack from civilians and children, but the rules of engagement were not to be changed.

The Red Army High Command, on the other hand however, knew all too well from experiences such as the terrible siege of Stalingrad, that in war sometimes every resource has to be pooled in order to survive, let alone emerge victorious, even if it does defy acceptable grounds of morality. The Red Army was also sending its female soldiers into battle, and some of them would fight units of German female combatants pressed into service in the *Volkssturm* or the Werewolf Project.

The scene was now set. As the Allies approached Aachen from the west – just across the Dutch border – with the intention of taking the first major city in Nazi Germany, the Russians were rapidly clawing back the German-occupied territories from the east.

The reality of the German situation was conveyed to the people by changes in the methodology of the German propaganda machine. The message had dramatically shifted emphasis from that of great nationalistic pride and conquest of weaker nations, to that of the preservation of the Fatherland, regardless of cost. By means of Nazi propaganda newsreels and films, the German nation was warned of what awaited them should they ever fall under Russian occupation.

With the Allied air forces now ruling the skies over their country, and the rumble of distant Russian guns in the east now audible, even the most misinformed of Germans could not help but be aware of the seriousness of the military situation.

The *Volkssturm* and Werewolves would soon get the chance to prove themselves in battle.

Chapter Twelve

A Playground with Guns

After the remarkably successful but equally costly acquisition of their Normandy beachhead on 6 June 1944, the Western Allies began to break out from the invasion beaches to begin their difficult advance inland into enemy-occupied territories. The battles that followed clearly illustrated to the Allied forces that the liberation of Europe would be both costly in terms of material and human casualties – a task that would be anything other than easy. It was also clear that the German forces were prepared and willing to contest every square kilometre of ground.

The youth of Germany had also proved themselves fanatical in some respects when Canadian forces engaged the 12th SS Panzer Division-Hitler Jugend in Normandy. This unit of Hitler Youth boys fought with a ferocity never before experienced, or indeed, expected by many of the battle-hardened Allied soldiers. The conduct of the 12th SS Panzer Division-Hitler Jugend in the field of combat can only best be described as barbaric. In their wake, they left only murder and mayhem.

The first real test for the *Jung Madel* and BDM girls of the Hitler Youth operating as Werewolves would come in the battle for Aachen. The battle developed as a consequence of the United States First Army's offensive to break through the Westwall fortifications, the German term for what the British called the Siegfried Line. Aachen was the first German city within the Third Reich to face an attack from the Allies, and was therefore from many perspectives a target of immense importance. Space does not permit what would be a lengthy narrative for the attack on Aachen, but there is much material available online and in print, which explains the Allied plans in their entirety should the reader wish to research the battle further.

In the city itself, prior to an inevitable American attack, the atmosphere was said to have been intense beyond description. Many of the young women in Aachen, with young children and babies, had gone to shelter in cellars and air-raid shelters, while Werewolf groups, made up of older children and those enlisted with the *Volkssturm*, were busy preparing and taking up positions within the city. Weapons had been distributed amongst the population and all they could do was await the inevitable storm that was to sweep through their city.

Barbie Densk was born and raised in Aachen, a city and its people she loved very much. After turning fourteen in August 1943, she had also joined the BDM with many of her school friends. She had also volunteered to become a Werewolf, and was now with a large group of girls and boys preparing to defend Aachen, lying in wait in a trench with a loaded rifle by her side.

She periodically picked up a pair of binoculars to scour the terrain immediately in front of her, her piercing brown eyes searching for signs of movement amongst the barricades of upturned commercial vehicles and city trams. Beyond the barricades lay a railway line. Enemy movement had been spotted within that area, so it was presumed that the enemy might choose to simultaneously attack from that direction. Barbie wore a whistle on a length of black lanyard around her neck. At the first sign of enemy soldiers approaching, she was to blow the whistle as hard as she could to alert everyone. She explains the general plan of defence and what the waiting was like:

> Waiting for something to happen, that was the worst part. I had left my mother and father during the early hours of 10 October, as I had volunteered to help defend our home and our city. All *Volkssturm* and Werewolf members had been mobilised as a result of German intelligence that had warned of a possible enemy attack on the city, but we were given no suggestions as to when it might happen, and were just told to prepare ourselves.
>
> The preparatory shelling and bombing by the Americans had probably been warning enough to most that the Americans were going to attack soon, and we wondered if they were going to hit us from everywhere at once. Mother, Father and my two young brothers and younger sister had moved long ago with other civilians to the safety of the main air-raid shelter a short distance from our homes. Mother in particular was very unhappy with me being involved in any possible defence or fighting in or around the city, and said that maybe I should hide somewhere. My father offered to go in my place, but because of a physical impediment, the local authority flatly refused this request. I told them both not to worry about me, and that I was not foolish, and besides, nothing might happen after all.
>
> We travelled to the various weapons-collection points in the city and were each given a weapon. There had been some heavy sporadic bombardment so we were forced to move quickly around

the city, making use of any cover. A long snake of old men, boys and girls trudged their way to the weapons-collection points. At the collection point, I was issued with a rifle because I had proved during the great mobilization that I could shoot. I had trained using an air rifle, firing small lead bullets at paper targets and empty tins. I had only fired a proper army rifle a few times previous and I found the kick rather painful to my shoulder area. Other girls within my group had grenades and rocket launchers.

We were also offered steel helmets and I decided to take one of these. I was later told by one of our soldiers to make sure I did not have the strap done up too tightly under my chin. He told me if possible to leave it loosened or completely unfastened, and when I asked why, he explained that if I were shot in the head, even with just a glancing blow, because of the force of impact the helmet would get blown backwards off my head and the strap could break my neck. The soldier had learned this from his father who had fought in the Argonne Forest at the end of the First World War.

Our defences had been prepared to the far east of the residential area of the city near to the main railway track. Anything and everything had been used to form defensive features, including barbed wire, upturned cars, lorries and trams. We had prepared holes and ditches and could fall back farther amongst the buildings if necessary. If our position came untenable, we were to fall back farther, and if necessary would fall back into the main reinforced-concrete air-raid shelter that lay one thousand metres south of the industrial area near to our homes.

Our task was to cause as many enemy casualties as we could and to remain elusive. Those were the basic orders we were given. There were a large number of our soldiers and Hitler Youth around the city and we felt confident that we might prevent the enemy from capturing the city. Just before the Americans began their attack on the city, I recall a reading that took place at our very last meeting with our maidens' league about a week ago. Our group head explained about the virtues of being either a *Volkssturm* or Werewolf member.

She said:

Girls, German girls, you are like the grey slender wolves of our nation. As she-wolves in the great wilderness, the human female is also a natural predator, provider and protector. She will provide, protect and kill according to her needs. As wolves you shall roam the shadows and leave no enemy safe, our enemy shall drown in their own blood and that of ours if necessary.

That was something I have never forgotten, it was funny, because when the fighting started that group head was nowhere around. I found out that she had donned civilian clothing and had gone to ground, surrendering to the first American patrol she encountered – so much for her being a leader of wolves!

On 11 October, American artillery fired 5,000 shells into the city, which was followed by aerial bombardment by the USAAF until the 13th. The 1st (American) Infantry Division could only afford one infantry regiment to take on the task of taking the city – the understrength 26th Infantry Regiment, commanded by Colonel John Seitz.

As planned, the attack on Aachen began at 9.30am on 13 October 1944.

The 2nd Battalion, the 26th Infantry Regiment had taken up position along a fifteen- to thirty-foot-high railway embankment that bordered the city to the east. At 9.30am, the American battalion threw grenades over the top of the embankment, before throwing themselves over the top with guns firing. The German defenders were caught completely off their guard. All hell broke loose as bullets and grenade shrapnel flew in all directions. It took over thirty minutes for the Germans to organize themselves and begin to return effective fire.

Already, the screams of wounded civilians, and American and German soldiers could be heard over the sounds of battle. Two American Sherman tanks then came over the railway embankment and entered the fray, followed closely behind by the battalion's remaining vehicles, which drove through a railway station concealed beneath the track and sited within the embankment itself. The German forces defending the periphery soon found themselves in an untenable position, coming under sustained and increasingly heavy rifle, grenade, machine-gun and artillery fire.

Barbie Densk vividly remembers the onslaught that began to draw ever closer to her *Werewolf* unit:

The night of 12–13 October had been relatively calm, and I do not recall any artillery fire either during the night or the early hours prior to the American attack of that morning. We had been moved out of some buildings that we had been using as temporary shelter and had to take refuge in a series of small trenches. It was pretty cold and we had huddled together as a group with our blankets and were trying to sleep. We were not accustomed to having to sleep in a trench out in the open air, and we had not had the chance to get used to this. It was an unpleasant experience in many ways and the sanitary conditions were also very poor. We were warned to take great care when going to defecate or urinate, as American snipers might shoot us dead. Men of the *Volkssturm* had often used mess tins or helmets to defecate in, and they would then throw the contents out from their positions – it was not pleasant at all for a female.

The American attack was very sudden, loud and startling. There was a series of muffled explosions, followed by the sound of rifle and machine-gun fire, followed by shouts and screams. We threw the blankets from off ourselves, and as instructed, I blew my whistle several times and grabbed the steel helmet and put it on. There was a tremendous commotion in the positions ahead of us that were occupied by men of both our navy and army forces, and bullets could be heard ricocheting above our heads. The steel helmet I had put on kept slipping over my eyes, so I took it off and threw it aside.

A short distance away, a field telephone began to ring, and an ageing *Volkssturm*, we had nicknamed '*Der Ratte*' [The Rat] because of his long nose and beady eyes, scrambled across to answer it. I watched his trembling frame and I could see that he was in a slight panic and was shaking from fear. After a brief exchange of words with whoever was on the other end, he slammed down the telephone and scrambled back out of sight before returning some minutes later.

In the meantime, we grabbed our weapons. The Rat came scrambling back along to us on his hands and knees, and he came over and said in a trembling voice, with a string of spittle running down from the corner of his mouth, 'The Americans are here and they are coming, they are coming now, we must not allow them to break through, now get your weapons and start shooting.'

We nervously peeped over the wall of our small trench, and The Rat shouted, 'For Christ's sake, start shooting, or God damn the lot of you!'

I slung the rifle to my side and looked through the binoculars and could see enemy soldiers spilling over the steep railway embankment. I could see the steel-helmeted heads of our soldiers in their holes firing away, though the view soon became obscured in the overcast morning gloom and by smoke.

My rifle was already loaded and ready to fire. I clicked off the safety catch and the other girls followed suit, and we then began to fire our rifles. I could make out figures darting from one position to another. The Rat was still panicking and shouting at us, and I shouted back at him, 'How the hell are we supposed to know whom we should be shooting at?'

The Rat grabbed hold of my head with both of his hands and said, 'Look, can you see the flashes directly ahead of you, those little fucking yellow sparks?'

'Yes,' I replied.

'Well, those are the muzzle flashes from enemy weapons, if they come any closer you will have an even better view of them as a dead person, now start shooting.'

I fired then reloaded the rifle again, swinging along to the next muzzle flash before firing again. I was surprised at how poor the light was, even though it was morning. I could not be sure if I killed anyone – I aimed at the flashes and pulled the trigger.

After a few minutes we were firing quite steadily toward the American advance. Because of the adrenalin, it was very difficult to keep the rifle sight steady and my hands shook as I pulled back the rifle bolt after each shot, and sweat coursed down through my dirty hair and into my eyes. I had to keep rubbing my eyes, which made things worse as they became very sore.

In what must have been a split second, there was a flash, followed by a very loud bang. I was thrown back hard against the back wall of our shallow trench, and fell – completely stunned with my eyes full of soil and my ears ringing – to the floor. Everything seemed to be swirling around me in slow motion, and the noises of battle around me seemed dull and distant. I stared around and saw the blood-spattered bodies of my friends; some of them lay across my legs convulsing violently with blood running from their mouths and nostrils, some of which spilled in a warm stream onto my legs. Little funnels of smoke rose out of the holes in their bodies and steam rose out from their torn stomachs. I felt winded and it was difficult to breathe, and all I could do was lie there and gasp for air. The smell of cordite burned my nostrils, along with the strong stench of stale urine.

Still in slow motion, I remember one of our soldiers looking down at me and then he jumped down into the trench, he stared into my eyes and slapped either side of my face with his hand. Realizing I was not seriously injured but severely concussed, he picked me up and threw me over his right shoulder and ran along the trench with me. I remember seeing the floor of the trench and pieces of skin and bone lying there with dark stains made on the brown soil by blood. The ground became a blur and I must have passed out, because I woke some hours later and found myself in the big air raid shelter back with my mother and father looking down at me with tears streaming down their faces.

My hearing had been damaged and was not very clear, and I learned that a shell had landed close to our trench and that I was one of the survivors in that particular section where there had been at least six of us. Apart from being severely concussed by the blast, I had received only a couple of relatively minor shrapnel wounds to my forehead and some bruising to my ribs and back. I developed a slight fever that quickly brought on a nasty cold, and I remained wrapped in blankets and was being cared for at the rear of the shelter where all of the wounded had been placed. I had been tended by a member of the *Deutscher Ritte Kreuz* [German Red Cross], and was told that I would be alright in a few days. The fever had probably been caused by being out in the trench the night before without adequate cover or bedding.

I could hear explosions and the dull crack of rifle fire. The only other recollections I have after that is of the 15th of October when many German soldiers began to cram themselves into the shelter and take up various positions within. I remember their faces, dirty and gaunt, and the dark blue metal of their weapons gleaming in the dull light inside the shelter, and the smell of unclean bodies mixed with cigarette smoke that grew ever worse. Because of the nature of my fever and lapses into deep sleep, I had missed all of the action.

When I awoke next, I found myself in a tent, and as Mother and Father had said, that the Americans later came and encircled the shelter. There were some exchanges of gunfire from our soldiers inside, but they gave up and surrendered when the Americans brought in flame-throwing guns and grenades and threatened to burn us all alive and throw the grenades in if we did not come out with our hands raised. Someone had shouted that there were wounded people and kids inside, and the Americans ordered that the wounded should be brought out one at a time and between two people only.

The fighting was still raging on in other areas of Aachen, but Mother and Father said the city would fall very soon, and they were right. It was strange really, as I remember, in between bouts of feverish sleep, receiving medical attention and being given medicine from the Americans.

I recovered quickly and was briefly questioned by a German-speaking American man. He wanted to know how I came to get wounded; it would have been useless to tell lies and so I told him the truth. He said that he already knew that children of the Hitler Youth had been involved in the fighting in and around Aachen as he had seen their dead bodies. He also asked if the Nazis had encouraged and taught me to shoot and I told him that yes, they had. Lastly, the American wanted to know if I liked Hitler and if I wanted to continue fighting. I told him that I only wanted to stop enemy soldiers from killing or hurting my friends, family and to stop them from destroying my city, my home. The American said that no American or British soldier would shoot innocent Germans or deliberately destroy our property. Asked again about whether I liked Hitler I told the American that I did not really know as I had never met him, and had only seen him in films and pictures. No further questions were asked and all civilians had to be moved out of the city into camps.

My war was over, and in a way I was glad, but was also very fearful for what the future of Germany was to be and what was going to happen to us now.

Other Werewolves had been more successful, and in the face of superior firepower had still managed to inflict substantial casualties upon the Americans. As the fighting progressed farther into the city, the Werewolves split up and hid inside ruined buildings. Some even disappeared into the underground sewerage network, where they would wreak further havoc upon those sent down to flush them out. In many cases, the American forces were compelled to block up sewerage manhole covers, as the German defenders were using these underground networks to infiltrate the enemy's rear.

Reports began to flood back to the Allied command that boys and girls as young as eight were participating in the defence of Aachen. Many of the American soldiers were unsure of how to deal with these youngsters, even though they posed the same deadly threat as the adults.

Willi Anderson, who had served as a young private with the American 26th Infantry Regiment recalls:

It was a shock to see kids shooting at you. The saddest thing of all is that you were faced with no choice but to return fire and kill them. We encountered a number of young females during the operations to secure central Aachen. They had succeeded in taking down a few of our guys. Things like that did not go down too well with the guys, and they would aim and shoot to kill. One incident sticks in my mind today, and that was when we were advancing up a side street. A shot rang out and one of our guys was killed. For some minutes, there was panic as we tried to find out where the sniper was.

In the meantime, this guy had died slowly, drowning on his own blood as blood filled his lungs; there was nothing we could do to save him. A second shot was fired at us, and as we had rolled out of the way behind some rubble, one of our platoon had observed and made out a faint puff of smoke from the cellar area of a ruin some 250-300 yards in front of us as the shot was fired. This was masonry dust thrown up by the muzzle blast of the sniper's weapon. Any self-respecting sniper would have taken such a thing into account, but not this one. As usual we had to think quickly and get the sniper neutralized so as we could move on up the street. You have to bear in mind that the enemy is all around and you cannot hang around in any one place for too long and allow your enemy to converge his fire onto you.

We took the only course of action that we could under the circumstances and fired a bazooka at the small entrance of the cellar. The round went straight in there and burst with a loud 'puff'. We then ran like hell firing as we went into the hole of this cellar. We waited for a few minutes for the smoke to clear inside and shouted '*Achtung, Grenate!*' [Watch out, grenade!]. If anyone was in there alive, then the idea was to flush them out by threatening to throw a grenade in. Nothing happened so one of our guys pulled out his pistol and crawled inside to have a look. He came out in a state of shock and said, 'Jesus fucking Christ, there's a dead kid in there, a girl.' We didn't believe him at first and asked if there were any other bodies in there, and he lit himself a smoke, spat and then said again, 'Only a fucking kid, a girl that's all. Why don't you take a fucking look?'

We all had a look and came out of there silent, in disbelief almost. We had all seen some pretty bad things, but this was something we just hadn't expected and it made us all feel physically sick. We had guessed her age to be around thirteen maybe. A commercial non-military type big-bore hunting rifle, fitted with a small and relatively inaccurate telescope, lay close by her body, along with several expended cartridge cases. That kid's death had a very demoralizing effect upon us, as some of us had kid sisters back in the States, they could easily have been our sisters, that is how we looked at them. We all felt like we had committed murder, even though we had no choice but to kill her, it just felt bad. She had no ID on her so we never knew who she was.

Before we moved off, we stuck a rather crude wooden cross, formed from two sections of floor boarding, and placed it against the outside wall of the cellar hole – we hadn't time to act as a burial party for anyone, not even this kid.

As numerical superiority lay with the Germans, the fight for Aachen called for the intelligent use of the various weapons systems available to the US forces, as they fought their way inside the city. Particularly stubborn pockets of resistance were dealt with by the utilization of such powerful and highly efficient weapons as the 155mm Howitzer M1. These big guns with, their 100lb high-explosive shells, made short work of the makeshift pillboxes and concrete reinforced defensive positions around the city. As the Americans pushed farther into the centre of the city, the fighting intensified greatly, and there were still reports of German forces popping up in the rear of the American attack.

In one such incident, the Germans, using their advanced tanks, managed to push the Americans back several blocks, before the attack was countered, causing the German attack to stall. This then allowed the American forces to regain the initiative. The bloodiest fighting was now starting to take place amongst the ruined buildings, as the Americans were forced into close-quarter fighting with the Germans as they attempted to clear each building in every street of Aachen.

Willi Anderson explains further:

The fighting amongst the buildings near to the centre of the city was particularly intense. There were many diehards who were determined to try and push us back. We had to clear each room of every damned building in every street, and you cannot even begin to describe or even imagine the state of pure bedlam going on all around. There is the continual clatter of machine guns, the pop of grenades going off, the whoosh of incoming artillery, both enemy and friendly, and the ricocheting screams of bullets and shrapnel and screams from people.

Our strategy was brutally simple, and we threw a grenade into each room and burst in firing our guns as we went, and if any Germans were in there who were still alive, we killed them with our bayonets – that was the way any enemy lying in wait was eliminated. One of our guys ran up the stairs of one building and was shot and then bayoneted somewhere near to the top, and just before the enemy made their escape, they tossed a stick grenade down to us. Fortunately for us, the grenade failed to explode. Often we would use a flamethrower to get the enemy out of buildings, and sometimes they would come out, while other times we had to cook them. On one occasion we flamed out one building and several German soldiers came out shouting in German, enveloped in flames. As they fell down we shot and bayoneted them.

We managed to take some prisoners and these were both soldiers and civilians including women and children. They had to be disarmed and removed to the rear as quickly as possible. Many of us were by this time aware of just how deadly even the children could be.

One of my good friends told me a shocking story shortly after Aachen had fallen. He told me that a friend of his had seen a German tank roll over a group of young Hitler Youths in the confusion of battle. The youths, including girls, were crushed to death as they were lay down firing rifles and it appears that the tank crew didn't care and just went over them, the thing just kept going.

A short distance away, the German tank was engaged and put out of action by one of our tank-destroyer crews with a fifty millimeter. Our guys were on it in seconds, firing their guns through the tanks viewing slits to kill anyone who might still be alive inside. They pulled up the lid and discovered that that tanks crew consisted of senior Hitler Youth boys and a girl, which explained to a good degree their terrible driving. My friends laughed about it, but it illustrated perfectly the measure of desperation that we were facing. I was shocked that young girls were involved in the fighting, but we were warned about them, and they proved every bit as deadly as the male soldiers. Some of the girls carried knives or bayonets hidden in their clothing, and they knew how to use them.

Corporal R. Marshall, also of the 26th Infantry Regiment, relates a rare account of German Hitler Youth girls in battle at Aachen:

> The ones which we encountered fought very well considering they were after all only young ladies. They sniped at us, threw grenades at us, and generally did their best to kill us, yet when we captured them they would drop their weapons, spring up and raise their hands shouting '*Amerikaner! Amerikaner!*'
>
> They also became subdued very quickly and asked us for sweets and chocolate bars. That's one of the funny things, they knew that we Americans always had chocolate bars, and they were just kids and they should never have been used in any fighting at all.
>
> In general, we were ordered not be social in any way with any of the Germans, and not to smile or be friendly. We did talk to some of the girls through interpreters and discovered that they had been trained as saboteurs, while others had been trained to use anti-tank weapons. One of the little ones I talked with said that she had spent weeks learning to handle and use a *Panzerfaust* and had been very disappointed that we had not brought more tanks forward into the battle so as she could shoot at them.
>
> She had explained that the girls of the *Jungvolk* were promised Iron Crosses from the Führer for every tank they killed. This girl was fifteen years old and had gone to war purely for accoutrements, a pretty badge to wear on her clothes, which is kind of crazy, isn't it. Just brought it home to me how much war stinks.

As the nature of the fighting had gradually turned into hand-to-hand combat amongst buildings in the inner-city area, the dangers only increased for the American forces. Around every corner danger lurked. One classic example of this is where Hitler Youth girls and boys hid inside buildings that the Americans thought to be empty. Any careless soldier entering without firstly discharging several rounds from his weapon into the interior areas of the building, could find himself on the receiving end of a stick grenade, pistol or bayonet. You did not have to be a particularly good shot to use a pistol at close quarters.

Barbie Densk remembers:

I knew of at least one girl, a friend of mine, who was in Aachen during the battle. She quietly stayed huddled up in the corner of a room inside one of the buildings. When any enemy soldier entered, she raised the pistol that she kept in her hands at all times, and fired. She killed a few enemy soldiers in this way, until she had no more bullets left in the gun.

She was captured later and she told me that the Americans were very angry with her and they slapped her face and kicked her hard up the backside before moving her away from the fighting. When she was reunited with her parents, she told me that an American shouted at them in German language, something like, 'You are fucking sick cowards, how do you people allow your children to fight for you, you are sick, where's your German pride now?'

I also heard from another friend of an incident where a Hitler Youth boy was trying to shoot a tank with a *Panzerfaust*. The boy was shot dead by an enemy soldier's bullet, and one of the girls ran across the street, picked up the dead boy's *Panzerfaust* and fired at the tank he had been trying to destroy. She succeeded in firing the weapon and destroying the enemy tank. She then threw down the weapon and ran back across the street to where her friends were. The Americans quickly moved in and fired at them with a small artillery gun, but did not manage to kill them as they had escaped through a maze of rubble.

In many cases, as the Werewolf groups retreated, they left trip-wire booby traps behind as they had been taught, and these certainly slowed down the American soldiers.

R. Marshall confirms what has been said above:

It was unwise to chase kids up alleys and we soon learned to use flamethrowers and grenades instead. There were many incidents where our guys had chased bands of Hitler Youth girls and boys, who had been throwing stones and rocks, up alleyways within the city. The kids would run up the alley, and in many cases, the chasing soldiers ran into booby-trap devices like grenade trip-wires, or were shot or stabbed from behind. The kids, having rigged up the grenade devices, knew exactly where the trip-wire was located, and were able to jump over them as they ran, but the pursuing soldiers in their heavy boots often tripped right over the wires and set the grenades off. Such booby traps were often fatal for one or more of our guys.

One of the nastiest devices was the anti-personnel mine used by the Germans. There were a few of these in Aachen and you did not know they were there until you stepped on one, where they would then shoot out of the ground to shoulder height and then explode, spraying steel ball bearings everywhere at high velocity. One of our guys stepped on one of those things and there was not much of him left, or the four other guys who were unlucky enough to have been near to him. One of them had been decapitated in the blast, while the other four had been perforated and torn up by steel ball bearings.

I reckon in most instances girls were used as decoys, so we quickly learned, rather than chase them, it was safer for us to use grenades and flamethrowers as these could shoot massive streams of burning, jellied petrol right up the alleyways and inside suspect buildings. Burning to death is not a good way to die as it's slow, but sadly, there were occasions when we did have to use them to flush out the pockets of armed resistance, and sometimes kids too ran out, enveloped in flames, screaming as their flesh began to melt on their bones. Some of us wanted to run and help, but we would have faced certain ambush had we done so.

War is an incredibly evil thing, and after Aachen I prayed every day that we would experience nothing like it ever again; it was like a butcher's shop, with pieces of human meat lying everywhere, dead bodies of men, women and little children. The fact that the Nazis had even encouraged young girls to fight their futile war for them seemed obscene to me.

In later years, my memories have faded somewhat, but the nightmares, oh yes, I still get the nightmares even after all of these years, and my wife will tell you all about that.

By 21 October, the battle for Aachen was effectively over.

On that day, elements of the 3rd Battalion, 26th Infantry Regiment, were preparing to destroy an enemy bunker emplacement with their 155mm Howitzer. One of the Germans inside the bunker was none other than garrison commander, *Oberst* (Colonel) Gerhard Wilck. Wilck soon grasped the predicament he was in, and, facing imminent oblivion from the 155mm, decided to radio his high command to inform them it was his intention to fight to the death. After making the call, he promptly emerged from the bunker and surrendered to the Americans.

After the surrender, 5,600 German defenders were taken prisoner. The US 26th Infantry Regiment had sustained 498 casualties during the course of the battle, a relatively light figure owing to their exceptional resourcefulness and skill. As for the beautiful city of Aachen, some eighty per cent of its buildings had been destroyed in the fighting. For those involved in the battle for Aachen, there are many lasting memories and anecdotes to tell, some very touching.

R. Marshall confided in me during my last interview with him in the summer of 2000:

Our intelligence guys had learned some pretty shocking stories during their many interrogations of soldiers and Hitler Youths captured or wounded in Aachen. On the way back home after the war, we talked quite a lot amongst ourselves and swapped information and stories, even though it was supposed to be secret information.

I heard one story of an old *Volkssturm* member who had been captured inside the ruins of a beer hall in Aachen. There were four dead Hitler Youths in that beer hall with him, three boys and one girl. Under interrogation it appeared that the old *Volkssturm* man had told these kids that if we captured them alive we would scalp them just like American Indians did to the white man, so the kids shot themselves with their own weapons rather than surrender to us. That *Volkssturm* could thank his lucky stars that he was an old broken man, or he would have probably received a punching – our guys didn't like Germans like that at all.

However much we tried to hate the kids of Germany, we couldn't, as they were victims themselves in many ways, and people today must understand this. Before many of us left for home, we came to like some of the kids, who had very likely been trying to kill us in the past fighting. Many of them could not speak very good English, but one of them came to me shortly before we moved on, she was a young, fair-haired girl, very pretty, with lovely blue eyes. She just came over to me and said 'sorry' and gave me a rather wilted flower, which she had picked especially for me. Her eyes were vacant and empty, totally devoid of happiness and I didn't know what to say really, and it sounds stupid when I say that I took that flower from her and I had a lump in my throat. I gave her my packet of chewing gum and my wristwatch, though don't know to this day why I gave her my wristwatch. I did not know what to say to her as I was just a young guy, so I just told her to take care of herself and to keep out of trouble, and that she should now go away and learn all about the real world that is waiting out there for her.

Of course, I never saw her again, and I put that flower inside my cigarette case and placed it in my pocket. The flower dried out completely, yet I still have it to this day, kept in the same cigarette case. In fact, my son now has it, and it was the only souvenir I had from Aachen.

When I last interviewed Barbie Densk, and showed her the content of the above interview, she carefully read through the text and said:

It does not surprise me at all. Those Americans were very good considering what they had been through, seeing their friends killed and wounded. Some of them never tried to talk to us or show us kindness, as I believe they were ordered not to by their commanders, but there were always those Americans who would sneak us chocolate bars and other sweets. I remember most of them searched our clothing looking for badges and things, which they could take as souvenirs or trophies. I gave one of them my small Hitler Youth badge and my older friend gave one American a RADwf work services badge that had the ears of corn motif on it.

I often wondered what they really thought to us, if they really hated us, or thought us monsters, or even felt pity for us. Either way, I think we girls earned their respect, as some of us had fought better than our own soldiers, and with bravery also. In reality, Aachen was like some kind of a big playground for many young Hitler Youths cowed into defending the city. I do not think many of us really knew what we were in for, what it was really all about.

For months after the battle I suffered from nightmares, I still have them now, nightmares about corpses and body parts and blood, and I have relived the battle over and over in my sleep. Aachen at the time though, seemed like a kind of playground, a playground where the children carried guns.

The American forces in Aachen conducted themselves in a highly professional manner. The author could find no instances of any American committing war crimes against any of the German prisoners of war, or against any of the civilian population in the city during the occupation. There were some relatively minor assault cases where American soldiers had either kicked or punched German soldiers and civilians, but these instances were very few.

According to Red Cross and other formerly secret military files, there had been no reported cases of rape or sexual violation of young girls or women in Aachen under the American occupation, and, under the circumstances, most of the inhabitants were treated with respect. With Aachen now captured, the Allies could breathe a huge sigh of relief and continue their advance into Reich territory, while the Russians pushed towards Berlin. There were however many other as costly battles that would be fought in and around small villages and towns in Germany while on the road to the major target of Berlin, including the last great Nazi gamble of the Battle of the Bulge. The Battle of the Bulge was the last German ground offensive of the Second World War, and although initially successful, the German forces soon lost the initiative against their superior Allied opponents.

As far as the Russians were concerned, Berlin was the biggest prize of them all. They were determined that they would be the first to occupy the Reich capital.

The seriously depleted remaining fighting elements of the German army had already fallen back from the Russian advance, as were tens of thousands of fleeing German refugees and wounded soldiers. Both soldier and civilian were now literally running for their lives. This defeated army began to prepare for what would be the final battle, the battle for Berlin.

This was the twilight of Hitler's twelve-year Reich. It was also a time of reckoning for Germany's female youth operating as Werewolves, or recruited into Gertrud Scholtz-Klink's female guerrilla units. The civilian population of Berlin had already heard the death knell of the distant Russian guns. The city had been reduced to rubble from the constant pounding from the air, and many of her citizens were now hiding in cellars, subways, sewers and any other place that might offer some degree of safety from the coming onslaught.

Many others had no choice but to fight, and began to prepare themselves to meet the arrival of the feared Soviet soldiers. The old men and women of the *Volkssturm*, and young Hitler Youth boys and girls had also been mobilized in readiness. The Red Army was advancing at a fast pace, virtually unhindered. They knew that the Germans were technically beaten, but they also knew that Berlin was not going to succumb without a fight. It would be a last-stand battle, a battle of annihilation of the die-hard remnants of Nazi Germany's armed forces.

The drug-addicted Hitler still attempted to evade the reality of the now hopeless situation. In his delusionary state of mind, he still believed that it was possible at any time for Germany's military fortunes to change miraculously. The already defunct Luftwaffe and *Wehrmacht* would emerge like a phoenix from the ashes to destroy the hated invaders from the east. The Führer could no longer separate fantasy from reality, marrying mistress Eva Braun as a final token of capitulation before ending his own life. History, however, had already decided the fate of the German people.

Chapter Thirteen

The Fall of Berlin

As the German forces began to retreat from the Red Army, they were ordered to destroy railway lines, bridges, food stores and shops, and indeed anything else that might prove to be of material use to the Russian enemy. The Germans were now having to do exactly what the Russians had been forced to do at Stalingrad.

With their Aryan biological duties now almost completely suspended, many German girls, including those of the *Jung Madel* and BDM, had little choice but to arm themselves and join the fight against the approaching Russians. It is therefore pertinent at this stage, to briefly examine certain aspects of the conflict, prior to the battle for Berlin, in and around Warsaw in Poland. It was here that the German female guerrilla units, organized by Gertrud Scholtz-Klink, first fired their weapons in anger at the enemy.

Little is known about Scholtz-Klink's all-female guerrilla units, other than the fact that they were hastily trained but well-motivated individuals, ranging in age from girls as young as thirteen to young women of twenty-four years of age.

From the examination and translation of documents that have lain in archives in various institutions in the UK and Europe since 1945, one is able to build up a slightly better picture. Russian documents appear to confirm that there were definitely female guerrilla units deployed by the Germans in and around the Warsaw area in 1945, and that they did in fact engage in combat with Russian forces, inflicting casualties on them.

Whilst the author could find no information on any unofficial or homemade insignia, as mentioned later by Theresa Moelle, this does not mean that such insignia did not exist. The emblem in question apparently consists of a dark-blue or black wolf's head on a white background.

The girls within the two guerrilla units were employed in much the same ways as male riflemen and were used mainly to augment the *Wehrmacht* forces within the Warsaw area. They were also actively employed as snipers, saboteurs and to keep guard over prisoners. There are no casualty statistics available for these female combat units. It is clear, therefore, that they had never been intended to be anything permanent, but were more of an expendable means of filling in the spaces left by German soldiers badly wounded or killed in action.

Young girls were sent to fight the Nazis' war under the orders of both Hitler and the Hitler Youth leadership. The fighting at Warsaw was extremely fierce as the Germans fought desperately in vain to halt the Russian advance. The ensuing close-quarter combat with bayonets, rifle butts, boots, fists and knives was a sign of things to come, and it would only get worse. The Germans again suffered defeat, and those not killed or taken prisoner were forced to run. The jubilant Red Army forces of Marshal Georgy Zhukov's 1st Belorussian Front, liberated Warsaw on 17 January 1945. An estimated 800,000 of its population had perished during the course of the Second World War.

Before the Russians could launch their first assault on Berlin, they firstly had to take the strategic high ground known as the *Seelower Höhen*, or Seelow Heights. The Russians had been over-optimistic and a little ignorant of the difficulties that they may encounter when they had set forth their ambitious plans to take Berlin by 15 April. The fighting to secure the Seelow Heights would clearly illustrate to the Russians that even at this apparently terminal phase of the war, the Germans could still deliver some clever tactical surprises and offer very fierce resistance. It is not possible to cover every military and tactical aspect of the Russian assault on Berlin in this publication, but an examination of the general anatomy of the battle is important.

The Russians began their massive offensive towards Berlin on 16 April 1945. The Russian command had over 2,500,000 men and 6,500 tanks allocated for the assault. Masses of artillery guns of all calibres were brought in, along with mortars, machine guns and Katyusha 'Stalin's Organ' multiple rocket-launchers.

At 3.00am on 16 April, the 1st Belorussian Front was the first to strike. Marshall Zhukov devised a plan where he would unleash a pre-dawn barrage from 10,000 artillery guns and 400 Katyusha rocket-launchers, that would effectively pulverize the German front lines on the Seelow Heights, also referred to as the Gates of Berlin. The bombardment was one on a truly epic scale, the heaviest in the entire history of land warfare.

The German commanders had predicted such an assault, so had therefore deployed a second defensive line of troops and weapons farther back and out of immediate harm's way. As the Russians began to advance, German artillery began to exact a heavy toll on the Russian attack which, together with the swampy terrain, began to stall at the foot of the Seelow Heights.

This was only a temporary setback, however, and with a combination of sheer weight of numbers and the dogged persistence of the Russian soldier, they were soon able to recover and continue on to eventually take the Seelow Heights. Once this valuable elevated position had been secured, the Russians could then position their heavy artillery to mount accurate bombardments of Berlin.

On the morning of 20 April 1945, Hitler's 56th birthday, the Red Army was only twenty miles away. It was also on that day that bombers of the USAAF flew their final sortie of the war against Germany with a last crippling blow. Their objective was to sever the last remaining gas and water supplies into the city. As the last of the bombers began to turn away for home, Hitler emerged briefly from his bunker to address a small group of Hitler Youth boys.

One of those boys, Otto Krische, recalls the event:

> How gaunt and sickly looking Hitler was. He was black around the eyes and his limbs appeared to shake in an uncontrollable spasm. There was a drying beard of spittle around the corners of his mouth, and his eyes – the fire had gone out in his eyes. He smiled, but it was a dead man's smile; he looked a frail, beaten old man, and nothing like the Führer of the past years.

In the 22 April issue of the Nazi publication *Das Reich*, Propaganda Minister Goebbels appealed to the youth of Berlin to resist at any price. He asked that every German boy and girl fight with unequalled fanaticism. It was to be his last hypocritical bluff to the youth of Germany, as he chose to hide below ground with the remainder of Hitler's shameful band rather than fight. Two weeks, later Goebbels and his wife Magda would poison with cyanide their six children, aged from four to twelve, before committing suicide themselves.

There were 500,000 German soldiers trapped inside Berlin, together with around 2,000,000 civilians. Many wanted the opportunity to leave, but were told if they tried, they would be shot as deserters. Lynching, performed by members of the Gestapo and the SS, began all over the city. Corpses could be seen hanging from lampposts, trees and buildings. These were often the victims of unfortunate misinformation due to the confused nature of the situation in the city and lack of communication. Puppet courts dispensing rough justice, were responsible for the murder of hundreds of ordinary Berliners.

Almost incessant propaganda boomed out across the city through loudspeakers, reminding the civilian population of what would happen to them if they were captured by the Bolshevik enemy.

There was even a radio station dedicated to the werewolf groups around the city. Appropriately named Radio Werewolf, the station began broadcasting on 1 April 1945, the brainchild of Propaganda Minister Goebbels. The broadcast could be heard continuously calling for the boys and girls of Berlin to fight, and die if necessary, for the Fatherland. One of the inane broadcasts called for all unarmed boys and girls to throw bricks and stones at the enemy, quoting the legend of David and Goliath. Though the main message that was continuously repeated was '*Besser Tot Als Rot*' or Better Dead Than Red.

The Russian guns began to shell the city, much of which was already in ruins. Those who were not able to fight, for whatever reason, usually the very old men and women and young children, sought safety in air-raid shelters, subways and cellars beneath buildings.

For the young girl members of the Werewolf groups, who would now have to fight alongside *Volkssturm* members and German soldiers old enough to be their fathers, the battle for Berlin would come as a nightmare. It would be unlike anything they could ever have imagined, the sights and sounds of which are indelibly etched deep in their memories to this day.

Heidi Koch:

> I had never known fear like it, I was petrified. Loudspeakers around the city were asking the citizens of Berlin to remain firm and not to run like cowards, and that relief would arrive soon. The dead bodies of traitors were hanging from trees and lampposts; it was like everyone had gone mad. Russian shells began to fall around the city that could only mean that the Russians were getting closer to Berlin. Soldiers and civilians spent much of their time preparing defences by digging holes, making walls of rubble and by upturning abandoned motor vehicles and trams. At this point, we had been issued with weapons, and had been told not to go far from our refuge areas. If needed we, along with *Volkssturm* units, would be sent to reinforce German army positions and to give first aid to our wounded.
>
> During this time, I talked with some of our soldiers; these were veterans of the fighting in the east, their uniforms were torn and filthy, and their faces were dirty and grey looking, and they were

as scared as the civilians. There were many members of our SS in the city, but many of those I met did not speak very much and often ignored questions. There was one man in particular I kept asking questions and he turned and shouted at me, 'Do you know what will happen if the Russians get here? Let me tell you, shall I, they will probably fuck you then shoot you, now do you understand?'

His eyes were wide and staring and he frightened me, so I turned and ran. After that, I talked very little with the soldiers, besides they were busy with their own tasks and absorbed within their own thoughts, I think many knew it was the end for them.

Theresa Moelle who had been serving with a flak unit recalls the seriousness of the German situation that April of 1945:

It was very bad, and over the months information kept filtering back about the *Wehrmacht* and its failures in battle, and how the Russians were pushing our army back up against Berlin. Our unit was encountering more and more Soviet aircraft that were employed in low-level cannon firing attacks against our positions in and around Berlin, and we shot some of them down as they were not very good fliers like the Americans and British. We received orders to dismantle our position and report to the anti-aircraft garrison commander in Berlin on 8 April 1945. We were told to prepare immediately, and take with us only our essential belongings.

I arrived at the Moelles' house during the late evening, as the darkness provided cover from fighter-bomber attacks. I quite literally ran in and grabbed a bundle of things and threw them into an army bread bag. Walter Moelle had been preparing to abandon the house and leave with the family, and had assumed I was going to go with them. When I told him I was staying and had to report to my unit, he went quite hysterical.

He shouted, 'Have you gone mad? You will all be killed! Do you think we want to see you dead?'

I replied 'No, but I am going with the others, as they are my friends.'

As I dashed outside the house and ran to the lorry, he followed, and I remember how he kept shouting my name, and for me to come back and that he loved me. I did not stop or look back and climbed into the back of the lorry with the others. As we drove off up the drive, I shouted to him, 'Don't worry, I will be alright.'

By the 10th, we had been deployed to the northern sector of Berlin, along with hundreds of *Volkssturm* members to reinforce defensive positions, and our *Flak 38 kanone* was to be used in the ground role against Russian soldiers and vehicles should they attack and break through. For the most part, there was much confusion, fear, panic and general disorganization in the city. Food was becoming very scarce, and ruptured water mains were the only source of drinking water, but this was becoming contaminated by the sewerage system, which had also been ruptured in the bombing raids.

The first Russian perimeter incursions into the city of Berlin were made to the east and north. German units given the task of defending these perimeter sectors consisted of the remnants of those units pulled back after the fighting on the Seelow Heights, including the 18th, 20th and 25th Panzer Grenadier divisions, the Panzer-Division Müncheburg, 9th Paratroop Division, and the Nordland and Charlamein SS divisions. These units, once combined with the *Volkssturm* and other armed units of the civilian population, meant that there was a combined garrison of 300,000 ready to engage the Russians. The reality was that barely 50,000 of that number were experienced combat veterans.

The Russians were going to use the same tactics as those adopted by the Americans at Aachen. The commanders formed their masses of soldiers into effective assault groups utilizing tanks, light artillery, mortars, flamethrowers, grenades and machine guns to punch a hole through the city's defences. Once the initial breach had been made, heavy artillery, tanks and infantry would be brought forward en-masse to begin the capture of Berlin, street by street. Waves of Russian soldiers would then follow and overwhelm the German defenders. It was a brutally effective plan, and as the first assaults were made, fierce fighting developed, particularly around the Templehof aerodrome that lay to the south of Berlin. Here members of the *Volkssturm* and Hitler Youth boys and girls, backed up by elements of the German army, fought against the Russians.

Dana Henschell, twenty-one years old at the time, recalls:

We were told that we must not let the enemy take the aerodrome and that it was of great strategic importance. Many of the *Volkssturm* were old men who just could not cope with what was going on around them. One of them threw down his *Panzerfaust* and started to run away. He was shot in the back a few seconds later, presumably by one of our own soldiers for desertion. I heard the shot and saw this old man fall down, and he did not move after that. I watched this happen and it's true.

We had to hide amongst the damaged huts on the airfield perimeter and the soldiers were constantly updating us on what was going on, and every so often we had to move out from our positions to other ones as they shouted out their commands to us. As a *Heckenschütze* [sniper], I had to move away from our group of girls and *Volkssturm* and get to the far side of the airfield, where I would wait and shoot dead any Russian who appeared to the right side of the aerodrome, which is where the main attack was apparently coming from at that time. The Russians were firing artillery and mortars at the airfield, and as I got up and ran, I frequently stumbled over in panic, as a bomb came in and landed nearby, sending earth and shrapnel crashing down around me. I was worried about damaging the rifle, which sounds silly, and I actually hesitated to rub the dirt off it before carrying on running. I jumped down beside a destroyed vehicle that was lying on its side and was full of shrapnel holes; I noticed that oil saturated the ground and that I was now lying down in it. This position, though uncomfortable, gave me a good view and field of fire to cover, and if I needed I could withdraw to the rear with the others.

When the Russians did appear, firing and throwing grenades, there was just commotion all around. The *Volkssturm* men began to surrender without even firing a shot. I watched them jumping up to surrender, though some were shot and bayoneted to death by the Russians as they surrendered.

The next few seconds were the slowest of my entire life. I cocked [loaded] the rifle and with a pounding heart, I looked into the telescope with my right eye, while closing the other tightly shut. All I could view now was the black cross inside the telescope. Resting the rifle on the vehicle's broken axle, I held the black cross steadily on a Russian soldier who was crouching down and firing his rifle at our soldiers positioned to my far right. As taught, I held my breath for a split second and slowly squeezed the trigger. As my rifle fired I saw the Russian thrown back by the force of the bullet's impact;

he twitched and convulsed momentarily then lay still. I quickly pulled back the bolt, and remember the empty bullet case flying out onto the grass. I again pressed my right eye into the telescope and scanned around for a target.

This time, a Russian, lying down and sneaking along the ground on his belly like a snake. Again, I held my breath for a second before slowly squeezing the trigger. As the rifle fired, the Russian rolled over onto his back and appeared to have been hit in the side of his body. I whispered '*Verdammt*' [damn it] as I reloaded and fired a second shot into him, and after that he stopped moving.

More and more Russian soldiers were appearing and began to fan out around the ground in front of me. One of the Russian soldiers ran to help the man I had just shot, and so I aimed and fired and killed him too. I looked over my shoulder as I thought that they might try to come around our rear, but all seemed to be alright at that stage and I received no warning from my comrades.

The Russians must have discovered where I had been as, after some minutes had passed, a mortar bomb fell very close to where I was hiding. I heard the muffled explosion of the bomb and the shrapnel striking the vehicle and several small pieces landed near my legs. Another two bombs came in seconds later, and these appeared to be much closer. In the belief that I had been discovered, I quickly backed away from the vehicle and crawled away through the grass and small trees around the boundary.

Moments later there was a loud 'whoosh', followed by an explosion as an artillery shell came in and must have landed very close to where I had been as I felt the earth shake and saw a large chunk of the vehicle I had been hiding under sailing into the air as the shell exploded. I got up and started to run as fast as I could as more shells came in. The rattle of machine guns and crack of rifle fire grew more intense now as I became fully aware of what was going on around me. I came running through some trees and startled three of our soldiers manning a machine gun as the one aiming the weapon swung it around towards me and screamed, 'Halt!' and must have been ready to shoot me dead in an instant.

He drew a deep breath and just said, 'Go on – fuck off, get out of here.'

As I moved back to the rear, I remember the cries of wounded men and how other people were trying to treat their wounds.

I remember the look on their faces as men were being brought into one of the huts at the rear that was being used as a first-aid post. Men who had arms or legs blown off, or fragments of their skulls missing exposing their brains, all kinds of horrific injuries. Blood was everywhere, even up the walls; it was like a butcher's shop for human beings. Some of our girls could not cope and some were outside vomiting and crying hysterically and calling '*Mutter, Mutter*' [mother, mother].

A young soldier came in and shouted, 'Get these fucking kids out of here now!'

'Where do we go?' we asked and the soldier just said, 'I don't care where you fucking go, go home if you like, but get away from here now.'

I helped two of the girls to their feet and decided that I should go with the soldier and help him to get the other girls away from the aerodrome area, even though it was against the Führer's orders, I don't think anyone cared anymore. We left in a civilian baker's van, which the soldiers had commandeered and was one of a very few which had fuel. Shells landed around us as we jumped into the back of the van and drove off, swaying from side to side.

Many Hitler Youth boys and girls remained behind at the airfield, but it was useless and the Russians soon captured the aerodrome. We headed back into the nightmare of Berlin with its cratered roads aligned with hideous ruins. One of the girls was still hysterical and I did my best to try to comfort her. She was covered in the blood of dead and dying German soldiers. The baker's van pulled up outside a makeshift first-aid station, and we were all bundled inside it. At that point, I realized that I had left my rifle behind at the aerodrome. Nausea coursed through my stomach and I retched violently, but nothing came out. My whole body ached and I was sweating heavily and trying to get my breath. I was given a small metal cup of water, which had sugar in it and drank it down. I was told I was suffering from shock and this would help calm the effects.

The fighting around the peripheral areas of Berlin continued with an ever-increasing ferocity, and by 24 April, the city's fate was sealed – there was no escape from Berlin as the Russians had now completely surrounded the city.

Just two days prior to the Russian encirclement of berlin, Anna 'Tiny' Dann, her mother, father and two brothers escaped the hell of Berlin through Nauen, via a road to the northwest of the city. Her two brothers, Franz and Josef, who had been attached to a Berlin flak battery, had taken a military vehicle under the pretence that, under orders from their commanding officer, they were going to collect ammunition resupplies. It was an intensely risky undertaking, but the two brothers were determined that their little sister and parents would not be sacrificed for what had become Hitler's lost cause. Anna and her parents were stowed away under a tarpaulin sheet in the back of the lorry, only emerging once they were safely out of the city.

The Dann family had to leave everything behind but they had made their escape, ditched the lorry, and continued their journey to safety on foot. A short while later, the family surrendered to the first American forces that they encountered to the west. The Americans treated them well, and no doubt, after being interrogated, gained much-needed intelligence on the situation in Berlin from the family.

At 5.30am on 25 April, central Berlin came under extremely heavy bombardment from Russian heavy artillery, and for the first time, the Reich Chancellery received direct hits from Russian 175mm shells.

Hitler, languishing deep below ground in the bunker beneath the Reich Chancellery, was still trying to convince himself that the German 12th Army under General Wenck could soon arrive and relieve Berlin. However, the awful truth was that the 12th Army no longer existed, at least not in its original form. Although Wenck and the considerably weakened forces under his command made some determined advances, the general just did not have the resources and numbers required to come to the rescue.

In other rooms of the bunker, Hitler's staff, including Martin Bormann, bickered amongst themselves, accusing each other of treachery and poor conduct, while SS soldiers sat in the passages, resigned to their fate. SS officer Gerhard Boldt recalls how two women orderlies in the bunker shouted at the SS soldiers:

> These two female orderlies shouted at the SS soldiers, 'There are boys and girls of the Hitler Youth up there fighting and dying, while you lot hide down here, maybe you should have our aprons and do our job while we go up there and help fight the Russians.'

As the fighting raged, German soldiers, *Volkssturm* recruits and Hitler Youth boys and girls fought in the city, which had by now become the ultimate environment in which to wage their guerrilla war. The remains of the 11th SS Panzer Division had positioned their latest, deadly *Panzer VI Ausf.B Königstiger* 'King' Tiger tanks in the vicinity of the government buildings in central Berlin. The inner city was now little more than a ten-square-mile zone where nothing remained but broken buildings and piles of rubble. In almost every street, flames from ruptured gas pipes poured out from broken roads and pedestrian walkways, as did water contaminated by raw sewerage.

Dora Brunninghausen:

> The scene near to the central area of Berlin, particularly in the vicinity of the Dorotheenstrasse, was unbelievable. Open sewers strewn with dead bodies that had been blown into pieces by the shells, and had started to rot in the April sun. Flames poured out from buildings and the holes in the ground, and I could see bodies of dead people crawling with maggots, partially covered by fallen masonry and the stench was overpowering. Many buildings were burning furiously and it was like Dante's Inferno, the heat generated by these fires, coupled with the increasingly warm April sunshine, made it so it was the nearest that one could come to hell on earth.
>
> We could not find any food and the soldiers who were with us taught us how to skin and gut dead cats and dogs so as we could eat the meat to survive. It utterly revolted me to have to resort to such actions, and I have to admit that after eating the meat I vomited and cried.
>
> The sewer system was a terrible place to have to hide and fight from, but it offered a greater degree of safety. We moved through the sewers that were crawling with vermin and insects and came up through manhole covers in the streets, where we fired our *Panzerfausts* at Russian T-34 tanks before fleeing back to safety. On one occasion, the Russians sent dogs down the tunnel after us, the dogs were quickly shot by one of the *Volkssturm* men with us. The Russians threw down grenades into the tunnel, but by the time they had exploded, we were long gone, though the explosion seemed to rattle all the way through the tunnel system.
>
> We often came out at night as it was not healthy to stay down in the tunnels continuously, but we never strayed far from the safety of those tunnels. They were hellholes, but we were desperate to remain free and safe from the Russians, and it is strange what

you can be prepared to suffer to remain free and safe under such circumstances. Anything was better than being captured by Russians.

Sophia Koertge, who had joined other Hitler Youths, soldiers and *Volkssturm* fighters, remembers killing a Russian soldier with a Luger pistol:

We fought together often in groups of twenty to thirty individuals, and there were kids who did not have any weapons, and they picked up bricks and things and threw them at the enemy, not that that was a very good idea. I am not proud that I had killed somebody, and it is with some reluctance that I am telling you now.

It happened on 26 April, sometime around noon, when our group had become scattered by quite heavy fire from Russian small arms up a narrow walkway in the area close to the Wilhelmstrasse area of the city. It didn't look how I remembered it from the days when we had paraded here, much of it was now destroyed and on fire. Firefights with the Red Army were breaking out almost continually. We instantly scattered and ran into buildings to try and find cover to fire from; some of us ran upstairs while others hid downstairs. I ran and sat down in a corner by a window and could hear excited Russian voices coming down the walkway outside, they were firing their weapons continually. I could also hear a whooshing and crackling noise, but did not know what this was until I could hear the sounds of something burning outside in the walkway, it was the noise made by a flame-throwing gun. It happened so quickly, this Russian soldier leaned in through the blown out window that had no glass or frame, I raised the pistol towards this man's head and recall the expression on his face just before I pulled the trigger. I saw his head and shoulders thrown back as I fired and the blood spatter the walls near to the broken window.

I immediately got up and ran like hell out of the back, as I ran I stumbled over and cut my knee open badly on some glass that was on the floor, at the same time I dropped the pistol, but did not go back to retrieve it. I felt no pain, only panic, as I got up and continued to run. My lungs felt like they were going to burst I ran so hard. More shots were being fired and many came very close to my head, and made a *zup, zup, zup* kind of sound as they hit the ground near to me. Some Hitler Youths across the street were shouting frantically across to me. I could see that they had *Panzerfausts* and I ran over to them. We greeted one another like old friends and one of the boys told me that his name was Willi Meyer and one of the others then quipped, 'Meyer, isn't that a Jewish name?'

Willi turned to them smiling and said, 'I assure you, my friends, that I am a perfect fucking German, now shut up.'

One of the others, who introduced himself just as Kurt, commented that I had blood on my face, and he asked me if it was my own or that of the enemy. I told him that I thought it was from the enemy as I had just killed one of them in a house.

He then said, 'Here, let us wash away that filthy stuff.'

Kurt then pulled out a piece of white silk from his jacket pocket spat into it and then preceded to wipe the blood off my face with it. The nausea and shock had by now welled up inside me and I sank down to my knees and was sick several times before we were forced to get up and run again for our lives. We were being slowly pushed further and further back into central Berlin and we knew that soon there would be nowhere to hide.

One of the boys said, 'These bastard Bolsheviks will kill us for sure, where do we go to escape these devils?'

Theresa Moelle and her comrades of the flak battery had also engaged a strong Russian force in the northern sector of the city.

We used our gun, a flak Type-38 anti-aircraft weapon with four barrels against the approaching Russian infantry. It was an amazing and awe-inspiring sight to see such a weapon being fired at zero elevation towards soldiers on the ground. The tracer bullets streaked out like rain and we could clearly see the bright yellow flashes of the exploding 20mm rounds hundreds of metres ahead. I had to load the right-hand ammunition magazines onto the gun, and as they ran out, I slotted a fresh one in its place.

One of our other girls, an 18-year-old named Anneliese, had the job of filling the empty magazines up with fresh 20mm ammunition. Anneliese had only been with us for three weeks, and was one of many girls drafted into the fighting under Hitler's emergency plans. We fired at the Russians until we had used up all of our ammunition, in fact by the time we could fire no more, the empty shell cases were piled up high on the ground. After we had run out of ammunition, we had to reluctantly abandon our gun, but before we left it we made sure it was totally useless, so as the Russians could not use it. We had only managed to hold the Russians off for what seemed a short while. We then picked up our *Panzerfausts* and rifles from their collection point.

A while later, a Russian T-34 tank came over a piled-up embankment of rubble some 180 metres to our front, the noise it made as it came towards us was terrifying. Some soldiers to our right flank fired at it with an MG42 [*Maschinengewehr Modell* 42 machine gun], and I remember seeing the bullets hitting the tank, including tracers that bounced off into the air. A second later and the tank fired its cannon at the machine gunners and scored a direct hit. We dived to the ground and began to panic a little as rubble, dirt and steel splinters came raining down on our backs.

Anneliese was shaking and began to babble, 'Someone is going to have to stop it or it will kill us all.'

I am sure she was on the brink of becoming hysterical; as the tank was coming closer we could feel its vibrations through the ground, and the grinding and creaking noises as it moved along on its metal tracks. None of the men would do anything, they just seemed to freeze.

I then said, 'Anneliese, give me the *Panzerfaust*,' whereupon she just stared at me wide-eyed with tears running down her face and began to tremble even more.

I was forced to shout at her and I said, 'Anneliese, we cannot afford to lie here and do nothing, now give me that thing before we all get bloody killed!'

She quickly grabbed the *Panzerfaust* and chucked it at me. I picked it up and the instructions on how to use the thing began to go through my mind, and I whispered them to myself. My hands trembled as I removed the safety device from the trigger unit and the sight flipped up, it was now ready to fire. I crawled around to the left and had to crawl over the quivering Anneliese and several soldiers and *Volkssturm* men. As I crawled over the men I muttered 'Bastards!'

There was a brief rattle of machine-gun fire but I do not recall where it came from, maybe from the tank, I am not sure. I got up, sprinted a few feet and knelt down before this huge metal monster, which was coming directly towards me. It was less than one hundred metres now and well within range, I framed it in the sight as best as I could and fired. Surprisingly, there was little to no recoil from the *Panzerfaust*, and in slow motion I watched the little rocket projectile streak towards the tank and impact it between the turret part and the body with a loud clank. There was a flash followed by a puff of smoke and small explosion and the tank veered to the left and looked as if it were out of control. It ran into the side of the remains of a building and stopped in a shower of bricks and rubble, and for a few seconds there was nothing. Suddenly the lid of the tank blew off into the air followed by a rush of bright red and yellow flame and sparks, it looked and sounded like a roman candle firework going off. I felt a momentary sense of total elation, as it was the first tank that I had ever killed. I stood up and then jumped up and down and shouted with my arms raised in the air. There were popping noises, and by this time the others had got up and started running away.

The next thing, there are these Russian voices coming from out of the smoke and haze, and one of our soldiers fires a couple of shots at them and hits one of them. Anneliese has recovered her composure enough to throw a stick grenade before we all run like hell as the Russians start firing in all directions. In the ensuing confusion we separate, we become like rabbits caught in headlights not knowing where to run. Rubble and fires obscure our escape, I hear a girl screaming, I recognize the screams, its Anneliese, I run a little way back to see what is happening to her, through the haze of smoke I see that the Russians have got her. What happens next is horrific, they are all over her like ants, pinning her to the ground, ripping at her clothing, hitting her face, they remove everything and then one of the brutes squeezes himself between her legs and starts raping her.

I run at them screaming, 'Leave her alone you bastards, get off her!'

I collide with the two of them who are holding her down and manage to kick one of them in the face hard and he falls back holding his nose that is streaming with blood and possibly broken, as I recall the crunching noise as I kicked him. I struggle with the other one, and I instinctively try to grab hold of his hair but he has no hair to grab hold of. My only recollection after that is of being hit very hard from behind. I knew some time afterwards that I had been hit with a rifle butt.

I came around some time later and found that I had been bound and gagged. I had been caught and just wondered what was going to happen to me next. As I came to, everything was a blur and I found that I was surrounded by objects on the floor. I focused hard to try and make out what they were, and as my vision slowly began to clear, I could see that they were the severed heads of German soldiers neatly arranged in a circle. Five Russian-speaking figures stood a few yards away urinating over a poster of the Führer. My head hurt so bad that I shut my eyes and probably lapsed into unconsciousness again through shock and my head injury.

I remember thinking that everything our leaders had said about these Bolshevik scums was true, so very true. Escape crossed my mind, but I was in too much pain to rationalize at that point. I wondered what they had done with Anneliese, and learned a while later that after I had been hit and knocked unconscious, they had finished raping her and afterwards they had shot her. One of the bastards took great pleasure in telling me what a good fuck the 'bitch' had been, and maybe I would be next.

By 27 April, the mixture of German soldiers and civilians trying to defend Berlin from the Russian onslaught had been pushed back into a corridor area running from east to west, ten miles long by three miles wide. With every passing hour, the area was being systematically reduced by heavy fire. German soldiers and civilians within this zone nicknamed it 'The Meat Grinder'.

It was also at this stage that Hitler issued his vilest order. Hitler was concerned that the Russians were able to suddenly appear behind the German defensive pockets around Berlin by means of the underground tunnels and tube networks around the city. To counter this danger, Hitler insisted that a special group of soldiers be organized and assigned with the task of flooding these tunnel and tube networks by opening the locks of the River Spree. The fact that thousands of wounded German soldiers were seeking refuge in these underground structures with civilians, including young children and elderly people who were also sick or wounded, mattered not to Hitler. This order even sickened hardened SS soldiers such as SS *Leutnant* Gerhard Boldt, who described this order as completely insane. As the order was executed and the locks of the Spree opened, an unknown number of people died a horrible death by drowning in the darkened caverns below the city. There was absolutely no means of escaping the torrent. A German soldier reported that the entrance to one of the many tunnels was awash with the bloated corpses of dead children, babies and adults. This was one of the most tragic episodes of the battle for Berlin, clearly illustrating the depths of madness that Hitler himself had stooped to. Hitler had earlier retorted that, 'Any Berliner worth his or her salt would be dead anyway by now, and that only the dregs and the useless of German society were still living, and they were the unfit of German society.'

On 27 April, ten-year-old Elsa Lantz lost both of her parents. It was an event that still haunts her to this day. She remembers that terrible day:

I was with my mother and father and we were hiding in the cellar room of one of the many partly destroyed buildings in the city, when a shell came in and hit one of the upper floors. There was a tremendous explosion and pieces of concrete, plaster and brickwork came crashing down. We were forced to flee the safety of the cellar and we ran outside into the street. Outside there was thick black smoke billowing out, which filled the street and there was the sound of automatic gunfire. In the confusion, I became separated from my mother and father.

A short distance away, the Russians were going from house to house firing their guns into each building and killing the people hiding inside. I could hear the screams of children also. I began to panic and began to shout for my mother and father, '*Mutter! Vati!*' but I could not see them or hear them anywhere. I ran down the street and kept stumbling over lumps of debris. I came across the body of an old man lying out in the middle of the road. As I approached the body I could see that the old man was still moving. When I got to him and looked down, blood and red foam were oozing from his wide-open mouth as he gasped for air. There was a wide gash in his throat that went from one ear to the other, and he was surrounded by a pool of his own blood. It appeared that the Russians had slit his throat, and the reason was probably because he was wearing a *Volkssturm* reservist's armband on his long black coat.

A nearby building was on fire, and flames were billowing out from the windows and I could feel the heat on my face. As more shells came in, I found a small gap in one of the walls of one of the buildings and I crawled through into the space to try to seek safety from the shrapnel. Inside, a man and his family, a wife and three small kids, were all huddled together in a corner. As I crawled in the man jumped to his feet and started to shout at me, 'You cannot come in here, now get out, get out!'

He pushed me out and I fell backwards onto my backside and began to sob, and I again shouted, '*Mutter! Vati!*' My legs were covered in gashes and I picked pieces of glass out from one of the wounds. I had also lost two fingernails from my right hand and these wounds were very sore. As I got to my feet, a group of figures appeared at the end of the street, and after only a few seconds I knew they were Russians. The Russian soldiers had four large dogs with them, and it was the dogs that spotted me first and began barking and snarling and straining at their leashes to get at me. The soldiers began to run down towards me, and in fear I shut my eyes tightly then raised my hands into the air and called out, '*Aufgeben! Aufgeben!* [I give up].

As they drew closer, I could hear the thud of their boots on the ground and they shouted commands to each other. I also heard the dogs and their growling noises grew louder. I kept my eyes shut as I thought that I was going to be killed. One of them grabbed hold of me and began to search my clothes. I think he was looking for hidden weapons, but I had no weapons on me at all. He then held my face in his hands and I slowly opened my eyes to see this big unshaven face staring at me. I remember the Red Star badge on his uniform and some medal ribbons. He said something in Russian to his comrades, and the soldiers with the dogs then went off with the others and the sound of gunfire resumed.

The Russian then said to me in broken German, 'I will see to it that you are removed from here and away from danger.'

I told him that my mother and father are here somewhere and that I lost them a short time ago in the area.

The Russian replied, 'Oh, no there are only dead Germans around here, and now I will see that you are removed, please do as I tell you to and you will be safe.'

I had no choice but to go with the Russian, and we frequently had to crawl along the floor as we left the area because of the rifle, grenade and machine-gun fire that was raging around us. Suddenly, he dragged me into one of the empty buildings, made me take off my underwear then forced himself on me, he raped me. The rape hurt and I screamed out and he put his fingers in my mouth so I couldn't scream out anymore. In a few minutes, he had finished and then got off me like nothing had happened. He later handed me over to another group of Russians and I was taken to a civilian holding area, where we were given a white number on our clothing (mine was number five).

We received very little food and water for the next two weeks. I never saw my mother and father again and never learned what happened to them. Bodies just vanished in the rubble and shellfire and they were just two of many thousands who went missing during the fall of Berlin. It is believed that they had been killed either by shell or rifle-fire and may have been hastily buried in an unmarked grave somewhere.

I told the Russians holding us that I had been raped, and they laughed and told me, 'Raped eh, you are lucky we did not kill you.'

While everyone else around them began to flee, Helene Rischer recalls how she, her father and mother prepared to defend themselves. Aged twenty-four at the time, she remembers the subsequent engagement with the enemy and the rape of herself and her mother.

The rumble of distant shells had been going for days. At night, the sky was alive with flashes as Russian guns came ever closer to our city. After the battle for Seelow, the bloody Russians were able to fire their guns directly onto the city. Shells fell all over the place and as they took more ground around the city, the shelling got much worse. In our home, Father had collected our furniture tables together and used them to try and make a barricade for our downstairs windows. A space was left so as my father could shoot his rifle. My father insisted that 'No bloody Bolshevik will ever drive him or his family from their home', and instructed me and my mother that if the Russians came down our street we were to go outside into the air-raid shelter in the tiny garden space and hide in there, and not to come out under any circumstances. He lastly instructed me to protect Mother with the small-calibre pistol that I had been issued with under the people's mobilization. The pistol was an old Czech made design that seemed ironic under the circumstances.

When the Russians did come, they came like a whirlwind in the night. There was intense commotion outside and people were running and firing weapons, and we heard many people outside our house.

Father shouted to one of the people 'What is happening? And what is going on?'

A voice simply replied, 'They are coming; the Ivans are coming, hundreds of them.'

Father shouted for me and Mother to get out of the house and into the shelter. Mother and me questioned what good that would do and maybe we should run with the others.

Father told us to 'Shut up and do as you are told or else!'

The sound of gunfire seemed to steadily die away over the next hour and it felt as if we were the only people left in our now deserted street. Nothing happened and we began to think that maybe the Russians were not coming after all, maybe they had retreated or something. Against Mother's wishes, I crept out of the shelter, as I wanted to go and see what was happening with Father. I crept like a cat slowly into our yard. I was just turning the corner of the house to go around to the side door, when I was confronted by a man holding a rifle. We both froze like a cat and dog meeting one another. I reached for the pistol that I had placed inside my waistband and the soldier that resembled no more than a dark silhouette before me in an instant drew up his rifle to his shoulder. I was the quicker of the two of us and fired three shots into him from no more than ten feet away. He sank to the ground dead and his rifle clattered down by his side. Father came bursting out with his rifle at his shoulder and we almost collided with each other in the doorway of our house. He swung me around the door and slammed it shut.

'Why the hell did you not do as I told you to, and stay in the shelter with your mother?' he raged at me.

He could not get another sentence in as the door burst in and shots followed that almost hit both of us. We dropped our weapons and fell to the floor in terror and found ourselves staring down the muzzles of Russian Mosin–Nagant rifles with long, pointed bayonets on their ends. The Russians began to kick us and we huddled together, they then grabbed my father and dragged him outside where they continued to hit him. I shouted for them to stop and kept telling them '*Nein, Nein*' [no] but they wouldn't stop.

Mother had by this time run out of the shelter and she was also screaming at them to leave her husband alone. They then grabbed Mother and got her down on the ground. One of the Russians then muttered something in his own language, and grabbed my wrists and held me tightly from behind while the other unbuttoned my blouse and slid his hands inside. I tried to kick the soldier holding me with the heel of my shoe, but he bent me further backwards so as I could not kick. Mother struggled and shouted at them to leave me and take her instead, but this one man continued to rub his hands inside my clothing. The grip upon my wrists seemed to tighten even more and then my legs were kicked out from under me and I fell to the ground. One of the soldiers grabbed my wrists and pinned my arms down while the other tugged until my clothes were removed from me. This man then removed his belt from his trousers, unfastened them and they fell around his ankles. It was absolutely horrifying for me. I could not believe this was happening and I tried again to struggle, but could do nothing at all to stop this.

As I continued to struggle he got on top of me and I felt him nudging at me and then he put his penis inside me. I tried and tried to struggle free but it was hopeless, I began to scream out as loud as I could, then another one of them slapped his hands over my mouth, and I tried to bite his hand, so he took a belt or something and tried to put it into my mouth. He shouted something at me in Russian and hit me in the face. I was being raped by this man and had no way of stopping him. I tried to focus my thoughts on anything other than what was happening to me now. The worst thing of all is that they forced my parents to watch this. The man was rough and the ordeal hurt, the smell of his dirty body and breath and the feel of sharp facial hair were just horrible, it was the worst thing that ever happened to me. His sweat was dripping from off his face and into my eyes and mouth. I turned my head to the side with my eyes shut and he started to bite and kiss at my neck.

When he had finished he lay down looking at me, panting heavily for a few seconds and then just got up off me, pulled his trousers up, put his belt back on, picked up his rifle and walked away. The man holding me down then leapt on top of me, entered me and began to rape me also. All I remember afterwards is my parents screaming hysterically for them to stop it. When they had finished some of those Russians who had stood by watching then raped my mother while my father and I were forced to watch.

We were then taken away at gunpoint to a place where the Russians had started to gather all those captured during the fighting, mainly civilians, I was not the only one to be raped in the city; Russian soldiers had systematically raped many girls and looted their parent's homes of jewellery and valuable household items. Those Russian soldiers who did the raping and could speak a little German often said to their victims, 'Why do you struggle, we are liberators of German vaginas.'

I do not know how I was able to cope with what happened to me. We never ever talked about it after the war as Mother and Father strictly forbade it, and it was one of things you looked upon with great shame. I did report the rape to the German Red Cross [*Deutscher Ritte Kreuz*], though this was much later, and by which time the physical evidence of the rape had gone. It was only by a miracle that those who had raped us had not made either my mother or me pregnant. Both my parents are dead now, but I hope that they can find it in their hearts to forgive me for telling this to you all these years on. The Russians didn't destroy us or ruin our lives as they had hoped to do by raping and beating us. We were lucky to have survived our ordeal, as many had not been that fortunate. I suppose that the rape was a small price to pay for being allowed to live after shooting and killing one of their comrades, but I was only young and they were grown men who should burn in hell for what they did to me. Maybe they are burning in hell at this very moment, though they tell you God forgives all those who do such terrible things.

The account of this rape was by no means easy for Helene to recall for this publication. This interview, recalling the rape, was the longest I had to conduct during my research. With the help of her husband Bernd, who was constantly at her side consoling her and holding her hand, she was, after some considerable time, able to present all of the terrible details.

Helene said afterwards, 'Anyone with a daughter should read this, as this is what happens in war when one country conquers another and women and girls become the spoils of war.'

Anita Skorz and her close friends from the Hitler Youth were also caught up in the madness of war during the street fighting in the city.

We called Berlin the 'Dying City' because that is how it had become. It was in total ruin and we were being hailed to fight for what were no more than ruins. Our parents were going hysterical with worry and, as we left them to join the Berlin defenders, one of the local police rounded them together and told them to seek shelter along with the other families and women with small children and babies in the little chapel. I remember the calls of reason such as 'What about our sons and our daughters?' and 'Why don't you cowardly men do the fighting for them?'

Uproar amongst the parents began to break out and the policeman drew out his pistol and threatened them, 'Don't make me have to use this.'

We collected weapons from what had been our local NSDAP offices; there were not many left apart from some grenades and some rusted handguns of various types. I tied my hair up into a ponytail with a piece of shoelace to keep it from out of my eyes and picked up several grenades. We joined up with the reservists who had much better weapons than we did, and were told what we must do and to wait behind a barricade made from the remains of a tram and some sandbags. This was bisecting one of the narrow streets, and there was a Tiger tank and machine gun at the two other bisecting points. Our task was to try and to stop any assault from reaching the area of the Reich Chancellery, a very special task we were told. There were many very heavily armed *Waffen* SS soldiers occupying the ground to our rear in dug-in positions. They called out words of encouragement frequently to us, though a girl named Maria, who had been one of our BDM deputy or junior leaders, whispered under her breath, 'Oh, shut up will you, your turn will come soon enough.'

She then turned to me, and with a concerned look on her face said, 'Anita, if anything happens and we become separated, and if I should never see you again for whatever reason, I want you to remember that we were sisters in life, and we will be sisters again in death.'

She then kissed me softly on the cheek and began to stare into the big open space in front of our position. One of the young men warned us against allowing ourselves to be captured by the Russians. He said, 'If you become captured you must not co-operate or smile at them and you should avoid any eye-to-eye contact with them, do you understand me?' We replied, 'Yes.'

He then walked away and we watched him pick up a field telephone and he began to talk to someone on the other end. He called across to one of the soldiers who was smoking a cigarette, and when the young soldier took the phone and began to talk into the phone, he became quite irritated and began to raise his voice. After a few minutes he slammed the phone down and walked away, cursing to his comrades. Maria asked me to find out about this telephone conversation, and I said to her, 'How on earth am I going to do that, he will not tell me anything, who am I to know?'

Maria dug me in the ribs and said, 'Go on, you are a pretty girl, you can charm him.'

I got up and walked over to the soldier who was sat down with his rifle looking at a photograph. 'Is that your family?' I asked him.

'Yes' he replied.

I then asked, 'May I have a look at the picture?' He passed it to me with a deep sigh.

'Your wife and children are very pretty,' I said as I passed him his photograph back, he then put it back into his wallet.

I then asked him, 'Do you think we will ever get out of here alive? Was that what the telephone call was about, as I noticed you were upset.' He looked up at me and replied,

'I had phoned earlier to ask about our reinforcements. That phone goes to the Führer Bunker and I had spoken with Bormann [Martin Bormann] about our reinforcements.'

'What did he say?' I asked.

'Well', he said (putting on a grumpy voice), 'Bormann said to me in his sarcastic voice, "My dear comrade, the people are your reinforcements now." And that is what upset me so much. What does Bormann understand of this situation, he is no military man, and he will not let me speak to anyone, he just hangs up.'

He then asked me my name and said his was Peter.

He also said to me, 'You should not have to be doing this, this is our war not yours.'

I replied, 'Yes, but Berlin is my home and it is my city also.'

Incidentally, that field phone connected to the bunker building was never used again, and later during the brief fight with Russian forces, I picked it up and the line was completely dead. We did everything possible to hold the Russian assault, but we had no decent weapons. I threw several grenades as our position was stormed and one of them failed to explode. We were overrun in a well-coordinated and heavy attack; many of our defenders were killed including Maria. Maria was stabbed with a bayonet as she tried to fire a rifle. She went down and this brute jabbed his bayonet into her belly three times, even though she had shouted a surrender cry. Many were taken prisoner as combatants. We were kicked, punched, spat upon and roughed up before being bundled off with our hands in the air.

The SS had the best equipment and were able to continue to fight and fall back into the Chancellery building, where they continued to inflict heavy casualties on the Russians. At the end, some shot themselves with their last rounds of ammunition rather than be taken alive.

As we were moved away, we could see the extent of the Russian attack, they were everywhere, and T-34 tanks and artillery were pouring in from all directions. They were possibly heading for the Reich Chancellery. As we walked with our hands on our heads into captivity, the Russian soldiers were still pulling frightened people from basements and cellars and had mixed reactions to us. Some just looked, others smiled and swigged from bottles in a gesture of victory, and there were those who shouted things at us and spat. As we passed alongside one of their tanks one of the crew hung his penis out and urinated upon us as we walked by. My thoughts then suddenly turned to Mother and Father, are they alive? Did they remain safe? Where are they?

Suddenly, it was like the end of the world, and I have to admit, as I trudged through the streets with the others in a long line I cried, more out of frustration and anger than anything – frustration at not being able to do anything about it and anger at perhaps letting my parents down, and the strong possibility that I may never see them again.

At this stage of the battle for Berlin, only the government sector around the Reichstag and the Reich Chancellery, with its subterranean bunker system, remained under German control. Everything else was now in the hands of the jubilant Red Army.

By the evening of 29 April, the fighting was less than a quarter of a mile from Hitler's bunker. The last days in the bunker were filled with an almost surreal air of madness as Hitler's moods constantly changed. One minute he was euphoric and cheerful with much rejuvenated spirits, and the next he became a raging madman shouting at his staff. He blamed them and the generals for treachery and incompetence.

There were few things to console Hitler in the depressing air of the Führer Bunker but he found solace in his pet Alsatian dog, named Blondi, and her puppy, and the Goebbels children. Joseph and Magda Goebbels were among the few who had elected to stay with their beloved Führer and to die with him. Hitler had a particular affection for Heidi Goebbels. The little girl, with her blue eyes and long blonde locks of curling hair, could frequently be seen sat on Hitler's lap, talking to him and putting her little arms around him in genuine shows of affection. She was one of the very few who had access to Hitler's private apartments at all times. He adored the little girl who often helped him to overcome his many melancholy bouts.

As the rumble of the incessant shelling crept ever deeper into the Führer Bunker fifty feet below the ground, one of the German army officers present during those last days remarked how he heard the muffled cries of some of the Goebbels younger children, who were obviously becoming alarmed by all of the noise above them. Their nightmare would, however, be a short-lived one, as Magda and Joseph Goebbels decided that they would kill their six children and then themselves, rather than be taken alive by the Russians. Magda Goebbels had commented earlier, 'What terrible things do you think that the Russians would do to us and especially our girls if we allowed ourselves to be taken alive?'

On 30 April, Hitler and his bride of only a few hours, Eva Braun, killed themselves. Finally, after all those years, and now as the dream of ruling the world had come to its final logical, but equally insane conclusion, did Hitler feel he could give Eva Braun the commitment for which she had yearned all those years – the privilege of marriage.

The reality of the situation for both Hitler and Eva Braun dictated that death by suicide was the only remaining option available to them. What unimaginable horrors and tortures would Eva Braun have had to endure if she had been taken alive by the Russians? Rape, torture, interrogation and then inevitable execution may have been a certainty for Eva Braun. Hitler would, no doubt, have been dragged before the world stage, a crumbling wreck of his former self to be publicly ridiculed, humiliated and made to face trial for his Nazi-fuelled genocide. Hangmen would have jostled and vied for the honour of being the one to execute the most hated man on earth.

All that remained of Hitler now was the ghost, and the last will and political testament as dictated to his secretary Traudl Jung during the final hours. The resulting paperwork expresses, amongst other things, no remorse for the murder and persecution of the Jews, the overall conduct of the war, as well as encouraging the Nazi stance on the Jewish question. As it happened, the bodies were removed from the Führer bunker and placed in a shallow grave where the bodies were doused with fuel and set alight. There were also many unsubstantiated reports that Hitler had fled to Argentina. To this day, this is still subject of debate amongst historians, but the theory is wholly unlikely.

The last Soviet artillery assault came on 1 May 1945, when Russian patience with the stubborn defenders making their last stand from the Reich Chancellery building, ran out. At 6.30am that morning, virtually every Russian mortar and rocket launcher in Berlin opened fire on the Reich Chancellery and the surrounding streets. After a vicious ten-hour fight, troops of the 1st Battalion, 756th Rifle Regiment, hoisted the Russian flag upon the roof of the Reichstag on 2 May.

The following morning at 6.00am, *General der Artillerie* Helmuth Weidling, the last commander of the Berlin Defence Area during the battle for Berlin, surrendered to the Russian forces, and at 3.00pm, 2 May 1945 the Russians had formally achieved their final objective and had captured Berlin.

The loss of life had been colossal due to Hitler's persistent refusal to surrender. The Red Army had suffered 360,000 casualties, including 81,000 dead. At the time, Soviet estimates gave the number of German forces killed at just on 460,000, but extensive post-war research by the German authorities put the figure at a maximum of 100,000. German civilian casualty figures were put at an estimated 125,000 dead. Considerably more had been wounded, raped or driven to insanity by the hell surrounding them.

On 7 May , Chief of Operations Staff in the German High Command, *Generaloberst* (Lieutenant General) Alfred Jodl at the Supreme Headquarters Allied Expeditionary Force (SHAEF) in Reims, France, signed the instrument of surrender. SHAEF Supreme Commander, General Dwight D. Eisenhower signed on behalf of the Allies.

Moscow, however, declared the Allied-sponsored German Act of Surrender unacceptable, mainly for the unspoken reason that the Soviets, as self-proclaimed conquerors of Nazi Germany, wanted the 'pleasure' of accepting the German armed forces' capitulation. A second surrender ceremony was therefore arranged by the Russians, to take place in Berlin itself. Presided over by Marshal Zhukov, *Generalfeldmarschall* (Field Marshal) Wilhelm Keitel signed the definitive German armed forces instrument of surrender just after midnight on 9 May. This redraft of the Reims document, however, was backdated to 8 May, to fall in line with the Reims surrender.

The Second World War in Europe ended officially at one minute past 11.00pm , Central European Time, 8 May 1945. For many German combatants and civilians alike, however, the war did not end on 2 May 1945.

Russian brutality was at fever pitch, particularly in Berlin the former capital of the vanquished Third Reich. The Russians, their hearts filled with hate and high on Vodka, continued to rape, murder and loot the now defenceless inhabitants of the city. In fact, the rape and murder began to spiral out of control, and it was only after Russian dictator Josef Stalin himself issued orders for the rape of German women and girls to stop, that the Red Army soldiers halted their barbarity in the city. Stalin only ordered the rape and murder to stop because he was anxious about later problems arising from the Soviet occupation. He realized that he could not afford to have thousands of German civilians grow to hate the Russian forces, and had to work quickly to capture the hearts and minds of the German people, before the Americans and British succeeded first.

Chapter Fourteen

The Soviet Rape of Berlin

The atrocities committed by the Soviet incursions into Berlin, particularly against German females, provide some shocking and disturbing reading, and is not for the fainthearted. It appears that, at the time, the world excused the Russian army for its grotesque behaviour in Berlin, as the Russians were always quick to mention Stalingrad whenever the issues of atrocities were raised. It is certainly true that the Russians, civilians in particular, did suffer terrible cruelty at the hands of certain units of the German army during its victorious early successful campaigns on the eastern front, especially the SS, who were responsible for the murder of thousands. However, there was nowhere near the number of sexual violations carried out against very young girls and women, as there were by the Red Army in Berlin and surrounding Soviet-occupied territories clawed back from the Germans in the Second World war.

During almost every campaign fought by the Germans in the east, each German soldier participating in the action were reminded of what would happen if he were found to have carried out any sexual assault or molestation of females in the occupied areas. During the French campaign two German soldiers had been found guilty of molesting (not raping) a French woman, both were quickly court martialed and shot by firing squad as a warning to the others.

Firstly, with the issue of war crimes, one has to examine what constitutes such an act. Certainly, the maltreatment, abuse, and/or shooting of civilians, unarmed or disarmed combatants, those who have expressed a clear wish to surrender whether military or civilian personnel, all constitute war crimes. The rape of young girls and women cannot be condoned under any circumstances whatsoever, regardless of the reason. Rape is a totally bestial and abhorrent crime, whether carried out against a man or a woman, and is sadly one frequently encountered in situations of war even to this day, as we have already learned from testimonies given in the previous chapter.

The abuse, torture, rape and murder of young girls and women in Berlin from April 1945, were carried out not only by the many hundreds of illiterate Russian peasant conscripts, who had joined the fight against the Germans, but also the regular Russian forces. Another little known fact is that, under Stalin's direction, convicts were released from Russian jails on the condition that they volunteer for immediate military service within the Red Army. As a result of this rather unorthodox policy, many hundreds of dangerously psychopathic and unstable characters were unleashed upon the inhabitants of Berlin during the fall of the city. The only convicts excluded from this policy were those said to have been political prisoners. Stalin was well aware of the consequences of such an action, and it was to serve as yet another reflection of the evil that was to soon surface in all of its obscene glory before a supposedly better post-war world.

German girls and women were viewed as just one of many of the spoils of war to be taken by the Red Army, along with the contents of German homes in the city. Under Stalin's authorization, the Russian army high command was initially given a shameful three-day window where its soldiers, high on alcohol and hatred, could loot, rape and murder with an indiscriminate brutality. In fact, the rape and murder only stopped when Stalin and his army commanders became concerned about the possible effects these crimes would have on future Soviet-German relations after the fighting had stopped.

The mindset of many Red Army soldiers at the time was to make as many German girls and women pregnant, in revenge for the suffering of the Russian people, as well as to teach them a lesson, as it was bluntly stated, 'for giving support to Hitler and the Nazi Party'. Nevertheless, many girls and women were gang raped by as many as five to ten men, and then shot dead afterwards. Even girls as young as eight years old were raped, without any regard whatsoever for the physical wounds caused by the ordeal and their psychological state of mind afterwards. Some suffered worse by having bayonets, knives, broken bottles and gun barrels inserted into their vaginas. However, the average Russian soldier considered the rape of German females as being the ultimate humiliation that could be meted out. Young boys and men also fell victim to the sexual brutality of the Red Army in Berlin, as Theresa Moelle can testify:

While held in internment, I heard many horror stories of what some of the Russians had done to people in Berlin. One woman told me of the fate of her 9-year-old son. The boy was hiding with his mother when the Russian soldiers discovered them. They were both ordered out of their hiding place at gunpoint and came out with their hands raised in the air. The Russians then attacked the boy and, after removing his underwear, they circumcised him with a sharp blade of some description, possibly one taken from a razor. The Russians laughed and told the boy's mother, 'Now your boy is a Jew.'

As in Germany, circumcision had been outlawed by the Nazis as it was seen as an exclusively Jewish practice for Jewish males only.

Thankfully, the boy mentioned above, who fell victim to this horrifying assault, survived the ordeal and was later given treatment by a Russian medic who disagreed with the conduct of his comrades.

Theresa also mentioned another incident while in Russian captivity:

The soldiers were constantly drinking alcohol, some of which had been homemade by distilling boot polish. They often fought and squabbled with one another, and it was during this time that they became especially violent towards us. They would threaten the girls by pointing at us and shouting '*Fick*' which meant fuck in German language. They would often urinate and defecate in front of us. In fact, they took great pleasure in defecating upon a large portrait of Adolf Hitler that they had taken from one of the houses in the city.

One of them tried to kiss one of the German girls and she turned her head away from him. He tried again to kiss her and again she turned away. While this was going on the others, including officers, just walked away and let him carry on with what he was doing. He became angry and pulled his pistol out from his belt, and placed the barrel right against her forehead. He then unzipped himself and gestured for her to conduct a sexual act upon him. When he had finished with her, he walked a few feet away turned around and then shot her dead with the pistol. We thought that we were all going to go that way, one by one, even the German men with us. I had made up my mind that they would never rape me and they'd have to kill me first so they'd be raping a dead body.

The Russians also employed women into the ranks of their armed forces. Many had fought with great bravery in the battles alongside the men of the Red Army. The Russian male soldiers often abused their female counterparts, and seemed to have very little respect for them, and often enjoyed belittling them in public. Some of the women were employed to guard the captured German combatants and civilians.

Theresa Moelle remembers more than one encounter with a Russian female soldier who had recently joined the men. She recalls that the camp was situated somewhere near Mi–dzyrzecz, a town in Poland to the east of Berlin.

> The women soldiers of the Red Army came and joined us after several days had passed. We thought that they might be better being women, but this was not the case. One of them was a bully and a big-built bitch that liked to hit us girls. She often entered the long hut, which was actually a cow shed, where we were kept during the hours of darkness, deliberately mumbling in Russian and German and stamping around to keep us awake; we were tied up and could not move.
>
> She came to me one evening and grabbed hold of my hair and yanked my head back. She pushed her big face up against mine and whispered sarcastically, 'I want to know, when you masturbate yourself, do you see your dead Führer's face?'
>
> She then brushed her lips against mine and I felt her tongue. I did the only thing I could and that was to spit hard into her fat face. She reacted by calling me a 'Nazi scum' and 'German bitch', and all these things as she wiped the spit away with her sleeve. She then gave me an almighty slap across the face with one of her hands that was like the paw of a bear. That slap hurt me more mentally than physically. If only I could free myself, I knew that I could hurt her just as much back. But I had to sit there and take it.

Even elderly German women were not spared the indignity of being raped when caught by the Red Army. During the research for this chapter, the author was able to access many previously unseen documents and photographs that graphically illustrate the sexual violence perpetrated by elements within the Red Army. Almost all of the photographs I viewed were just too distasteful to have been included in this work. One of the black-and-white photographs held in a German archive, shows the body of a 60-year-old German woman who had been raped to death somewhere near the Warsaw area in 1945. It is believed that at least twenty men had been involved in that attack, and that the woman's only crime was that she was a German citizen. This particular scene was also filmed by German combat cameramen in the area, which was then used as proof of Russian atrocities taking place in the area at that time. It is small wonder that the population of Berlin fought so desperately when such films were shown to them in such graphic detail in cinemas around the city.

The Russians also used torture as a means of gleaning information from captured females, particularly those who had joined Werewolf and *Volkssturm* units around the city.

Dora Brunninghausen recalls:

> When captured, the Russians wanted to know what military information we could tell them. The men and Hitler Youths who refused to co-operate with them were beaten with rifle butts and had their fingers crushed and fingernails wrenched out. Some were bound with rope and had gasoline poured over them, and if they continued to refuse to co-operate they were set alight. I myself was interrogated and told my captors that I knew nothing of any military planning or anything.
>
> They said to me, 'Are you sure about that, Fraulein? You were involved in the fighting, and you were armed, surely you must have some knowledge.'
>
> I again told them that I knew nothing. They left me alone for a while and then came back and tied my hands behind my back with metal wire. I was held down on the ground and the clothing removed from the upper half of my body. I thought to myself 'this is it, they are going to rape me and shoot me.' After exposing my breasts, one of them reached into his jacket pocket and pulled out a cigarette lighter. He clicked the lighter with his thumb and a large yellow flame came out of the top. The one asked me again if I knew any information. I told him I did not know anything, and that I had been mobilized to fight under the Hitler Youth regulations, and that much time had been spent digging trenches and helping the *Volkssturm* to assemble defences.
>
> The one with the cigarette lighter then moved the flame towards my breasts, particularly the nipples, and threatened to burn them with the lighter if I did not tell them anything. I began to cry and pleaded with them to leave me alone. One of the *Volkssturm* who sat tied up with the others screamed at them, 'You are bastards, why don't you leave her alone, she doesn't know anything, she is just a child.'
>
> The attention of the Russians then turned towards this *Volkssturm* recruit. They walked over to him and said to him, 'You seem to have much to say for yourself, my friend.'

They then began to beat him. He could not protect himself with his hands bound behind his back and he suffered terrible facial injuries during the assault. When they left him, one of his eyes was hanging out of its socket and some of his teeth were lying broken on the ground around him; he was covered in blood – that man died shortly afterwards. Had it not been for him speaking up when he did, I probably might not have been here now to tell you this.

I began to suffer from nightmares during my sleep and we were often beaten for crying out in our sleep. The mentality of our captors was something we could not understand: why did they not just shoot us and get it over with, that might have been easier to take. I was so lucky, some young girls, particularly those who had been involved with the SS as auxiliaries, suffered terribly, and were always executed afterwards.

Burning the nipples of girls and women with cigarette lighters and lighted cigarettes seemed to be one of their favourite tortures, amongst other degrading things. Women with children also suffered, as the children were often threatened with knives at their throats and things. In fact, the Russians were often referred to by the German people as Ivans, after Ivan the Terrible, who ruled Russia in 1547.

Dana Henschelle was captured in central Berlin. After Templehof, she declined to fight again, and had decided that she was better employed in the service of giving medical aid to soldiers and civilians wounded in the fighting.

We had to move out of positions in danger of being overrun in the fighting, and had used the lulls in between the battle to move out to other safer areas of the city. We had to use the many dugouts and trenches to move around, as shells and bullets were flying everywhere in certain areas of the city. We ended our war on the Potsdamer Platz, and we were inside the Colombushaus. The Colombushaus was once the biggest department store in the world. I had never been inside this building before in my life, as my parents could never afford to go in there and shop. It was as good as any place to try to care for those who had been wounded in the fighting. I did my best to help the wounded, as our soldiers continued to shoot at the Russians all around the outsides of the building.

My years with the BDM had meant I was competent at first aid and nursing, though I could never have prepared myself for some of the terrible injuries, which I just could not deal with properly. Soldiers and civilians, along with women and children, were brought in with arms and legs blown off and serious gun-shot wounds and blast injuries. The children often died very quickly from the shock and loss of blood, often crying out '*Mutter*', '*Mutter*', which means mother in German.

We had no proper medicine for pain killing or anything, and we tried to patch up the wounds and stop any bleeding as best we could. Often we nursed people until they died in our arms; that is an awful thing for a young girl to have to experience. The fighting outside raged continuously, and with each wounded soldier that came in, they were warning of the approaching Russians.

When they [the Russians] arrived they stormed into the huge building firing and shouting and in the end everyone, including myself, was ordered out into the street. I explained that there were wounded civilians and soldiers in there who had a right to receive medical attention. I do not know if they could understand German or not, but several of them went inside the room. Seconds later there were shots fired from a sub-machine gun and the petrol-fuelled lamp, which was the only lighting we had inside the room, exploded under a hail of bullets and set the room on fire. The Russians came running out and gestured for us to move. Many Russians went into the building, probably searching for something to steal, as many goods were lying scattered all over the place. They prodded us with their bayonets and kicked our backsides as we were marched into captivity with other Berliners. I couldn't believe that they had just murdered wounded people, not just soldiers, but civilians also. There were women and children in that place, and no one got out of it alive. I often ask myself today, could I have done more to try and stop them from killing those people. My friends often say, 'Dana, you did everything that you could to help them, they are in God's care now, and their killers will be burning in hell forever.'

Anita von Schoener, a very attractive blonde who had married an SS soldier in May 1944, mainly due to the pressure put upon German women with the Aryan qualities of blonde hair and blue eyes to marry and produce children, had fled her home taking her baby son that she and her husband, Bruno, had named Anton. They had fled along with thousands of refugees from the eastern edges of Berlin.

Anita had seen firsthand the wretched state that many of the young girls and women were in.

The stories of mass-orchestrated rape, sodomy, and other acts of sexual violence were unbelievable to me at first, and I did not really believe that such things could be happening. I had lost touch with my husband Bruno, who had spent almost his entire career within the *Waffen* SS fighting in the east. His letters suddenly stopped coming and I had just assumed that he was unable to write because of the military situation.

When the train of refugees began to pass through our area and Russian fighter planes were seen in the skies over our homes almost every day, I packed what belongings I could and headed for Berlin, thinking that we would be safer there. For much of the time we were relatively safe, though the conditions in the city were dreadful, and disease was claiming the lives of many people in the city, so I was very worried about taking the baby there, but had few options.

In Berlin, there was little food and water, and many had taken to collecting the filthy water from the rivers and canals running through the city. This had to be boiled before it could be drunk. If you didn't boil it, then it would have poisoned you.

Later on, Russian snipers picked many people off as they collected water, and so it became too dangerous and we often had to go without a drink for days. When the city came under siege from April of that year, things grew worse, though we did try to share what we had with others. Strangely enough, only the SS soldiers refused to share their rations with us civilians. Our armies of volunteers were hopelessly outnumbered, and in the end were forced back further and further into the wrecked heart of the city. When the Russians came, there was fear and panic everywhere. Quite a few German soldiers fled and headed for the flak towers like the one in the Brunnenstrasse. Some SS soldiers took the clothes off dead bodies and put them on, and then threw their SS uniforms and dog tags away. They were trying to get away as ordinary civilians. Anton and me were forced to hide in the rubble and were left to fend for ourselves as the chaos of war broke out all around us. My only concern was for my baby boy, Anton, at that time, and most of the food we were able to find I naturally gave to the baby. Often we ate stale bread that was very hard, and I had to mash it up in my mouth before giving this to Anton, as it would have choked him. When the enemy came and found us, we were immediately taken away; thankfully Anton was too little to know what was going on around him. We were taken to a side street near the Potsdamerstrasse, where many Russian tanks and men had gathered in large groups. There had been very heavy fighting around that place and it was strewn with dead bodies and parts from dead bodies. I covered my little son's eyes so that he could not see this carnage, even though he would not have understood what it all was, it was just motherly instinct.

We had not gone far down this narrow street when I was shoved violently inside one of the many empty alcoves in the ruins. Anton was snatched from my arms and held outside and he began to cry. I knew what they were going to do with me, and I was taken into a corner, forced to take off all of my clothes, and thrown down. A gang of Russian males then raped me, one after the other. I could not stop them, as while one did the raping, the others held you down. I had to survive what these men were doing to me for the sake of my child, and I shut my eyes and just thought of my child. They were like a pack of wild animals, and when they had finished taking turns abusing me, I had teeth marks on my neck, breasts and my shoulders. My arms and legs were also covered in bruises. After the rape, they left me virtually alone to put my clothes back on, and I was then taken out to my baby who was still crying.

I later heard that some of the Soviets had sodomized little boys, and so I checked him myself. Thankfully, they had spared him from harm and had taken their frustrations out on me. When the Americans arrived, I spoke to one of their medical people, a young nurse, who said she came from New York. She examined Anton to check his health, and then afterwards she checked me, and she saw the teeth marks on my body and the bruises, then asked how I got them. I told her what had happened, thinking she would not believe me, but she was very kind and what I had told her made her visibly angry and she made a detailed report of this which she said would be passed to her seniors. She gave me some medicine as I had also contracted something nasty down below [VD], something from the Russian soldiers, which soon cleared up with the medicine.

The worst thing of all was that I later discovered that I was pregnant, pregnant with the rapist's child. I went ahead with the birth as many German girls did. Because of what had happened it was utterly impossible for me to bond or show any love or affection for the child, and I gave the child up straight after the birth. I did not even want to know if it was a boy or girl or even look at it. How could I possibly love the baby of those who had raped me? I would have only grown to hate the child, and it did not deserve to grow up being hated, so I had to let it go.

Bruno did not return from the war in the east. A comrade of his later told me that Bruno had been killed. The Soviets often executed SS soldiers. Those they did keep alive were refused any medical treatment and gave them literally nothing to eat or drink, and let them die slowly. I was also questioned briefly by the British shortly after the end of the fighting in Berlin on my husband, but could tell them little of his operational details, as he never wrote about them in any of his letters, though I did not have any of his letters with me to prove it. I only wish that the British and Americans had taken Berlin – that was a view shared by thousands of Germans after the war.

Kirsten Eckermann had planned to try to get away from Berlin before the Russian army arrived, but although she and many others made several attempts to break out of the city with groups of soldiers, all attempts to flee were scuppered by the speed of the Russian pincers which closed tightly around Berlin.

All that was left was to try to get out of Berlin; it was a question of self-preservation. Whole families fled into the night, and found that by daybreak they were facing an advancing army, a Russian army. Then they would turn and go back dejected and frightened. There was nowhere to hide as many of the city's buildings had collapsed and only the ruins remained. If you could, you crawled into a hole and stayed there, it was much better than staying out in the open when the shells and bombs came raining in. Only those driven insane by the exploding shells and bombs wandered around aimlessly in the streets.

Occasionally, a woman holding a child in her arms would run screaming across the street. We were basically flushed out like rabbits. The Red Army patrols would pass by shout '*Granate*' [Granate means grenades in German] into anywhere they felt that people could hide, and it made you think that they were going to throw in a hand grenade if you did not come out, so you did what you felt was the right thing and quickly obeyed them and came out with your hands up. Men were kicked and punched to the ground, and if they had dogs with them, they would let the dogs attack them. The Russians liked to set dogs on you very much, it seemed like a sport to them. When some women and children would run the Russians would let the dogs off their leads, and the dogs would chase and catch them. One little girl had her face bitten badly by one of the dogs, and a piece of flesh on her small face was hanging off and blood pumped out from the wound. The little girl just stood rooted to the spot convulsing violently and screaming. I will never forget that child's screams so long as I live. Her parents went down on their knees and cried hysterically for mercy and begged for help, when one of the Russians began arguing with his comrades. They had been constantly swigging from bottles and pointed their guns at each other during the argument, and the nasty one walked away while the others went to attend the child who had been bitten.

There were one or two German soldiers who were found still in their uniforms a few hundred yards from our hiding place. They were ordered out and they came out with their hands in the air, and were made to kneel down, dogs were set on them, and when the dogs had finished they were shot in the head, the bodies were then searched for valuables and money. My father and I began to protest and they came over and told us to 'fuck off' in German, before my father was punched several times in the face and I was called a 'fucking German bitch' and slapped. The slap had been hard and left marks across my cheeks.

While this was going on my mother noticed that the Russians were urinating into the open mouths of the corpses of the dead German soldiers that had just been executed, and, with bored expressions on their faces, they prodded their bayonets into the dead men's eyes. Mother later warned me and Father to 'keep your mouths shut in future, because I want us all to get out of this alive.'

The things that I had seen stayed with me and are still with me now. I wrote down much about it in a diary that I kept after the war, just so as I could look back through it all to make sure it wasn't just a bad dream. I was German, yes, but I did not do any harm to any Jew, gypsy or ethnic people and it took many years to restore my faith in humanity.

During the critical period of research, medical files retained by the German and Allied authorities in Berlin remain confidential and thus cannot be scrutinized, so there are doubts as to whether any of these still exist in document form today. Most of the material in Russian hands was burned after the war for reasons known only to the Soviets. The United States Army Medical Department (USAMD), and the British and German Red Cross organizations would have no doubt compiled material of a medical context regarding the rape of girls and young women in Berlin during and after April and May 1945. The official figures for rapes committed by Russian soldiers in Berlin do exist, but will probably never be released to the public. Berlin's former mayor, Ernst Reuter, quoted a figure given to him as 90,000. These were the treated, recorded and medically proven cases of rape that had taken place in Berlin during the early part of the Soviet occupation of the city. There were many more girls and women who had been attacked and had not come forward for medical treatment or support. So, in reality, the quoted figure is to be used as the minimum.

Amy Richardson was a 20-year-old nurse attached to the one of the US army field hospital units that had been hastily set up to give medical aid to wounded civilians and soldiers alike. When the Allied forces finally arrived in Berlin, they did so in huge numbers, bringing with them many resources and supplies to aid the suffering.

What shocked Amy Richardson more than anything else she had ever encountered throughout the war, was the number of rape victims she had to deal with in Berlin.

To be honest, I was absolutely furious and disgusted by it all. We had ten-, fourteen-, fifteen- and sixteen-year-old girls coming in time after time to receive treatment sustained as a result of being raped or sodomized. Now, I know that these were German girls who had probably shown support for Hitler and whatever, but they were basically children, very brainwashed children, and no one had the right to do that to children. In fact, I complained many times to the higher authorities of my profession about it, but was told to just get on and treat the people and not to get too emotional about it all. I was told 'these terrible things sometimes happen in war', but I replied 'this is the first time that I have ever come across this thing.'

To explain further the medical evidence of rape is very obvious to any trained doctor or nurse. Sometimes, the physical evidence disappears rapidly, depending on the severity of the individual attack. Many of the young girls that came to me for treatment had been brought in by their mothers, aunts, sisters, or whoever. Many had deep bite marks on their breasts, shoulder areas and their necks. Their wrists and arms were often badly bruised due to being violently restrained, and dried semen was often found on the clothing. The most serious cases I had to treat needed stitches around the vaginal entrance, clitoris and labial areas.

The one that sticks in my mind most, is a 10-year-old that was brought in to us, and when I gently coaxed her into removing all of her clothing, she had dried blood all the way down the insides of her thighs, and bite marks on her chest and shoulders. I had to wash and clean her and put several stitches into a vaginal wound. The degree of sexual violence exerted upon that little girl's body had been quite considerable, and it was enough for me to write a letter to Allied Command. I noted in my report, after seeing and dealing with so many depressing cases like that, I did not even feel safe having Russian soldiers nearby. My opinion was that if they could do that to a young child, then what might they do to someone like me?

At least we know these rapes did occur and possibly many more than the known ninety-thousand recorded cases. I was very relieved to have finished my work in Berlin as it was deeply upsetting. My superiors were often as disgusted as I was. We were instructed to not cause any fuss, as we had to keep good relations between Russians and Americans. Though I have always felt it was wrong that this kind of thing was deemed excusable, purely on the pretext that the Russians were our ally.

Carly Hendryks, another US army nurse, remembers the many young female rape victims:

We made reports such as their physical and mental state of mind, and documented their injuries and asked them as to how they had been acquired. The great danger with rape victims is they tend to blame themselves, which often leads to severe psychological problems, an inability to form future relationships with members of the opposite sex, and depression, self-abuse, and even suicide. I once had to remove half a broken bottle from the vagina of one German woman. Some brute had forced the bottle into the woman with such force that it broke off inside of her. It was a miracle that she survived such a horrific sexual assault.

I also know from reading up documents from Berlin much later, that many babies were born as a result of German girls and women being raped, and that many of the children ended up parentless, having been handed over to orphanages and convents. Only a woman will fully understand how rape can destroy you. It's sad that most of the medical reports and documents were destroyed after the war. Our Government was very sensitive to Russian needs and political obligations of the time. They put the Soviet authorities before the needs of little girls and women who had been raped and abused. To me, that was unacceptable as an adult. It's something that made me feel a bit sick at being an American, a member of the victorious Allies, because that sort of thing wasn't victory, was it? I do know that later on General Patton spoke out about his disgust of the Mongol hordes, and how they behaved in Warsaw and Berlin.

Margaret Neilson, also a nurse, had also seen the evidence of Russian sexual crimes in Berlin, and says:

I was not keen on some of the things the Germans had done to people. But, tell me this, what kind of creature gratifies himself upon the body of some pre-pubescent female child? Such things are totally disgraceful and are a criminal act of the most horrendous kind. I was very concerned indeed about it all, and I did make several complaints about it and hoped that maybe the reports would be made to the Allied commander himself, which is what I had suggested. The problem was we were just too busy to chase up these things, not that anyone bothered doing anything about it. Often we were told to 'get on with our job'. Being a nurse meant that I was neutral, and no, I would not shut up as I was told to. In the end, they threatened to have me removed from my duties, and I am sad to say that this was very typical of the attitude back then. I don't think anyone said anything to the Russians about it. There were far too many concerns about Russian sensitivity at the time, like don't go upsetting our Russian comrades, and things like that. The crimes committed though were very real and very ugly. It stays with, you things like that, when you have to put stitches into women who have been sodomized. Can you imagine having to do that duty, well I did. I saw firsthand the pain, helplessness and suffering.

While on the subject of war crimes committed by Russian soldiers against girls and women in Berlin, noted Allied war crimes after the D-Day landings at Normandy in France of June 1944, must also be examined.

As far as can be ascertained, there are no reports of any British soldiers ever having taken part in the rape of German girls or women. The British Tommy has always been, perhaps, the best disciplined of soldiers in the world, and in most cases conducted himself with great moral distinction throughout.

Research shows that the first Allied soldier to be executed for the crime of rape after the D-Day landings, was Private Clarence Whitfield, a coloured US soldier who had served with the 494th Port Battalion. Whitfield had been convicted of the brutal rape of Aniela Skrzyniarz, a young Polish girl who had been working on a farm at Vierville-sur-Mer just beyond Omaha Beach. This incident occurred on 14 June 1944, and Whitfield was hanged on gallows erected in the garden of the Chateau de Canisy, a castle in Canisy, Normandy, 5km south of Saint-Lô.

Two other coloured soldiers were also hanged for the crime of rape on 10 February 1945, in the village of Hameau Pigeon on the Cherbourg Peninsula. The two men, privates Yancy and Skinner, were convicted of the rape of 19-year-old French girl, Marie Osouf, and the murder of her boyfriend Auguste Lebarillier. Hundreds of black US troops were forced to watch the double hanging.

A total of 49 US soldiers were hanged for crimes of rape and murder that had been committed on French soil after the D-Day landings. It is noted that in the whole European theatre of operations, 109 civilians were murdered by US soldiers. It is also recorded, that US soldiers were responsible for the murder of at least 107 civilians and the rape of 552 in Germany. However, none of the German women interviewed for this work had any bad encounters or problems with soldiers of either the British or US armies, black or white.

Theresa Moelle can also testify to the shooting of at least one adult female, who was believed to have been involved in the fighting in Warsaw.

> She had been held by the Russians ever since they had swept through Warsaw and drove our forces out, though she was with us for only a short period of time before she was killed. I often tried to make a conversation with her, but she did not seem to want to talk to anyone. I remember that she wore a black and white patch on her shoulder. I remember it as plain as anything; it was a black wolf head on a white background and was roughly triangular shaped. I did once ask her what it was and she said that it was one that she and her friends had made themselves from pieces of rag. Was she one of the female Wolves we had heard so many stories about after the war? Though we all called ourselves Female Wolves during the fighting in the city.
>
> Soldiers came one evening and took her away, and several minutes later we heard shots being fired. When the soldiers returned they began drinking again and making dirty remarks about us again, and took great pleasure again in telling us how good it felt killing one of us fucking Germans. Looking back, I think that the woman had very likely belonged to one of the combat units set up by Gertrud Scholtz-Klink. Either way, it may be impossible to discover the truth now.

The terrible things revealed in this chapter, and indeed excerpts of material contained in the previous one, are just a very small number of a great many such incidents. The author felt an obligation to record at least some during the four years of his research for this book. It would be impossible to place too much documentary emphasis on accounts of Russian barbarity, as most cases seem to follow the same grotesque pattern.

To conclude, there will always be those that will say, 'Well, those bloody Germans deserved all that they got for following the cause of National Socialism.' Such comments, however, are usually the ignorant and venomous words of those who have no understanding of how a nation functions economically, socially and politically under dictatorial rule. Unless an individual has personally endured life within the regimented, often violent and controlled environment of a state like Nazi Germany, then judgement of those who lived through it all, whether they supported it or not, should be withheld.

Finally, one has to highly commend those women who, despite being sexually violated during that terrible time in Berlin, have very bravely stepped forward to discuss their experiences with the author. Added to this, they have done so with such immense dignity and in such detail for this work. It can never be a complete account of war, in all of its ugliness, without the warts and all approach essential for the production of this kind of work.

To some degree, the reader will also now be aware that the rape and violence perpetrated against some of the contributors to this work did not destroy their lives as was the obvious intention, and therefore, their continued strength and courage has to be admired.

Heidi Koch:

I don't think that any of us would be here now if it had not been for the BDM. The BDM had prepared us all for struggle and to overcome all physical hardship and adversity. We were brought up to do nothing but struggle. Artur Axmann [Hitler Youth leader] once flattered us all at a meeting in 1943 by saying:

'You are all butterflies, a butterfly emerges from its cocoon, to a short life filled with struggle, yet its beauty is so delicate. Let this delicate creature be your natural example.'

It was our physical strength that kept our bodies and our minds alive during the war, and particularly the hell of April and May of 1945. We did lose the war, but we did not lose our minds, and we are here now, though considerably older and wiser. In war everyone loses, even the victors lose something and that is the logic of it all. No sooner had Germany been beaten than the British and Americans were facing a new enemy in Communist Russia, just as Germany had warned. It started a new age of terror with the constant threat of instantaneous annihilation. World War Three came very close to happening for many years after World War Two had ended.

After the fall of Berlin, the uneasy peace between Britain and America and the Soviet Union would soon crumble under mutual distrust and paranoia, which would inevitably and ultimately lead to the political partitioning of Germany into two sectors, East and West, with a huge wall erected by the Russians and East Germans as the dividing line between the two. Before long, this edifice would become known around the world as the Berlin Wall, becoming the symbol of Communist tyranny.

Chapter Fifteen

After the Reich

With Hitler dead, the war lost, his army and air force decimated, and his dreams of a 1,000-year Reich in total ruins, the people of Berlin were as shattered and thoroughly beaten as their city. Berlin was now a city without infrastructure and in a state of complete turmoil. Once the raping, killing and looting had finally ended after three long days and nights, on orders from Josef Stalin, the Russian forces in the city were like angry bees, spending much of their time erecting all manner of unofficial memorials to their fallen comrades and patrolling the city streets. By 5 June 1945, the four victorious allied nations of America, Britain, France and the USSR assumed occupation power, and began working towards their plan for the immediate dissection of Germany.

Many thousands of ordinary German families had become displaced during the fighting, and groups of men and women wandered around the city, hopelessly searching for their missing children and relatives, many of whom were dead. The first American forces would not enter Berlin until 4 July 1945, so in the interim, many Berliners were just trying to come to terms with a now very uncertain future. German soldiers captured during the fighting were still being marched out of the city and into Soviet captivity. Those German soldiers accused of committing war crimes were held at a prison situated in the Pankow district of northeastern Berlin, a sector that joined the borough of Reinickendorf. This area later became the administrative centre of the Soviet occupation zone.

Theresa Moelle:

> It was the worst period of my entire life. Everything was uncertain at that time and I was not sure if I would ever see my family ever again. I thought that we would all be transported to Russia and sent to the labour camps, as the guards often threatened us by saying we would be sent to die in the Gulag [Soviet forced-labour camp system]. I recall wondering if the Americans and British would come and try to sort things out, as everything was in chaos.

I had very bad cystitis, brought on by the unsanitary conditions of the camp, and was given very little food or water. The food we were given often made us sick. It was also around that time that they began intensive questioning.

It was always two different German-speaking Russians, who took it in turns to try and break you mentally. They told me that if I failed to tell them the truth I would be sorry. I told them I had only been with a flak unit, and they asked questions such as the type of gun and how many planes we shot down, and did we shoot any Russian planes down? When did we join the fighting amongst the civilians? etc. Lastly, they asked me how I came to be wearing a jacket of the type worn by the SS. I said that the jacket had been given to me during the battles in the city. I do not think they were convinced and they kept asking me if I had been involved with the SS, and I repeatedly told them no. Upon reflection, I had been stupid in taking the jacket from the SS soldier, even though I was cold at the time. He was just getting rid of the jacket in order to save himself I think, that's how it looked when I thought about it, but I did not see it at that time. After quite a lot of questioning about my family and where we lived, what my father did, etc, they left me alone and bothered me no more. The atmosphere became a little more relaxed particularly when the Americans and British came.

On paper, Britain, France, America and Russia had agreed to divide Germany into four zones of occupation. These were to consist of a large Soviet zone in the east, a British zone in the northwest, a US zone in the southwest and a French zone, also to the southwest. Austria was to be separated from Germany again, and the territories located east of the Oder and Neisse rivers were handed to Poland as compensation for the loss of its eastern territories, which remained as a part of the USSR. The northern half of East Prussia was also annexed by the USSR. The German populations of these territories, including those of the territories located within the borders of the restored eastern European states, such as Czechoslovakia (Sudetenland, Hungary, Yugoslavia, etc, were forcibly expelled from their homes. This policy of what amounted to Soviet ethnic cleansing created a total of some 10,000,000 men, women and children refugees. They had nowhere to go and many headed for central Germany.

As the Four-Power occupying countries began the task of planning the reconstitution of the four zones in Germany, all manner of political and social problems became apparent, not just between the people of Berlin and the occupying Russian forces in the city. Tensions had begun to build between Russia and the Western Allies, the two camps expressing differences of opinion on many important issues, including those of the quadripartite control council and currency reforms. For example, the Russians refused to recognize the validity of the new Deutschmark in their zone of occupation, even though it had been introduced and was in use in the western occupation zones. Petty disputes were suddenly becoming a regular consequence. Things began to seriously spiral out of control when Stalin ordered his forces to close the roads, railway lines and canals connecting Berlin with the three Allied zones in western Germany. This was the start of what became known as the Berlin Blockade.

The Allied sectors in West Berlin had a population of over 2,000,000 people, who suddenly found themselves completely cut off, with no incoming food or fuel – especially coal – Stalin was optimistic that the blockade would be successful. To boost his quest to completely force the Allies from the city that he claimed was rightfully his, he offered to supply the beleaguered western Berliners with food supplies from the USSR. The offer was ignored by the Allied administrative governments, who immediately organized the famous Berlin Airlift to supply the city with all of the necessary supplies of food, fuel, clothing, and in fact all the necessities, and the odd luxury, from the air, an operation that would last for eleven months.

The Soviets became the victim of savage press reports and damning communiqués though the lifting of the blockade was almost entirely as a result of the success of the airlift. Britain and America would not yield to months of military posturing and provocation by the Russians, deliberate harassment of the airlift aircraft flying the mutually agreed flight corridors, endless covert shuttle diplomacy, and continuous Soviet-sponsored media propaganda. In spite of extremely hazardous flying conditions in the winter of 1948, the airlift tonnages continued to increase to seemingly impossible levels. The Allies facilitated a democratically elected city council in their sectors and, in spite of powerfully worded threats from the Russians, unilaterally introduced a new German currency. Out of concern that he was rapidly losing Russia's sphere of influence in the region, Stalin lifted the embargo. More importantly, and although Soviet forces on standby in neighbouring satellite states enormously outnumbered those of the Allies, Stalin was still three years away from the usable production of nuclear weapons. President Harry S. Truman, on the other hand had, at that time, the trump card. He had used the atom bomb against Hiroshima and Nagasaki with devastating success. He was not afraid to use the weapon then, and had the potential to use it again in the event of a Soviet-initiated war in Europe.

Although roads, railways and canals were once again opened, relations between the western allies and the USSR would never be the same again. In fact the situation deteriorated as the Western Allies made decisions often without involving the Russian authorities, something that caused Stalin and those closest to him within his political circle some great consternation.

Theresa Moelle, in the meantime, had been reunited with her adoptive family and clearly recalls in late July 1945 when their lives took a dramatic turn for the better.

> The Russians just came one morning and began selecting many of us for transfer. I thought that we were going to be sent to Russia and felt like fighting to try and escape, but with tied hands that would have been a useless idea. They came to each of us and unbound our hands and asked our names, which were then written down on a sheet of paper. The next thing we know we hear American voices and then see the first Americans we would ever meet. There was this young American man who quietly told us to get into the back of the truck and that we were leaving. I still could not believe this was happening and had to be helped into the back of the truck; we were just elated.
>
> The drive seemed to last for hours and we could not see where we were going because a tarpaulin sheet covered the whole of the back of the truck. We stopped occasionally and were checked, and then given a drink of water from a metal canteen bottle and, best of all, we were given chocolate. I could not even recall when I last ate chocolate and there I was with this big bar of chocolate, which I gulped down.
>
> We finally arrived at the western suburbs of Berlin and it was dark outside. We were taken into a building that had been a German house and was now being used by the Americans as some kind of Head Quarters. There were uniformed men and women everywhere. We were then separated and taken to our own room where we were searched and then given a medical check. A medical nurse, through an interpreter, asked me if I had sustained any injuries and began looking through my hair. She immediately found the wound on the back of my head, and gasped as she ran her fingers over it. She said that it was too late to put any stitching in the wound as it had already

scabbed over and was starting to heal, but she insisted that it was bathed and a bandage put on it. I also had a bruise underneath my left eye caused by the regular slapping routines from our Russian lady friend. My eyes were examined and I was then brought a meal consisting of potatoes, carrots and a little gravy and a cup of hot tea. I could not get the food down quick enough and drank the tea so fast that it burned my tongue.

The interpreter said, 'Hey, take it easy will ya,' in his American accent.

I then was given some nice clean clothing to put on, though it did not fit me too well as I had lost so much weight, but it was clean and made me feel like new. After that, I was taken into another room and asked questions about the fighting in the city and how I had been involved in it. I answered them as best as I could, and I trusted them more than the Russians, so this was not any problem. I asked them if I could have a cigarette, and one of my interrogators placed a packet before me on the table, took one out for me and gave me a light. I then handed the packet of cigarettes back, but he told me to keep them. I explained I couldn't as I would be in trouble if my family found out I had begun smoking cigarettes.

After the questioning I was taken back to my room and was told to try and get some sleep, and that if I needed attention in the night I should knock on the door of my room, as the door had to be locked from the outside. I told them I wanted to find my family and the interpreter replied smiling 'We know who you belong to, your father, or rather your guardian, has been looking for you for many weeks.'

'Where is he? and 'can I go to him?' were my replies.

The interpreter then said, 'Please, rest now and your father will be here to see you within the next few days.'

I found it very hard to settle that night and the night was the longest of my life. I stared at the reflection of the moon that shone through a small stained glass window high upon the wall, and tossed and turned until the early hours. I finally fell asleep and was woken at around 10.00am in the morning by the interpreter and the nurse, who firstly knocked on my door before opening it with the rattle of keys. There, standing right behind the interpreter and the nurse, was Walter Moelle. We threw ourselves at each other and sobbed like children.

'Where have you been? What has happened to you?' were the words tumbling from his heart. He pulled back to look at me and said, 'Look at you, you are so thin, and your face is hurt, and what have you done to your head, did they [the Russians] do that to you?'

I nodded, and then told him they had hit me on the head with a rifle and one of their women had slapped me, and that I had got my own back on her by spitting in her face. He again threw his arms around me and said something that changed my life and my attitude about him forever.

He told me that he had searched for weeks to try to find where I was. He was unsure if I was dead or alive, but had not given up hope of finding me. After the fighting had stopped, he talked with the British and American Red Cross authorities that had come into Germany with the Allies. He gave my name to them and a photograph on the chance that the Russians might have taken me prisoner or something. Though I was one of thousands of missing girls in the city at that time, my name was noted and later cross-checked with Russian documentation concerning civilians, combatants and injured, etc. A name Moelle was listed as being held in Camp Three. My father had to give information that proved I had not been recruited into the SS and that I had been an auxiliary, which of course was the truth. Many phone calls were made and the documentation was cleared, and we were allowed to return home along with many others in the same boat, so to speak, providing my father agreed to collect me and be responsible for me afterwards. My adoptive father hugged me continuously and then told me that he knew we had immense difficulties in the past, but I was his daughter and he loved me like the others. I then said to him, 'Father, take me home.'

We then left to go back to our home to see what remained of it. When we arrived, the old farm and surrounding buildings, including our home, was still intact, like nothing had happened. The doors and windows had been broken and some of the belongings removed, including some furniture, which my father later discovered in an American office. Though he let them keep it for being so kind and helpful.

The soldiers had defecated and pissed in some of the rooms and there was all kinds of discarded rubbish, but this was soon cleared over the weeks that followed. An old lady, who remained behind at the farm when everyone else evacuated, looked after the place. Most of the animals had been killed, the horses lay rotting in the fields and the old lady said that American planes dived down and shot anything that moved, including the farm animals. What happened to the horses had made me cry. Why did they kill our animals? The old lady thrilled us with her story of how the Americans swept through as the Soviets began to encircle Berlin.

It was still early days and there were many problems, but we were trying to get back to normal, even though we had never really lived in normality, me especially having been adopted with no real family and then schooled under National Socialism. It was not a good start in life really, but I was determined that I would make good use of what life I had left.

Life had to begin again for many Germans. The nightmare world created by the twelve years of National Socialist rule under Hitler had created all manner of problems, which German society would have to overcome. Three quarters of its 1,500,000 residential units had been destroyed, while the Soviets dismantled and removed some sixty-seven per cent of Berlin's industrial capacity. Other cities in Germany had also suffered some seventy per cent ruin, indicating that most of these were not habitable and were in a dangerous state. The population had to be crammed into what buildings were still intact and safe to live in. In these conditions, up to four families had to live together in a single apartment. The situation was exacerbated by the Russian ethnic cleansing taking place in the eastern territories.

The collapse of both the state and the economy had been total, and though there was plenty of money in Germany at that time, there were hardly any goods to buy. Children often went out into the streets amongst the ruins searching for small pieces of coal or any other useful items they could find. Many families sold what few possessions they had in order to buy such luxury items as a few potatoes to eat. Many German people were so hungry that they often ate the potatoes raw.

After first entering Berlin, US soldiers were at first briefed by their superiors not to fraternize with, or be friendly to the people of Berlin and Germany in general. To aid this issue, a film was shown to the troops in which a section of its narrative contained the quote, 'The German people are not your friends!'

As time passed by though, the atmosphere became more relaxed and US soldiers often gave German children their chocolate and sweets. Chocolate was supplied freely to the US troops in Germany along with cartons of cigarettes. Cigarettes soon became a valuable form of currency on the thriving black market.

As a direct result of six years of war, the German population consisted mainly of boys, girls, women and the elderly people. As a consequence, adults between the ages of eighteen and fifty-five were in very short supply. Many were dead, missing or crippled in the fighting. The many tasks of rebuilding Germany would, ironically, fall upon the shoulders of the German women. All over Germany, gangs of girls, boys and women were organized into clearing-up groups and helped to clear away the detritus of war. The scars left by war, however, would remain for many years, and for some, for a lifetime.

The winters of 1945–47 were some of the worst recorded in Germany, and as many homes were still in a state of disrepair and without adequate fuel for even the most basic of heating facilities, hundreds froze to death. The US Red Cross made valiant efforts to prevent the misery by distributing blankets, clothing and care parcels. The British also chipped in to help, and the Germans gradually came to view the American and British forces as liberators rather than an occupying force. Even so Germans still had to work for the food given to them.

Perhaps the most important task faced by the Western Allies was that of the complete denazification of Germany. This had come too late for many adult Germans. As the youth are the future of any country, it was they who had to undergo re-education to rid them of the evils of Nazi philosophy.

As the political and social reconstitution of Berlin and Germany began, a scheme was implemented by the Allied powers to address the process. The authorities directed that any German male or female wishing to hold political offices, or to work as public servants such as teachers, judges or police officers, were required to produce the necessary documentation stating that they had not been active Nazis, nor were sympathetic to the National Socialist cause. A document was drafted for the introduction of German re-education, referred to as the *Persilschein* after a well-known brand of detergent. To possess a 'Persil ticket' meant the owner had been given 'a clean bill of health' to pursue a business or activity without fear of arousing suspicion.

Research on this subject was very enlightening. Many of those given the task of re-educating boys and girls in post-war Germany, including some who had been expelled by the Nazis after 1933, were impressed by how enthusiastic boys and girls were. They wished to learn of the outside world and its many differing races and cultures, all of which had been denied them during the six years of the Hitler regime. Once Germany's youth became fully aware that things could operate on other levels, without affecting one's own culture or cultural beliefs, and that other races and religions could live with one another in a state of relative social and political harmony, the foundations of recovery could be set in place for Germany. After being introduced and exposed to genuine education formulae, many German girls and boys expressed a wish to achieve academic status. When questioned, many said that they now wanted to become teachers, doctors, writers or scientists. Great emphasis was placed upon the thorough understanding of subjects of racial tolerance and how other cultures differed very little from that of many German citizens. The boys and girls were shown detailed films of the death camps such as those as Belsen, Dachau and Auschwitz, along with film and photographs of Nazi atrocities. In fact, many German citizens had been made to visit these places and to see for themselves the thousands of corpses of Jewish men, women and children – there could be no room for denial in the new Germany.

As rebuilding and re-education continued at a steady pace in Germany, the fraternization between Allied soldiers and German girls was becoming embarrassingly apparent to many of the commanding officers of the occupying forces. Allied soldiers, unable to resist the charms of the German girls and women, had taken a German girlfriend. Many relationships would eventually lead to marriage. There were, however, also a huge number of unwanted pregnancies that resulted from the illicit relationships between soldiers of the occupying forces and German women. This, under the circumstances, was inevitable.

Heidi Koch remembers how handsome the British and Americans looked in their uniforms as they went about their business in the city:

> There were a few very good-looking boys, but I felt that I was still too young for that kind of thing. I did think that they were very nice, and they understood those that genuinely had nothing to do with the Nazi attitude to Jews, gypsies and Slavs and the killing that had taken place. They did not blame us all or hold it against us and we co-operated with each other on a mutual basis. We liked the Brits and Yanks, but feared, distrusted and despised the Soviets in Berlin. Those bastards would not even let us visit friends or relatives in the eastern part of the city.

Anita Von Schoener praises the American and British forces that gave her much-needed support after her ordeal at the hands of the Russians during the fall of the city:

> I was offered much medical advice, and the American and British girl nurses were really nice people and helped me overcome my problems caused by the rape. The American and British soldiers were also very good to little Anton and they gave him their sweets and chocolate, even though he was a little too young for some of them, he liked the chocolate very much. I remained in touch with one American who had expressed interest in me, his name was Henry, and he wrote to me frequently and I had to get an English-speaking friend to read the letters to me. My family had helped me through the trial of being pregnant with a rapist's child, and when I gave birth, I gave it up straight away, as explained to you earlier.
>
> The war is no easier to discuss with people now than it was back then when my husband was listed as missing and I never learned the truth of what happened to him. I later married my American friend and I moved to the USA, where I gave birth to my second child. The nightmares persist, but I can face them with the counselling that is available today, which we did not have years ago. You have to be brave and face your demons in order to overcome them. Talking about my ordeal in full here for the first time was the final step in getting rid of my demons. They are now gone, like I shall also be gone at some point when God determines it is my turn.

Anita revealed that, during several discussions and tests held with physicians in the USA, they all concluded that she was still suffering from what is now called Post Traumatic Stress Disorder, a condition frequently suffered by soldiers who have been in battle.

Theresa Moelle and her adoptive family desperately tried to return to a degree of normality in the months and years that followed after the war. She explains:

> It must have been two weeks after returning home when the nightmares started. It was usually a mixture of things: a woman carrying the dead body of her child in her arms beckoning me to help her; the child was dead and had no eyes. The other haunting vision was that of the Russian tank that I had destroyed, and Anneliese

being raped. I had this reoccurring nightmare that the tank would not stop even when I had destroyed it; it kept coming, and it began to roll over my legs, I vividly remember feeling the weight of it and the air slowly being squeezed out of my whole body. At that point, I would be thrashing around wildly and shouting. Walter and Greta would come running into my room to find the windows wide open. I could never even remember opening them, it was terrifying. When they came rushing in I would be awake, trembling, sweating heavily and crying. I would be given a glass of water and Greta would fetch some water and towels to bathe my body that would be wet with sweat.

Things continued like that for several more weeks, and Greta was forced to sleep in my bed with me. They called a doctor to see me, but he could only offer tranquillizers, which Walter strictly disagreed with. He told the doctor, 'I do not want any daughter of mine becoming a drug addict.'

Walter later took us all away for two weeks holiday in Switzerland. The change of scenery and the fresh, clean air worked wonders and I felt so much better. When we returned home, the nightmares returned but not so bad, and they gradually faded away. The problem was that the things that I had seen and done were not things to have been proud of, and as a result you tried to avoid talking about them, and bottled them up inside your head, which often led to psychiatric problems later on in life. I was lucky as I was fairly strong-willed and was able to overcome the difficulties, and after some years, was able to settle down, find my direction in life and make my adoptive family proud of me.

When I learned of the atrocities committed by our forces, it disgusted me. I had nothing personal against Jews, other than the fact that we as Hitler Youth under Nazi rule were forbidden to have anything to do with them. We would have faced severe punishment, even death, if we had dared to try and integrate socially with Jewish people. And we did not question when they began to disappear from the streets in Germany. Living on the outskirts of Berlin, the only information came via propaganda and radio sets anyway. The propaganda told us that Jews had been deported – not murdered in their millions. We heard rumours, but saw nothing to confirm them. Only during and after Berlin had fallen did we really know what had been going on for sure. People stopped lying to us for once, maybe out of guilt, I don't know, but the lying stopped. The Russians told us, but we did not trust them, and thought they were lying too. I found out from the Americans when I asked them, 'Was it true about what I had heard about the Jews of Germany and Europe?'

A nod of the head confirmed that it was true, and I later saw photographs and film, and spoke with Germans who witnessed the death camps themselves. But don't forget, that many Germans died in Nazi death camps too, and the Nazis murdered many ordinary Germans, if only people today could see that side of it. This fact is all too often sadly overlooked by society when remembering the Holocaust. I hope that our world never sees anything like that again. Germany is different now; it is a unified country again and at peace with itself at last. Many of the ghosts are finally being laid to rest. Maybe they will only go forever once our generation has died and lives no more. No one can blame the modern generation for things that happened during our time.

The political and social tensions between Britain, America and the USSR reached their inevitable conclusion in 1961 when Communist East Germany began to erect what would become known as the Berlin Wall. The Berlin Wall was a grey and hideous monstrosity that would serve as the dividing line between East and West Berlin and Germany for over twenty-eight long years of what would become known as the Cold War.

By the early 1980s, the winds of change had started to blow, and few would have ever believed how much things could change for the divided German people over the next ten years.

The changes came with the Soviet government under President Mikhail Gorbachev. During the night of 9 November 1989, thousands of East Berliners approached the Berlin Wall at the Brandenburg Gate. Customs officials manning their station at the gate had not been issued with any clear instructions on how to deal with the rapidly unfolding situation. The numbers of people swelled over the two hours that followed. When the border was suddenly opened, thousands of cheering East Berliners poured into West Berlin, many for the first time in their lives.

Theresa Moelle watched the events taking place in Berlin on her television and recalls the event:

It was a very beautiful thing to see. All those people uniting against that wall and everything that it stood for. I watched as people met for the first time, kissing and hugging each other and celebrating. I never thought that I would live to see this happen, this was the beginning of a newly reunited Germany. My children phoned me and said that they had just seen what was happening on the news and were going to Berlin straight away to see it happening.

I said to them 'What are you going to see?'

And they all said at the same time, 'Mother, we are going to see the Berlin Wall come down.'

A week later, one of my grandchildren brought me a piece of the wall for a souvenir. It is hard to think that so many died trying to cross that thing into the West. We should not forget those people. I only wish that Walter and Greta Moelle could have been around to see it all happening, God bless them both. It finally felt that our war was over seeing that wall being torn down, it was strange to watch it all happening on the TV.

The only Western opponents to the tearing down of the Berlin Wall and the subsequent reunification of Germany, were British prime minister Margaret Thatcher and French president Francois Mitterrand. Though the two were prevented from airing their views in public, the opinions of people like these counted for nothing amongst the majority, who wanted to see the end of Communism and its oppressive history in the region. Finally, on 3 October 1990, East and West Germany celebrated unification.

After the unification, it became obvious that many, if not all of those in the former East Berlin and East Germany holding such offices as judges, administrators, professors and schoolteachers, would all have to be retrained or 'cleansed' of their Communist ideologies, much like the Hitler Youth generation of boys and girls after 1945.

The East German infrastructure of housing, roads, telephone networks and utilities were in a typically appalling state, much of it in need of complete modernization. Over the decade that followed, what was East Germany became the world's biggest construction site, as the rebuilding of its infrastructure began.

Reunification, however, was not without its problems of a social and political nature, but with time and patience, these were things that could be overcome. The commitment was there amongst the people who were now able to enjoy their lives in a state of freedom, democracy and self-determination. Today, the German administration is back where it belongs in the heart of

Germany – Berlin. One wonders what Adolf Hitler would make of Germany as it is today.

Many of the contributors to this work have managed to lead peaceful and rewarding lives after the turmoil of childhood and youth in Hitler's Nazi Germany. The nightmares of their youth had surfaced frequently over the years, but now well into their twilight years, they have thankfully grown lesser. They still have many questions that will never be answered. Perhaps one of the most intriguing was that asked by Theresa Moelle the last time we spoke:

> I heard that during Hitler's last days in his bunker that he would not sleep at night. He would spend the whole of the night pacing around in his room, only retiring to sleep for a few hours at daybreak. I have wondered all these years, what did the Führer dream about in his sleep during those final hours? I often wonder whether his dreams became consumed within the madness of his reality.

This last meeting with Theresa was memorable, as for the first time since starting the *Hitler's Girls* project, we did not talk about the war. We both felt that this would be the last time we would see each other, though we did not know why. Before she left to return to Germany where she was still living, she gave me a memento in the form of a fired 7.62mm Russian cartridge case which she had picked up off the street in Berlin back in April of 1945.

'It's not much, but I don't have anything else left from the war other than this.' She placed the small brass cartridge in my hand and gave me a hug and we said our goodbyes. Just a few months later, I received the news that she had passed away peacefully at home.

There are still so many stories to be told, but space sadly does not permit this within the context of this single volume. Perhaps the hardest part of this work was to devise a method that would draw it to a suitable close, with so much still remaining to be told.

I very much hope that, by this stage, many of you will have a greater understanding of what forces drove me to research and write this book about the female youth of Nazi Germany. Even as these words are written, there are conflicts and wars claiming innocent victims all around the globe, while governments of the supposedly civilized societies stand by and do nothing. There are also children of all religions and cultures, both boys and girls, fighting and dying in these conflicts under the direction of their so-called governments and educators. Living in the relative safety and comfort of our own homes under our democratically elected governments, with decent jobs and decent standards of living, it is all too easy for us to become ignorant.

It was after conducting the first few interviews with these German women that I felt I had discovered an appropriate title for this work should it ever be completed and become a book as I had intended, or rather hoped, that it might. And now, in lateral reflections when I think of the many German women I had talked with and interviewed, I think of them as the young girls they once were, particularly when Hitler came to power in 1933. They were not politically minded evildoers. A Nazi was not born – he or she had to be made, created and nurtured. I likened the girls in particular to doves being thrown amongst eagles.

Index

About the Author

Tim Heath was born in 1965 in Redruth, Cornwall to a military family. Both grandfathers and great grandfathers had fought in the two World Wars; one was badly wounded, losing both his legs in Belgium. His father Trevor was serving with the Royal Navy at the time of Tim's birth, and later relocated the family to the Cotswolds when he left the armed forces. From a young age Tim's passion for military history flourished, leading him to research the air war of the Second World War. Focussing on the German Luftwaffe in particular, Tim has written extensively for *The Armourer Magazine* as a regular contributor. During the course of his research he has worked closely with the German War Graves Commission at Kassel, Germany, and met with German families and veterans alike. Born out of this work, *Hitler's Girls* is his first book. He lives in Evesham, Worcestershire, with his partner Paula, two children and six grandchildren.